Who Can Afford Critical Consciousness?
Consciousness?

PRACTICING A PEDAGOGY OF HUMILITY

D1607757

RESEARCH AND TEACHING IN RHETORIC AND COMPOSITION
Michael M. Williamson and David A. Jolliffe, series editors

Who Can Afford Critical Consciousness?

PRACTICING A PEDAGOGY OF HUMILITY

David Seitz
Wright State University

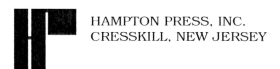

HAMPTON PRESS, INC.
CRESSKILL, NEW JERSEY

808.042
Se 45w

Library of Congress Cataloging in Publication Data

Seitz, David
    Who can afford critical consciousness? : practicing a pedagogy of
    humility / David Seitz.
        p. cm. -- (Research and teaching in rhetoric and composition)
    Includes bibliographic references and indexes.
    ISBN 1-57273-580-5 -- ISBN 1-57273-581-3 (pbk.)
        1. English language--Rhetoric--Study and teaching--Social
    aspects--United States. 2. English language--rhetoric--Study and
    teaching--United States. 3. Criticism--Authorship--Study and
    teaching--United States. 4. Report writing--Study and teaching
    (Higher)--United States. 5. Wright State University. I. Title. II. Series.

PE1405.U6S45 2004
    808'.042'0711--dc22

                                                            2004054322

Hampton Press, Inc.
23 Broadway
Cresskill, NJ 07626

Contents

Preface

A few weeks into the quarter at Wright State nearby Dayton in Ohio, a few of my students in English 101 disappeared from class. I e-mailed them to let them know they were in trouble in the course. Amy replied with this message:

> As of Monday Feb. 4th I have decided to drop all my classes. I am no longer happy at wright state and feel like i am stuck in a car going nowhere. I have a plan that I am going to start working on to achieve a goal that I have. Thanks mostly to your class and that essay I have decided to follow what I really want to do.

Amy's reply unsettled me. The work of my class had obviously achieved some persuasive effect, but I did not expect or desire for her to just pack her bags and drop right out of school. I e-mailed Amy back asking whether I could meet with her and talk about why she made this decision and how the writing in my class had influenced her choices.

Unlike most other students I had met at Wright State, Amy had come here from out of state, all the way from Vermont. In her work memoir essay (the pedagogy of which I detail in chap. 5), she had written about the satisfaction that she received from working at a nursing home there. Although I didn't keep that draft, I remember it for the pleasure of an unexpected turn in the narrative. Like other papers I have read about working in hospitals, it opens with a scene of Amy caring for a senior patient, leaving me to think the tone and focus of the piece would emphasize the warm values of work in a caring profession. Yet just as the older woman begins to tell a story to nursing home aide Amy, Amy the writer interrupts with something like, "blah, blah, blah, the old bat just wouldn't shut up, none of them would." Thwarting my initial expectations as a reader, Amy throws the patients into the background and instead foregrounds the good times of her relationships with fellow workers. Contrary to any of my friends who ever worked at a nursing home, Amy felt at home there.

When Amy and I finally talked about why she chose to leave school, she told me my work memoir assignment made her ask, "What am I doing here? What do I want and why?" As I show in chapter 5, I designed the assignment sequence to help students articulate their cultural values of work, their local social meanings and material histories, which underlie their common sayings about work and identity. Using the language of past, present, and future selves that memoir writing offers, I encourage them to consider their future selves at work in light of the complexities they see in their and others' work histories. Apparently for Amy, this process brought to the surface the disparity she saw between her future self as a nurse and the lack of vocationally appropriate courses she could take in her first years at Wright State. Like most teachers in the liberal arts, I first inwardly bristled at Amy's view of the purposes of higher education. Yet Amy was also paying for her own out-of-state tuition costs, having lost her parents some years earlier. She told me she had always been around hospital settings since she was five because of her mother's health. "We would always go with her for treatments or stay nights when she was hospitalized. Then two years after she passed away, I had to move." She lived with her aunt and uncle, an arrangement she did not care for. When she was 17, she began working in a hospital near her home.

Amy's reflections on her experiences and cultural values of work helped her understand why she constantly complained about all the required general education courses to her new friends. She also longed for the familiar environment and expectations of hospitals that had been her home for so long. So Amy left Wright State and took a job as a nursing assistant at a nearby hospital, working more than full-time hours for part-time wages, a work situation she critically assessed with me. Soon after, however, she landed a full-time position that would also pay for nursing courses at a local community college known for a strong nursing program. She wrote to me that she enjoyed her job, was learning more every day, and firmly believed she made the right decision to leave Wright State.

When I told this story to Mary, one of our MA graduate students, she replied, "Well, that's a success story."

"Don't tell that to the administration!" I countered.

"No," she added, "certainly not a success story for the university, but for the student, and for you. That assignment meant something for her."

Mary had received her BA from Wright State; she knew these students' struggles better than I ever could, and so I trusted her judgment. Mary and Amy reminded me of the humility necessary if teaching critical writing is to have any internally persuasive authority for students.

Now *humility* is a difficult word to put into print without sounding like a pious ass. So let me define what I mean here. Humility in my role as a teacher of critical writing is to recognize that I have minimal control over what happens and that the students' goals will likely differ from my own. In the case of Amy, she made the assignment her agenda following from her motivation. She granted me the role of generally unknowing catalyst, but that's about all. So this kind of humility for the teacher is a willingness to live with and learn from the unpredictable. Like other writing teachers whom I admire, I need to have enough flexibility, built on self-confidence in my teaching and identity as a teacher to recognize that students' learning, particularly the learning that I can learn the most from, often happens beyond the domains of my control.

I would claim this aspect of humility as maintaining a certain disposition—in some regard, a particular ethos—toward the rhetorical situation of teaching critical writing. But the more I have reconsidered my teaching from the perspectives of the students in my ethnographic research at the University of Illinois at Chicago and the students I have taught since at Wright State, the more I have come to see how humility in teaching critical writing must be a continuous balanced stance among ethos (as disposition), method, and theory. As this book will assert, methods of inductive theorizing, particularly ethnographic methodology, help discipline me, at my best, to remain continually attentive to the local situations, motives, and understanding of the students. In this way, adhering to main tenets of inductive methods helps constrain the possible theoretical arrogance of the critical pedagogue. Inductive theorizing helps me maintain a disposition of humility. If method helps me remain attentive to the moment, I view theory—as in critical theories of culture and language—as providing the tools for reflection necessary to learn from what does occur.

Although I only refer to humility once or twice in the whole book, I believe that this balanced stance underlies both my ethnographic research and my pedagogical responses to what I learned. Frankly, It's only as I complete this particular philosophical and political journey as a researcher and teacher that I have come to this language of humility (and I am not about to rewrite the whole book!). Yet I also think that the motives for this research grew out of some concern for humility. It began with my discomfort between critical teachers' published claims compared with the situations of students in my own critical writing classes at UIC (as I discuss in chap. 1). When I wanted to ask "who can afford critical consciousness," I was also asking how is critical pedagogy, and my teaching, a middle-class enterprise that provides cultural capital for some but may be a luxury that some working-class, minority, and immigrant students cannot afford. Yet the more I reflected on what I learned from my research, the more I realized that if I wanted to achieve some internally persuasive effect toward students' social change, I also could not afford "critical consciousness" in the form of fixed a priori theoretical assumptions. Along with other teacher-scholars reinventing critical pedagogy, this book is my contribution to that effort.

ACKNOWLEDGEMENTS

Back in graduate school when I read ethnographies, I wondered why so many of them took 10 years from the time of the ethnographer's participant observations to the book's publication. Now I know why. I also know I never could have finished this book without the deep collaboration of my good friend and geographically distant colleague, Julie Lindquist, and my mentor in academics and life, Nancy Mack. I find it impossible to untangle our conversations about teaching, our writings, and the details of our lives. Nor could I ever separate your two voices, minds, and hearts from this book even if I so desired. My wife, Daniele, is eternally grateful that I have both of you to turn to when I'm flummoxed. Daniele, your patient, yet not unconditional, love for me and Eli and Joshua reminds me what teaching should be about, and your anthropological view of the children you teach remains a model for my own understanding.

As I hope this book will show, I have learned so much from the students in my classes and those who have participated in my research. Their questioning of and ethical challenges to my teaching have enriched my views of the world, helping my teaching and writing to continually evolve. If any of you ever read this book, I hope you come away believing I earned my claims and your respect.

For the Chicago portion of this book, I am grateful for the tough love of our earlier ethnography writing group, Julie, Daiva Markelis, Jeanne Weiland, Raul Ybarra, and Richard Gelb. I always came away from our discussions with a clearer sense of what I was doing and why it should matter. For the chapters on my teaching at Wright State in Ohio, I thank the careful and creative readings of my second writing group, Deborah Crusan, Angela Beumer Johnson, and Alex MacLeod. More than anyone else, you all helped me see what was important for teachers who might not be "into theory," making the book far more accessible to a larger audience (we hope!).

Thanks also to Jim Zebroski and Seth Kahn for our conversations on teaching critical writing and ethnography that have influenced my thinking throughout this book. It's a pleasure to have such stimulating colleagues in the field to learn from. I also want to thank Marcia Farr for helping me shape the first stage of this project almost ten years ago and David Jolliffe for his encouragement and expert guidance throughout the long journey. Thanks also to Robert Brooke, who offered invaluable revision advice that have undoubtedly helped me write a better book, and to Bonnie Sunstein for her final reading of the manuscript. To Rich Bullock and Joe Law, you both have taught me much about good writing, good teaching, and expert copyediting, not that I am capable of it yet, but I will keep trying. And to the many colleagues in my department at Wright State, your good will and respect for teaching writing always made me feel welcome when someone would ask, "So, what is your book about?"

Provoking Questions

As any good teacher does, I tend to provoke questions. In this chapter, however, I want to foreground the questions that students in my classes at the University of Illinois at Chicago (UIC) provoked in me—questions that later resurfaced in my ethnographic research in Rashmi Varma's class also at UIC and have since guided the development of my teaching at Wright State. These questions arose because of the methods and theories for provoking questions that I had learned from the field of critical writing pedagogy.

When I learned about these teaching approaches during my graduate education, each philosophy resonated with pieces of my past and social background. I mention this because I want to first frame myself as a representative example of socially conscious middle-class writing teachers whose education in critical pedagogy may lead them to misread the different motives of their students, particularly those from nonmainstream backgrounds. As I present myself here as a researcher using ethnographic methods to reconsider the motives and strategies of my teaching, it is important for readers to know how my social background has influenced my interpretations of these students' situations and discourses. In providing some autobiographical background here, I am also briefly writing in the genre of work memoir alongside students in my first-year classes at Wright State to articulate my cultural values toward work and my future self—a pedagogy I discuss fully in chapter 5. Because I frequently refer to premises and commonplaces of critical writing pedagogies in this book, in this chapter, I map out the differences between these teaching approaches. I then analyze three situations from my own teaching at UIC that led me to question several assumptions in these pedagogies, shaping the questions of my research at UIC and eventually my future teaching at Wright State.

THE MAKINGS OF A MIDDLE CLASS CRITICAL WRITING TEACHER

I remember my father helping organize buses for the anti-Vietnam War protest marches in Washington, DC, before I was ten. For the next 10 to 15 years, I participated in several other marches in Washington, the most memorable being the 20th anniversary of King's 1963 rally because middle-class White kids like me were rightly the minority among African Americans and working-class unions. My father was a college professor, initially of French literature, but later film criticism and finally basic reading and writing courses, and we lived in Roosevelt, New Jersey, a town of 900 known among the other counties for its left politics. In 1936, Jewish garment workers living in New York who wanted to move to the country created the town with a cooperative garment factory and farming fields using support from the New Deal's federal resettlement administration. Although the cooperative ventures failed in a decade, the town's progressive politics attracted artists and writers who did stay. I grew up with shaggy long hair as a kid like most of my friends. I can only recall one to two African American families that attended the school or lived in town, although many people my parents knew suppported civil rights. Our segregation came more from cultural difference and economic opportunity than deliberate prejudices. As to our social class, I never felt my immediate family was wealthy; there were plenty of things we didn't buy. Our house, and the houses of most of my friends, did not sport any trendy furniture or big ticket appliances meant to convey social status. As one of my best friends in graduate school who came from a working-class background put it, my family "didn't have much economic capital, but heaps of symbolic capital." When I look back on visits to both of my grandparents, I now see their money and security which supported us later in life.

In the early 1970s, my father was denied tenure, and we moved to Wilkes Barre, Pennsylvania, a working-class city known for its anthracite coal mining. My long hair began to feel like a liability at the local public school. At home, we took in a series of students from the college where my father now taught, and I recall the thick waft of pot smoke from their parties as I lay in a corner grooving to George Harrison's Bangladesh concert over headphones. At school, I would shut my eyes as I heard the sharp thwap of teachers paddling children for simply not handing in their homework. In retaliation, I wrote an underground newspaper about this injustice to distribute to other kids. I clearly felt entitled, empowered, like a pint-sized SDS agitator taking on the repressive regime, unlike most of the children at the school. Although I cannot remember what the paper actually said, I fondly recall when my father offered to make the copies for me at his college. In my memory, we snuck into his stately campus building in the dead of night, leaving the hallways dark and lighting our clandestine activity with one overhead bulb. The cylinder of the ditto machine rolled off deep purple copies of my makeshift newspaper to be passed out like *zamisdat* writings in the Eastern Block. I doubt whether my father risked anything by using the machine especially because he was the chair of his department. Other boys remember their fathers playing ball with them or helping them with a difficult math problem; I remember my dad aiding the resistance.

Of course when I began distributing the newspaper on the playground, I was immediately called into the principal's office, who probably wondered where in the hell this weird kid came from. I remember he threatened me, although I don't remember with what, but it was enough to squelch my students' struggle then and there. Years later when I was in college, I found in my mom's apartment a large box of 1960s activist memorabilia she had saved. Out fell dozens of flyers and newspapers supporting the radical education movement, models for the kind of work that interested my father more in his first teaching job then the necessary academic publishing and department schmoozing that might have helped him get tenure. In my late 20's and early 30's, I would describe my father as an armchair revolutionary, an academic who spoke more about the politics of progressive action, such as how the Spanish anarchists were screwed by the Soviet communists in the Spanish Civil War, than actually did anything for social change as my mother did for a living. In the past decade, however, his actions have challenged my naïve dismissal, having worked hard for unionizing adjunct college teachers, like himself, in New York City.

If my dad was often the theory of social action, my mother embodied its practice as a classic case study of suburban mom as awakened feminist. After my parents divorced, a decision proceeded by their participation in several encounter groups before moving to Pennsylvania, my mother and I moved back to Roosevelt, just two years after we left. I remember waking up to a woman screaming in our living room during what I later came to understand were early consciousness raising sessions hosted by my mother. Before divorcing my father, my mom returned to college and finished the degree she forestalled after her marriage. She then helped campaign for the ERA and Title 9 legislation, worked for a government rental assistance program, and ultimately founded an innovative homelessness prevention program for New Jersey. Over several decades, she developed a social worker's savvy about state bureaucracy and its players without losing her commitment to progressive politics.

Over the years, I participated in mostly White middle-class political causes. Home from college for the summer, I burned my skin lobster red after eight hours of picketing with friends outside the local post office to protest Jimmy Carter's reinstatment of registration for a military draft. Later in college, as a member of the students for nuclear arms control, I lay down on the grass outside the student union as another radiated corpse of a mock nuclear disaster. My involvement with the nuclear arms issues led to full-time work with Physicians for Social Responsibility. A small minority of politically active students engaged in more local issues of working-class Waltham, Massachusetts, the town surrounding our progressive college on the hill, such as my wife and her best friend who volunteered in the women's shelter. But as I look back, I know that working-class issues and divisions of social class, much less race, never occurred to me then, nor did any of my teachers explicitly raise the question. From the framework of economic necessities, a middle-class kid can afford to be pissed off at big issues.

From these political causes and my love of reading and writing, it wasn't a big jump to critical approaches to teaching, calling on a range of critical writing pedagogies. Depending on each teaching situation I encountered, I have let these teachers' voices argue with each other in my head.

A RANGE OF CRITICAL WRITING PEDAGOGIES

Although there have been several overlapping strands of critical pedagogy in college writing classes over the past fifteen years, teachers influenced by these ideas hold one assumption in common. All of them believe the educational system, to varying degrees, promotes the cultural reproduction of social and economic injustice. In concrete terms, this has meant academic tracking in schools, policing of class and race through standard written English, and encouraging an ideology of individualism often at the expense of collective actions, to name a few examples. As their common rhetorical strategy, then, critical teachers seek to intervene in this reproduction of inequities sponsored by institutions, ideologies, and social discourses that support them. Most college writing teachers would agree with Nancy Sommers (1982) that our major job is to productively intervene in students' composing processes. Promoters of a critical writing pedagogy carry this process one step further, seeking out places to intervene in students' composing processes of the status quo through reading and writing.

Schools of critical teaching, however, differ in their larger assumptions about the ethics and methods of this critical intervention. In this respect, we can imagine a loose continuum of critical teaching philosophies and strategies based on commitment to enacting utopian ideals of social justice (see Figure 1). On one end, liberatory teachers such as Ira Shor (1987) claim their pedagogies should serve to liberate their economically and socially disenfranchised students. Thus, they imagine their teaching in the most utopian terms on this continuum. At the other extreme of this continuum, there are liberal realist teachers like Nell Ann Pickett (1998) and Marilyn Sternglass (1997) who believe educating nonmainstream students for mainstream institutions constitutes *by itself* a critical act against reproducing the status quo.[1] The critical liberation teachers might argue that liberal realist teachers like Picket and Sternglass accommodate to the system too readily, whereas the latter group might view the former's liberatory assumptions as colonizing and paternalist.

Significantly, the strongest arguments for both liberatory teaching and realistic liberalism come from teachers who work with working-class and immigrant students. In my teaching at UIC and Wright State, I have often shifted between these polar positions in my responses to students' writing and classroom

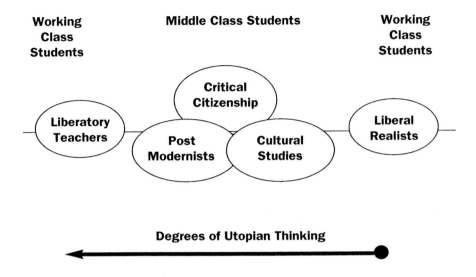

FIGURE 1.1 Mapping a Range of Critical Pedagogies.

dynamics. I have also tended to draw on critical teaching philosophies that, as I discuss later, originate more from teachers of middle-class students. I name these middle positions as the postmodern teachers, the teachers of critical citizenship, and the cultural studies teachers. As will become evident, the assumptions and practices of these middle positions overlap each other like venn diagrams rather than exact points on this continuum. Depending on the teaching situations and the students, I find myself justifying my teaching strategies from all these various camps as I am sure many teachers do.[2] To better understand how I came to the research questions that drove my study, it would help to quickly categorize these versions of critical writing because the rest of the chapter offers moments from my teaching that challenged my everyday use of their pedagogical assumptions.

When critical teachers like Shor have identified their aims as liberatory, they "have done so in the names of students perceived to be on the margins of school life" (Knoblauch, 1991, p. 15), most often working-class and minority students. These teachers aim to make marginalized students conscious of how the dominant power relations oppress their lives and collective opportunities. As Cy Knoblauch (1991) summarizes the position,

the goal is to enfranchise "outsiders" by making them . . .
more aware of the means by which power is gained, used, and
distributed in the professional and other communities they
may wish to enter; more aware of the ways to simultaneously
acquire that power and also subvert the structures that objec-
tify prevailing and debilitating power arrangements. (p. 15)

At best these teachers claim to enact this liberatory action
through shared dialogue, where teachers and students learn from
each other, with Paulo Freire's (1970) literacy programs as their
model.

Critics of these liberatory claims have challenged them on two
grounds—first, on assumptions of postmodern theory, and, second, the experiences of various marginal groups that did not fit
this model of universal liberation through rational discourse.
Informed by the postmodern theories of Francois Lyotard (1984),
Michel Foucault (1976, 1979), and revisionist histories of sophist
rhetoricians, composition scholars like Lester Faigley (1992),
Victor Vitanza (1991), and Susan Jarratt (1991a) endorse a pedg-
agogy that encourages students to value critical complexities of
discourse and the material world, but resists grand narratives of
emancipation such as the utopian neo-Marxist assumptions of
Shor, Friere, and Giroux.[3] These postmodern writing teachers
contend that truth is local and contingent, and so they reject
Marxist assumptions as a totalizing unity that can suppress different voices. Hence, the second ground of criticism. In an often
quoted article, Elizabeth Ellsworth (1989) offers an example of
how even in an advanced communications course on racism, the
Enlightenment aims of rational discourse underlying several liberatory teachers' critical pedagogies, specifically those of Henry
Giroux and Peter MacLaren, repressed different women's and
minority groups' modes of learning and activism in the class.[4] I
have yet to read of a teacher who thoroughly preaches the
antifoundationalist faith of postmodern pedagogy and also mainly
teaches working-class students. Perhaps the working-class students' more immediate material needs take precedence over the
luxury of putting into practice complex postmodern theories—a
situation I examine.

Other teachers of mostly middle-class students have claimed
their educational goal is to foster students as critical citizens for
participation in larger realms of public debate. Liberatory and
postmodern writing teachers sometimes espouse a similar goal.
Yet the teachers who emphasize notions of critical citizenship
and downplay the importance of Marxist and postmodern per-

spectives tend toward a more liberal understanding of education than these previous groups on the continuum. The critical citizenship teachers draw primarily, although sometimes tacitly, from two traditions: first, pragmatist traditions of American philosophy, particularly as developed in John Dewey's theories of education, and second, the rhetorical tradition of training citizen orators for participation in public life that held sway in American universities until the late 19th-century.

Stephen Fishman (1993) summarizes well Dewey's associations with American pragmatism: "that the individual's writing is always a mutual reshaping of author, culture, and text. It is never just private, but always private *and* social, personal *and* political: to change one's text is also to change one's self and one's culture" (p. 323). In his early histories of composition, Berlin (1984, 1987) lauds this transactional view of language as the "social epistemic" approach to teaching writing and engaging in public debates. Kurt Spellmeyer (1993) also draws on Dewey, among others, to argue for rebuilding a "public dimension" to writing in higher education that has been lost to the rise of 20th-century professionalization in academic disciplines. Spellmeyer principally imagines this dimension in students' engagements with other intellectual writer's ideas, promoting an "ethic of mutual understanding" rooted in difference and dialogue. I would also characterize the rise in service learning, or the more reciprocal goal of community-based, writing courses in the past decade, as another form of critical citizenship pedagogy.

In contrast, teachers who evoke oratorical traditions from the history of rhetoric encourage and model critical participation in public life through debates of public issues. Michael Halloran's afterword to his ground-breaking essay, "Rhetoric in the American College Curriculum: The Decline of Public Discourse" (1993), written ten years after the original essay's publication, may best represent this approach. In this revisit to his essay, he describes the efforts of the working class in the neighborhood of South Troy, New York, to prevent the city council from constructing an asphalt plant in their neighborhood. He compares the situations of South Troy and the privileges of his academic institution, Rensselaer Polytechnic Institute (RPI). Halloran claims that in the beginning years, RPI sought to promote a "populist science"—somewhat in the tradition of Dewey—to benefit farmers and mechanics, but soon established itself as a professional school. Through this comparison, he argues that although writing teachers should look to the rhetorical tradition for "its largely unrealized potential as an instrument of participation in the discourse that continues to shape American society" (p. 115), they must have students look critically at the politics of rhetoric and the promotion of citizenship. "American neoclassical rhetoric was among other things an instrument of patrician domination in the Federal period, and the economic interest of the academic rhetoricians of that time would have motivated them to align with those trying to build the asphalt plant, against those whose neighborhood will be degraded by it" (p. 114).

Teachers influenced by cultural studies, as in the later work of Jim Berlin, also argue for promoting critical citizenship, but they argue the structures of late capitalism have redefined our assumptions of citizenship in America (e.g., Berlin, 1996; Berlin & Vivion, 1992; McComiskey, 2000). As a major premise, critics in cultural studies assert that the machinations of late capitalism have transformed the role of citizen to that of consumer. In these social relations, group identities and self-definitions are formed around the commercialism of cultural products. Cultural studies pedagogy encourages students to question this transformation, and capitulation, of citizenship to reclaim a more active critical role. Not surprisingly, this approach has been predominantly a pedagogy for middle-class college students who perceive themselves as smart consumers of popular culture and material goods. Most teachers who espouse a liberatory pedagogy assume that marginalized students will acknowledge and may wish to interrogate material causes for their oppression. Because more privileged middle-class students often do not face these socioeconomic oppressions, cultural studies teachers push students to question the various consequences of their students' consumer privileges and pose alternative solutions. As Seth Kahn (2003) also argued, the danger here is that even if students buy into this faith, it can further reinforce their view of critical thinking as more shrewd consumption.

All three of these overlapping positions toward critical writing pedagogy—postmodern, critical citizenship, and cultural studies—originate more from colleges that serve middle-class student populations. As teachers, all three groups agree with liberatory teachers that their students should analyze social problems as complex systems of social injustice. At the final position of my posited continuum, liberal realist teachers of nonmainstream students may also encourage systemic criticism, as in the process of generally questioning their students' assumptions in the margins of their papers. Yet they assert the ends of their teaching is to assist working-class, minority, and immigrant students' entry into mainstream jobs with good wages and opportunities.

Nell Ann Pickett's (1998) keynote address reminded the membership of Conference on College Composition and Communication this aim serves disenfranchised individuals and can give back to their communities. Ira Shor (1987) critiques the role of many community colleges as middle-class society's holding pens for the disenfranchised that leaves working-class students to internalize their own failure. Contrary to this position, Pickett unashamedly argues why two year colleges are democracy in action that "have emerged as vanguard institutions in preparing an efficient, skilled, and adaptable workforce" (p. 98). Taking this view one step further, Marilyn Sternglass (1997) uses her longitudinal study of students at New York's City College to attest that the dominant society has much to gain by the inclusion of those people whom they have marginalized. She writes that over the course of her informants' college careers,

> Their writings reveal that they are capable of looking at the problems they must face in the society as members of minority groups in focused ways that can change the quality of their lives. They have developed analytical styles that lead them first to the questioning of existing assumptions and then to the recognition that they must be active participants in bringing about the changes they see are needed in the larger society. (p. 113)[5]

Over the course of my teaching at UIC, I came to wonder how much I might have misread some students' motives and social meanings in their work because of my experiences with middle-class political causes and my education in these critical pedagogies. In the following three moments from my teaching, I delve into the questions I raised as a kind of participant-observer in the membership role of urban university teacher. For this reason, I focus more on my responses as representative examples of larger issues in our teaching of critical writing. In the later ethnographic chapters, however, I focus much more on the contexts of UIC students' nuanced perspectives. Each of these three moments provoked questions of persuasive authority in my teaching and helped lead me to students' responses to the three keywords of critical pedagogy this book investigates: *instrumentalism*, *difference*, and *resistance*. Yet none of these three moments was unusually jarring or obviously revelatory at the time. I was not persuaded of their importance by each instance, but by the accumulated moments and memories of these conflicts of critical teaching and nonmainstream students' values. It is precisely the subtlety of these moments that motivated me to research this rhetorical situation from the students' perspectives.

CAN WE INTERPRET INSTRUMENTALISM IN STUDENTS' WRITING?

For their first formal paper, I asked my Comp 101 class to write about a powerful learning experience in or out of school and compare it with a critical analysis of an experience from their formal schooling. To analyze these experiences, they were to take on the critical perspectives from two of our readings on education—an article on "Connected Education" reprinted from Belenky, Clinchy, Goldberger, and Tarule (1986) *Women's Ways of Knowing* and Jean Anyon's (1980) article, "Social Class and the Hidden Curriculum of Work," a qualitative study of the cultural reproduction of social class in four fifth-grade classrooms of different socioeconomic status.[6] In the assignment, students needed to use the details of their narrative to examine the social structures and possible cultural differences of most institutional schooling.

George borrowed the definitions suggested by the authors of "Connected Education" to label the majority of his classes in a parochial high school as "connected learning" compared with the disfavored "traditional" education of his elementary and junior high schools.[7] Yet in the writing of his draft, George tacitly shifted from the term of *connected education* to his own language of *"communicative" education*, which borrowed more from managerial discourses. George chose to demonstrate the value of "communicative education" by comparing the communication skills he learned from his Catholic High teachers to the salesmanship skills demanded in his job at the Merry Go Round clothing store. For George, in this paper, the possible outcomes for future work in the adult world seem primarily instrumental—the means to an end rather than a questioning of those ends. The critical thought that is fostered in more "connected education" primarily serves to smooth over one's interactions with instructors and employers. The problem, George implies, is that the student—as future employee—doesn't know where the real authority for decision making should reside.

> For example, a person who had been taught by a connected educator will know how to interact with his employer. This

means that he may analyze decisions and possibly inquire about orders or tasks given to him by his employer. On the other hand, an individual who had been taught by a traditional instructor may simply follow instructions given to him by an employer even if he knows that there may be an error in his task. He, by no fault of his own, is deprived of a knowledge of communication, which, in my opinion, is a powerful learning experience.

The feminist authors of "Connected Education" did advocate a teaching based on relationships. Instead of assuming objective structures of authority, as George did here, their aim was to challenge the authority of institutional hierarchies. Up to this point in George's paper, his description of a communicative approach seemed an ad hoc application of the feminist ethics in "Connected Education" to the commonplaces of American values of education—better communication will yield better grades. It is when George compares his Catholic schooling to his job experience that his way of writing about the value of communication in learning takes a more instrumental turn.

As part of my duties I had to greet each person, perform a litttle "small talk," and somehow manage to make them leave our store with at least two items of our merchandise. We worked on a commission basis which made us work even harder. Our techniques ranged from sincere honesty to lying through our teeth, depending on our moods. Communication is the key factor to holding a job as a sales associate. If you could convincingly tell a person that an article of merchandise would look great on them you would make a sale and a larger pay check. My techniques were so good that I received a raise and a new title of sales consultant, along with a gold necklace and charm.

As I read George's efforts to equate his growing sales talent with the possiblities of critical learning, I thought of Kurt Spellmeyer's (1991) reading of Habermas' terms *instrumental* and *communicative* rationality. Spellmeyer writes, "To think reflectively is, as Habermas contends, to suspend the constraints of 'strategic' or instrumental reason for the unrestricted exercise of a 'communicative' reason—the former asking 'how' from the limited standpoint of disciplinary practice, the latter asking 'why' from the standpoint of social life as a whole, a life in which everyone has a stake" (pp. 74–75). It is this managerial discourse of "how to" that

I thought gave George a way to patch over the contradictions between the world of sales, his Catholic high school classes, and readings that challenge the status quo of formal schooling.

Yet what strikes me now is how my analysis of his language use presumed a corporate, and consequently middle-class, identity for George. Ethnographer of education Douglas Foley (1990) claims the prevailing communicative competence of middle-class ideology operates from a "pecuniary instrumental logic, 'what sells is true.' The more one is or wants to be in the 'mainstream,' the more one uses instrumental communicative practices rhetorically to define and manage social reality" (pp. 185–186).[8] Based on George's use of this instrumental language, virtually free of syntactical errors, and his description of his "college preparatory high school in the suburb of Oak Park," a more middle-class educated suburb of Chicago, I assumed I knew George's social class position. Or rather because of these social markers, I had not considered what this writing could mean if George were not from an established middle-class educated background.

As George continued to write during the term, however, aspects of a more mixed social class background emerged. In a paper on family issues, a topic chosen by the class, George comically characterized the ins and outs of living with an extended Old European family. When he wrote about his community friends for a first-hand event analysis, he described their peer and family situations in ways that suggested to me more of a working-class ethos than the expectations of teenagers from more conventional middle-class homes.[9] How much was my critical reading of George's paper and my suggestions for developing it missing local meanings in his use of these dominant discourses? What was I not examining about my own social positioning by responding with these strategies?

Although my margin comments to George gave him openings to argue against the readings' assumed values of connected education based on his experiences, I am arrested now by the less open questions I posed—the questions that implied a more politically correct agenda. Robert Schwegler's (1991) political analysis of many teachers' responses to student writing illuminates some of these dynamics that I was caught up in. Invoking Bourdieu's (1984) study of distinction and cultural capital, Schwegler suggests that teachers may feel such a strong need to respond when a student's paper has violated expectations of aesthetic and critical form because the student's writing "may be perceived as calling into question the value of the cultural and educational capital that constitutes the teachers' authority" (p. 215). Although

Schwegler refers to how conventions of academic writing constitute the teachers' capital, his argument could also apply to the
critical teacher's symbolic capital of "critical consciousness."

Lad Tobin's (1993) study of writing relationships with his students reaches similar conclusions from a more personal level.
Tobin analyzes his "misreading" of his first-year student Nicki's
meta-essay on writing and personal voice. "I was also reading
myself. I had a vested interest in thinking that my teaching and
my course had provided Nicki with something that she did not
get in her humanities class. And perhaps most complicated of all,
by reading her in a particularly imaginative and integrated way, I
could use her (as I am trying to do right now) for my own benefit
in my writing and research" (p. 25). Like Tobin, the distinctions of
my professional identity are often invested in particular ways of
interpreting and responding to students' writing. As composition
scholars have borrowed from literary and critical theory, our critical readings of student writings and contexts are the foundation
of our professional authority within English departments and our
universities. It is this critical authority that allows me to claim
distinction from "undisciplined" writing instructors, Stephen
North's (1987) "practitioners," those teachers without graduate
education in the field. But this critical work, my disciplined distinction, may have been particularly unpersuasive for developing
critical writing meaningful for George given his actual background. Only later did I ask myself, how else could I have
responded, or negotiated the project, that might have been more
persuasive in the long run, that might have worked more from
the position of the "other"? Chapters 3 and 4 examine these
questions through the discursive positions and lives of other
urban students who also wrote or spoke from an instrumental
language in college.

WHAT POLITICS OF DIFFERENCE IN
STUDENTS' WRITING DO WE OVERLOOK?

Throughout my years at UIC, students from minority and immigrant backgrounds often responded well to themes of identity,
difference, and cultural conflict in my writing classes.[10] Still others like Kisha have made me question what is at stake for them
when their teacher expects them to critique positive messages
that their communities want to affirm, not complicate.

For my basic writing course, Kisha had to take on Richard Rodriguez's (1981) key metaphor of public and private identities to analyze a cultural conflict they had encountered between their school's expectations and their other social worlds. How did or could they negotiate these differences? The assumptions in my pedagogy here followed the conflict pedagogies encouraged by Min Zhan Lu (1992), Patricia Bizzell (1994), Joseph Harris (1995), and others in composition studies journals from the late 1980s to the early 1990s. From that frame, however, I rarely considered those students who may want to discuss why their intellectual development had thankfully not yielded difficult conflicts of self-identity.

The body of Kisha's draft, however, confirmed the worth of my teaching strategies because much of the writing did not flinch from addressing the complications of identity formation for an urban African-American female student. She writes of receiving mixed messages from family members. Her "grandparents would tell me about their horrible racial experiences and they told me not to trust Caucasian people, but on the other hand my mother taught me to 'gain trust you must give trust.'" In her narrative, these ambivalences play out in her associations with dominant White media images and her elementary school teachers. "I believed Caucasians had the perfect families, the perfect education and the perfect life. I hated having Caucasian teachers because they would degrade my race and community. As I got older, I started to lash out at them afraid of having the same racial experiences." The paragraph before this one suggests the divided loyalties these influences yielded for her when in high school. "I lived in a majority Caucasian community. I went to my new high school with the idea to make new friends but the conflict between African-Americans and Caucasian-Americans was consequential. . . . I would explain to my African-American friends misusing other races will not gain prestige. I was always caught in the middle of being 'problack' or a 'sell out,' but because my mother taught me to make my own decision no matter what anyone says or does." When she describes her public identity at work as a professional, her actions within the public eye of presumably White society further complicates her sense of self.

> I must conduct myself as a highly educated and mature adult because many people would prejudge me once they saw the color of my skin [. . .] Many of my friends would ask me why

> I act differently at work than at home. The answer to that
> question is the way I may act at home may not be acceptable
> in the workplace or to the customers. Eventhough my behav-
> ior is different, my values have not changed. I still believe that
> everyone should be themselves and not what people want
> them to be.

Here Kisha apparently feels a need to reiterate her hard-won values to her imagined readers and me, her teacher, because she
senses the social contradictions of public identity and perceptions to which she must cater to succeed in most public workplaces.

But when it came to the introduction and conclusion that
framed her paper, Kisha opted for simpler solutions. Although
her introduction initially suggests she will focus her inquiry on
the dangers of claiming what is authentic blackness, as much of
her paper does, she then turns to what many critical teachers
would view as an empty commonplace: "Everyone has their own
perception or stereotype of others, but it should not be enforced
on anyone." Similarly, her paper's conclusion attempts to preach,
rather than reflect on, the insights that writing on her situations
have unearthed. "Cultural diversity is a continuing issue in our
society. We must learn from our cultural experiences through
communication and understanding. We also need to cease prejudice and discrimination and accept others for who they are and
not what we perceive them to be."

Reading this first draft, I thought Kisha was at a loss for how
to open and conclude her paper in what she saw as a suitably
authoritative manner, as David Bartholomae (1985) might suggest. Yet after we met to discuss ways to reshape the paper, the
introduction and conclusion remained essentially the same as
her first draft. As Valerie Balester (1993) points out, some
African-American students with a religious background, like
Kisha, call on the African-American rhetoric of "talking
respectable" when assigned controversial writing topics in school.
When faced with the uncertain territory of college education,
Kisha may have used this default language to contain the complexities her situations implied to appear neutral.

In our conference, Kisha stressed that the situations in her
draft should serve as examples to prevent stereotypes and discrimination. As an academic reader, however, I was most interested in how her insights on her experiences could challenge
often unexamined solutions for racial harmony, like the ones that
framed her draft. When students rely on the ways popular media

have defined issues of racism, their arguments, to borrow a phrase from Marilyn Cooper (Cooper & Holtzman, 1989), "are primarily persuasive in purpose and rarely offer the scope in which to develop and analyze new insights" (p. 52). For this reason, I saw Kisha's draft as the first step toward that deeper investigation. Yet when I judged her stated position as only the first step toward stronger critical literacy, I also sought to maintain my field's critical "standards" and so my particular professional authority.

Nevertheless, remembering the writing teacher's credo, I shut my mouth and listened to what Kisha wanted to do with her paper. It was then I knew that her final draft would not reconcile or probe these differences between her interest in a direct positive message and the complexity of these situations as she had described them. Yet I also recalled an image of Kisha with Athena, a Greek-American student, in our classroom with their heads cozily drooping onto each other's shoulders in sleepy repose. Their public gesture, repeated several times through the term, of a fast-growing friendship was one of the few times I have ever seen such a deliberate sign of interracial sisterhood in a first-year classroom at this urban Chicago university.

For years after, riding home on the El, I would encounter young Black men rapping on the trains to earn money for recording time in a studio, first assuring their captive audience of mostly White commuters they meant no harm. The raps almost always championed unity and individual achievement in the face of urban violence. In this way, the rappers' line echoed the rehabilitated gangbangers or former junkies who also testified their religious redemption on the trains to raise money for their volunteer programs. I would often associate the direct style of their appeals with editorials that would appear in *Streetwise*, a weekly paper sold by Chicago's homeless people. Often these editorials would dwell on the same themes as the rappers and, like them, would stress a direct, if often stylized, approach to getting the message out.

Listening to the rappers, I would compare them to students' writing like Kisha's and consider how the goals of my class differed from these community literacies. In what ways did my goals of exploring contradictions and complexities of lived experiences privilege the individual reflection of the critic over opportunities to reaffirm the values of their communities—values that have sustained these students' education so far? Critical theory searches out the negative position, asking what are the systemic problems in society. Cooper (1989) argues for the students' engagement in negative critique to help them "criticize and change the world and thereby claim it as their own" (p. 58). "To see what something is, one must see what it is not and vice-versa" (p. 56). In this version of the writing classroom, "the goal of writing is not the comfort that comes with conformity but rather the unhappiness that leads to understanding" (p. 58). Of course Cooper would prefer that this understanding lead to aspects of a leftist agenda of social justice.

Cooper contrasts negative critique with more mainstream discourses of positive thinking that tend to close down inquiry and accommodate dominant power structures. Yet from the perspectives of some students like Kisha, particularly those with low socio-economic status, do they feel they can afford to "think negatively"? This positive faith that has gotten her to college when so many others she has known have not made it becomes necessary when economic conditions limit her choices and complicate her life. The academics' valuing of complexity may not be persuasive to some students if these individuals are looking for ways to make their lives easier, not more complicated. Perhaps Kisha wanted to structure her writing as a direct message of hope, despite the complexities she describes, because it helped structure the goals she saw for her path in life. In chapter 6, I examine these questions further with the students from Rashmi's class, and in chapter 8, I lay out my pedagogical response to this problem for teaching critical writing.

CAN WE REALLY TELL WHAT IS STUDENT RESISTANCE?

Kisha did not openly resist the purpose of my writing course. Other times, however, I have encountered inertia within larger group dynamics of the "underlife" (Brooke, 1987) in the class. In some of these situations in my classes, critical theory has led me to interpret these group dynamics, or rather lack of them, as sociocultural resistance. Yet in my most frustrating instance of classroom dynamics, an English as a Second Language (ESL) composition class that I discuss later, I often felt that I could not interpret how the class as a whole perceived my expectations of their class work. This experience led me to question more carefully how critical teachers define resistance in their classes.

Despite telling moments with students like Kisha, more often than not my teaching strategies, tempered by my real interest in dialogue, motivated students as critical writers. Quite often my student evaluations praised my class as "open minded" and helping them be better writers for college. So when I collaborated on the design of a composition course for non-native speakers, my colleague Ulrike Jaekel and I adapted these pedagogical assumptions of culture, identity, and the development of critical literacy to address the concerns of this widely varied student population.[11] Because the class had been a general success, I assumed I would use the same curriculum again two years later.

Yet when I received the roster for the class, I began to anticipate trouble ahead. Unlike two years earlier, the roster now showed what preparatory ESL classes the students had to take before they were eligible for the composition class. Almost all the students had taken both courses in the ESL sequence. I guessed, correctly it turned out, that these students had already pumped out much information about their cultures for these courses. Moreover, I imagined they would probably have to churn out more insights on cultural issues and their backgrounds for the mainstream first-semester writing course most would take after my class.

I was complicit with a kind of unthinking immigration and naturalization process that required ESL students to repeatedly drag out their cultural baggage before they would be admitted past the gate. I intended for students to mine their cultural experiences for semi-sociological and anthropological reflections, to develop academic habits of defamiliarizing the familiar. Yet I knew that from these students' view my carefully worded prompts would mostly be read as "tell us about your culture and the problems you have had in the U.S." Around the fifth week, the class confirmed my suspicions when I asked them to write down what topics they wrote about in previous ESL classes and how they felt about our class so far. More than half wrote they were dead tired of writing about their cultural selves. Sarah's comment stung the deepest. After saying she was kind of bored with writing about herself and her culture, as several other students had admitted, she exclaimed she "would rather learn more about American culture and society." I felt the purpose of my assignments was to examine American society, admittedly through the back door of their various social situations. But Sarah's comment implied I might be unwittingly positioning the student writers as the exotic, the ones who should be studied for their differences from the mainstream.

As I stalled until I could figure out my next move, I spent an agonizing class trying to initiate cross-discussion on our current course topic of social contexts for spoken and written language. I had first put them into groups to list what they saw as differences between spoken and written language that we would then address as a whole class. The small groups were floundering as they had several times already that term, so I opened up the full-class discussion, which went almost nowhere as well. I don't recall what I wrote on the board in response to their meager offerings at the time. But I do remember having that feeling all too familiar to teachers—that I was going through the paces, but saw no immediate way to redirect the situation and make it meaningful to this class as it had been for others in the past. When I returned to the classroom after the seven minute break, everyone who had also returned had their heads slumped on their portion of the large grey seminar table, looking as if they were deep in midterm exam depression, although it was only the fifth week. It looked to me as if everyone had abdicated any engagement—diligent, talented, and unprepared students all alike. The room was silent. They weren't even talking about what they planned to do that night or helping each other with math theorems. Looking around, I thought about those who hadn't come to class today or hadn't come back from the class break. Teaching further today would be a total joke.

Certainly, I had encountered this listlessness in a group before, but in the context of the cultural issues of this class I read this mood as tacit resistance, as if en masse they were telling me they would also go through the paces if they had to, but it would mean little. Swallowing my frustration, I too abdicated. Not fully explaining why, I told them I was through teaching for the day and they could find me in my office should they feel the need. To my initial surprise, six of the women and one man did show up at my office twenty minutes later to dutifully hand in their writing responses I had not collected. They almost all looked shamefaced and truly wondered how they had offended me, their teacher. Admittedly, I had secretly counted on the Asian stereotypical value of shame and losing face to make them reconsider their commitment to the class. In doing so, I had acted as if all had been equally responsible for this impasse.

The following week, I came to class prepared to give the class control over developing the rest of the syllabus, given the readings available in our common text, as I had sometimes done in mainstream first-year courses. As a group, they would not buy this openly democratic approach favored by writing teachers who see their authority as perpetuating institutional power. Finally, I offered a compromise where I would research available comp readers for readings that did not directly pertain to the study of culture. As I perused through many anthologies, I found out just how much culture had become a god term in the composition publishing industry. From the topics I could glean, a majority of the class voted to write on issues of technology and then media and advertising, although they had originally voted work issues as the runner-up. So once the class was able to steer away from the retelling of immigrant experience, I felt the aura of crisis for myself and the students diminish, although I now had twice the work creating a new curriculum. Still some of the classroom dynamics that I interpreted as resistance persisted throughout the term. For my part, I cannot finally discern what kinds of resistance might have played out in different formations at what moments. Did the students actually perceive themselves as resisting my assumptions for the course? I can only speculate on the possibilities.

Perhaps most of the students saw themselves as immigrant Americans. According to John Ogbu's (1987) theories of minority resistance and education, families that choose to immigrate to America often maintain an ideology of accommodation despite the prejudices and socioeconomic discriminations they may encounter. Gibson (1988) and Fu (1995) offer individual insider perspectives in a Siekh community and a Loatian family, respectively, that confirm the intensity of these immigrants' beliefs in the American dream of achievement and freedom. For students from these voluntary immigrant groups, the critique of dominant ideologies, or the extension of that critique to their social worlds outside college, may be too uncomfortable because their stakes for achievement are so high. Could these theories account for some students' occasional reluctance to analyze socioeconomic situations in their reading and writing?

Or was the resistance I sensed tied more to their cultural expectations of how teachers and students should behave, and what content should be appropriate for classroom discussion? Marian Yee (1991) writes how her mainstream students, influenced by dominant narratives of race and assimilation, questioned her right to be the teacher. Conversely, my students who internalized Asian cultural narratives of education and authority would not let me relenquish the teacher's authoritative role. I intellectually understood that unlike Americans, Eastern cultures value listening in public discussions, often being "very conscious of our image to others" (Fu, 1995, p. 198). This understanding made it even more difficult to distinguish or separate possible moments of resistance to social critiques from the students' enacting of cultural behaviors.

The gender dynamics of the group further promoted these cultural responses. In my previous ESL composition class, there were several strong Latina women who spurred the Asian women to speak their mind and not be silenced by the men in the class. Yet this class was two-thirds women of Asian origin, and the only non-Asian women were friends from Poland who felt like the European minorities. Most of the women allowed three to four men to break the silences that hovered over most attempts at whole-class discussion. I compensated as much as possible with online discussions and groups responding to their ideas on the board, which was difficult because they wrote very slowly in class. For the most part, the individual perspectives and development of ideas came out in their essay drafts, not in the oral interchanges.

Yet taking in this complicated mix of macrosocial structure and local cultural behaviors, how much was the students' limited language ability a factor as well? With a third of the class, I was very conscious of their struggle to formulate complex ideas with limited English vocabulary. I wonder now if I misread the language and behaviors of apparently more linguistically capable students as social resistance when in actuality they too were grappling with language problems. In chapter 7, I examine the students' perspectives on what teachers and researchers, including myself, claim as students' resistance.

THE PROBLEM OF PERSUASIVE AUTHORITY

As important as all this critical reflection may be for teaching, it still did not lead me closer to the students' understandings of these educational situations and the assumptions they encounter in writing courses like mine. Carol Severino (1997) summed up the critical teachers' ethical dilemma when teaching the first-year composition class:

> Is the purpose of a composition course to help students fit into the society or to convince them to change it? Should composition be a professional course that facilitates survival in academic or corporate communities—an instrumentalist

approach that fosters "cultural reproduction?" Or should it be a cultural studies course that teaches critical skills and crucial facts necessary for political activism in an age of "information overload and ethical burnout." (p. 74).

Severino's dichotomy between service and critical intervention captures the moral crux for teachers who primarily work with nonmainstream students, as Shor and Sternglass do. Victor Villanueva (1993) asserts that teachers who develop curriculum from Friere's philosophy have an ethical obligation to teach the dominant traditions that promote mainstream success—but with a critical emphasis. Analyzing the resistance of African-American teens to a critical liberatory agenda in an alternative high school, Villaneuva argues the teacher's efforts to foster critical intellectuals from the 'hood were not effective because it did not take seriously the individuals' perceived desire for freedom. For the learning to be critically meaningful, Villanueva contends by way of Friere's philosophy and practice, teachers must make the participants' individual dreams of freedom part of the educational process along with addressing social, political, and economic concerns of the particular community. As Villaneuva put it, these kids with so much at stake "were not in school to have their dreams destroyed" (p. 61).

In this respect, the question of the critical teacher's moral obligation is a moot point. For Severino's dichotomy of offering service or critique assumes that teachers always have the persuasive authority to convince different students the course is about getting into the system or dismantling it. As Gesa Kirsch and Peter Mortensen (1993) pointed out, students judge teachers on both their authority of office and authority of person. In Bakhtin's terms, the institution and its conventions endow the teacher with authoritative discourse. Yet how internally persuasive the teacher's discourses are depends on how individual students read the teacher's ethos. In these examples from my teaching, the students clearly did not grant me this persuasive authority of person in the ways I had intended. Moreover, because of their different social positioning with me, the university, and other students, their rejection of my critical authority took different forms. In contrast, Severino's dichotomy suggests that the meaning of the social critique will be interpreted the same way by all students. Instead, as I have shown here, the teacher has to be concerned with what all of the subject positions of different students might mean rather than trying to figure out the master strategy, an ur-persuasion if you will, that can work in all situations. That concern is the work of this book.

The chapters that chronicle my ethnographic research with the students at UIC focus on the perils of teaching critical writing. The UIC students critique some of our key critical theories. As my response to these perils, the two pedagogy chapters emphasize the promise of internally motivated writing with students at Wright State. Clearly I have only chosen to examine some of the students' strongest critical writing in the pedagogy chapters—the writings that have helped me learn how to teach better. Similarly, in my classes I now only bring in strong models of former students' writing for all of us to learn from. I have come to see the practice of using "bad" student writing in my classes as an insult to the students, and within these pages I am not about to dismiss that respect for the students' work.

I believe that both the ethnography and pedagogy chapters are necessary for the development of critically reflective teaching. Together they show the students' situations as both local and systemic, and they demonstrate the experiences and questioning that led to my current teaching approaches. In terms of structure, the ethnography chapters first define and generally historicize the term I foreground from critical pedagogy and composition studies before situating it in the students' perspectives and social motives. The pedagogy chapters first offer a critical rationale for the approach as a response to the problems raised by the ethnography chapters, then reflect on the processes of the teaching approach, discuss models of students' work, and briefly address problems encountered in the teaching.

In chapter 2, "Class Contexts," I briefly describe and analyze the institutional, historical, and material contexts of the UIC. I then define the UIC students in terms of socioeconomic situations and their various orientations toward school, work, and "critical literacy." I articulate why I use the terms *working class, minority,* and *immigrant* as critical tools to analyze the attitudes expressed and discourses employed by my key participants. I then address how and why I chose Rashmi Varma's class for my study, delineating her aims for the course and general classroom practices. Finally, I describe the complications of my participant-observer role and profile the key student participants in my study.

Chapter 3, "Reconsidering Instrumentalist Motives," and the one that follows it look closely at four students' local meanings of work and education in comparison to general critiques of instrumental thinking in students' approaches to the social structures of American education. To do so, I first define instrumentalist thinking as both a technical rationality and communicative practice. For UIC students who take an instrumental view of their education, economic necessity clearly influenced a practical vocationalism. For some working-class and minority students, like Mike and Peter, respectively, they may also take this approach to distance themselves from the social capital of mainstream education and certain forms of an institutional identity.

Chapter 4, "Immigrants and Instrumentalism," highlights the sharp contrast between critical teachers' expectations and educational anthropologists' studies of immigrant groups' instrumentalist strategies for achievement in school despite the racism these groups often encounter. I then show how this framework can apply to Min Wei and Gita, two rather different immigrant students from Rashmi's class, and reflect on what they taught me over the course of our interviews.

In chapter 5, "Making Work Visible," I offer my pedagogical response to some of the issues raised in the chapters on instrumentalist motives. The participants in my research at UIC repeatedly taught me they could articulate complex understandings of their local cultural and material situations that underlay their common sayings about work. I designed the work memoir project for Wright State students to aid their articulation of this complexity and validity embedded in their conventional language about work. This chapter lays out the process of the work memoir project and reflects on several students' writings on their prevailing cultural theme of control in the tensions among work, family, and social identity.

Chapter 6, "Social Meanings of Difference," returns to my ethnography at UIC to compare critical writing teachers' "politics of difference" to two respective cultural values in students from Rashmi's class: the individual and unity. First, I show how Mike's and Diana's understandings of individualism reveal complex issues of working-class solidarity and resentment, rather than the general manipulations of mass culture as critical teachers might assume. Using other studies of working-class students, I suggest how this resentment of identity politics emerges from a working-class ethic of solidarity in contrast to middle-class ways of seeking individual status and prestige. In contrast to Diana and Mike, Lilia and Shianta articulated deep understandings of racism toward their communities and sexism within them, yet both argued for a religious message of racial or interracial unity that thoughtfully challenges postmodern critiques of unity.

Chapter 7, "Reconsidering Resistance," identifies the difficulty teachers and researchers may have in correctly discerning resistance in students' responses to critical writing pedagogy. I reinterpret my understandings of particular moments with Shianta, Diana, Peter, and Gita by considering factors of their material situations and their rhetorical strategies not addressed in previous chapters. I then analyze the microdynamics of Mike's positions in the writing for his final paper to show that, although the teacher may perceive resistance from the student, the student may believe he or she is meeting the teacher's expectations in a way that also engages his or her own concerns. Indeed in some instances, students' responses and strategies may not wholly be a case of accommodation, opposition, resistance, or simply a negotiation of positions, but instead a fluctuating interchange of these responses and cultural interpretations depending on the immediate circumstances and contingencies of the rhetorical situations.

Chapter 8, "Social Affirmation Alongside Social Critique," offers my pedagogical response to the issues raised in the previous two ethnographic chapters. I argue how students' ethnographic research can offer a more persuasive version of cultural studies' aims in teaching. Unlike cultural studies' approaches that expect students to apply critical theories to their experiences, ethnographic research encourages an affirmation of students' local situations and understanding, which often motivates students toward a more internally persuasive social critique of local cultural groups and their larger contexts. Using examples from ethnographic projects of Wright State students, I outline some of the process I teach for students' ethnographic projects. From my theorizing of this pedagogy, I show how we need to see the ethnographic habit of mind as critical literacy for life-long learning, which may hold more internally persuasive critical use value in students' future lives than the claims many critical writing teachers make for more text-based critical analysis.

Finally, in my afterword, "Who Should Be Building the Theory?", I demonstrate how the ethnographic methodology's emphasis on inductive theorizing also helps discipline me as a teacher to remain continually attentive to the complexity of varying local situations in the students' projects and in our classroom learning. I then briefly show how several other teacher-scholars have designed courses that encourage inductive theorizing, but do not call on ethnographic methods of inquiry. Ultimately this teaching approach of inductive theorizing, and particularly the humility I have found that the ethnographic frame of mind fosters, must become more of a philosophy, rather than a technique to necessitate continual rethinking of critical questions that may foster students' internally persuasive learning.

NOTES

1. In chapter 2, I elaborate on a definition of *nonmainstream students* to better historically situate the lives of many students at UIC. For now I would claim that both Shor and Sternglass would agree that nonmainstream students are those on the margins of mainstream opportunities for middle-class education and employment.
2. Unlike most composition scholars who have drawn theory maps, I do not intend this map to claim an evolution toward a more advanced pedagogy. I agree with Elizabeth Rand (2001) that critical pedagogy is indeed a faith—a belief that often takes on religious overtones. I draw this map, then, to help us understand the different denominations we have ascribed to and to consider from what pews we are preaching from. I also mean to broaden the definitions of what can count as teaching critical writing, particularly in terms of what practices may be most ethical given students' positions of social class.
3. To be fair, Giroux and Shor have always recognized the intersections of other subject positions, such as race and gender, with the opressions of social class. Giroux (1991) also adopts a postmodern stance in his later writing's borrowing of the critical term borders. In general, however, the pedaogies of Giroux, Shor, and Friere maintain a greater sense of unified purpose than postmodern composition teachers.
4. With marvelous acuity, Amy Lee (2000) analyzes the rhetoric of Giroux's and McLaren's dismissal of Ellsworth's critique of critical pedagogy. Ironically sounding like high modernists, Giroux and McLaren refute Ellsworth on the grounds of the "tradition" of critical pedagogy, falling back on techniques of classical argumentation that attack Ellsworth instead of unpacking the issues she raises. McLaren further claims Ellsworth operated in "bad faith" (the religious metaphor revealing the dangers of the arrogant believer) and "self-doubt" (a contradictory view given the goal of critical pedagogy is critical reflection).
5. In 1998, the opportunity for nonmainstream students to attend the CUNY colleges was, and still is, in serious jeopardy as the republican-run city and state government voted to eliminate all remedial education at the city colleges. This move may force many underprepared, but very capable, students into the city community college system, which is already overworked and understaffed. At moments like these, the finer theoretical points of critical pedagogy do indeed seem the privilege of middle-class intellectuals. As Bertolt Brecht said, "first feed the face, then tell right from wrong."
6. Because these readings came from the anthology, *Rereading America*, the most popular text for first-year critical writing courses at the time, I would consider my teaching approaches to the class fairly representative of many other critical writing teachers.

7. All the names of students from UIC and Wright State are pseudonyms to ensure their anonymity and eliminate the repetition of several students' names that would hinder readability and a clear set of stories for the reader.

8. In chapter 3, however, I examine how Mike and Peter, two students in my study, operate from these assumptions to distance themselves from some aspects of mainstream identity, contrary to Foley's categorical position.

9. In chapter 2, I explain more fully how I use the term ethos in relation to social class to describe and analyze the situations and positions of the students in this study.

10. Borrowing from education anthropologist John Ogbu, I use the terms *minority* and *immigrant* to specifically refer to students' historical and socioeconomic situations. See chapter 2 for specific definitions of these terms.

11. The first assignment and group of readings implicitly asked students to explore issues of Americanization by comparing their family's expectations to various influences on their lives in the United States, such as different friends, media, school, and possibly church. At its most successful, the assignment led students to reexamine the benefits and problems of American values and roles through the lens of their own cultural values and vice versa, often refracted through gender and social class. From there the class examined ways they speak and write in different contexts and how they shape different selves in their identity. After they had inquired into their individual histories, they wrote a dialogue on what makes up a national American identity, cutting and pasting from different writers in the readings. The course ended with the cultural interpretation of oral storytelling, where students recorded, rewrote, and contextualized an oral tale passed on in their families or community.

2

Class Contexts

READING THE CONCRETE

On a bad day of cold Chicago weather in the early 1990s, the main buildings of the UIC campus, with their massive concrete slabs, sheer face brick, and dark windows, would loom over the small scale of people scurrying about on the cement and asphalt below. Students and faculty alike had difficulty distinguishing each classroom building from the myriad clumps of gray concrete rectangular boxes, each with equally nondescriptive concrete signs outside their door. Across the street from the subway entrance to the campus, University Hall housed most of the administration and all humanities faculty. As a series of perforated boxes piled on top of each other with only gothic slit windows for natural light inside, it rose up 28 stories. By the last eight floors or so, the building grew larger as it ascended to the university's administrative seat of power on its final three floors, despite the original campus design's claims of egalitarianism befitting urban education. The main Science and Engineering building on the opposite end of the central campus, and to lesser degrees the student center and library that flanked the other two sides of the space, repeated this imposing scale on a horizontal axis. The experience of navigating the institutional hallways in these build-

ings was often a series of wrong turns and false starts in a geo-
metric maze.

The leftist English graduate students used to joke that UIC
undergrads didn't need to read Foucault to understand discipline
and punishment. When students criticized the campus design,
they most often described it as a factory or prison, invoking two
possible fates some of them sought to escape. Students' discussions of the campus architecture easily demonstrated their
understandings of the systemic exercise of power on their education.[1] In the first section of this chapter, I examine the various
dynamics of historical, architectural, and socioeconomic contexts
that helped shape the interactions between students and writing
teachers in the classrooms at UIC.

The organization of the campus buildings and space was originally structured for the "commuting student body," as its archi-
tect, Walter Netsch, put it in 1965 when the new design was
lauded for its urban form as function. Yet more than Foucault's
model of disciplining the social body, Netsch's design embodied a
late modernist version of Frederick Taylor's ideas of capitalist efficiency as applied to urban planning. For Netsch looked to prevailing social theories of urban renewal in the "Great Society" of
the early 1960s, as well as styles of late modernism to manage
the "problems of urban education" with results that remind many
UIC students of their working-class status wherever they turn.
Instead of a place for lingering over critical conversations, the
"hard architecture," drawn from the brutalist school of urban
buildings, figures students' time on campus as a job.

Netsch designed the campus in terms of systematized functions, so lecture buildings, classroom buildings, labs, and
administration were all built as separate entities, rather than
groupings of academic disciplines. Drawing more from an industrial or corporate model than the traditional German model of the
modern research university, the university and its architects
sought the most efficient means to channel the largest population of students ever anticipated on an urban campus through
"the system."[2] Because the budget could not afford to replicate a
traditional campus, the modernist logic of "totality" demanded a
hard-line aesthetic of abstract form throughout the choice of
building materials and the mapping of space. Art critic Robert
Sommer (1988) argues the hard architecture of public spaces in
the 1950s and early 1960s was "designed to be strong and resis-
tant to human imprint" frequently employed to "cover up a desire
to maintain order, discipline, or control" (pp. 230–231). In effect,
the material structure of the UIC campus built in 1965 implied a

paternalist assumption that these predominantly urban working-class students would want the scene of their education to repro-duce the harsher sides of city life, rather than hope for a retreat from their commuter worlds. The architects' design made little effort to give the appearance of the privileges of time and space that residential colleges sell.

Whereas the architecture of UIC suggested paternalism toward its urban working class students, the history of the cam-pus' creation also reveals the university's ambivalences and con-tradictions toward the nearby communities whose sons and daughters attend the school. The construction of the UIC campus in the early 1960s, along with the development of the city's expressways that encircle it, clearly speeded the disintegration of the neighborhoods in the Near Westside area of Chicago (see Rosen, 1980; Royko, 1971; Severino, 1996; Terkel, 1967). Yet even community and business leaders from the earlier genera-tions of European immigrants in the area knew that change was inevitable.

Since the 1870s, Italians and Greeks dominated this neigh-borhood, bordered by Harrison and Halsted streets until the 1940s. After World War II, however, many of these earlier European immigrants moved into public housing, were pushed out by the construction of the expressways, or moved up and out to more prosperous neighborhoods and suburbs. From the 1940s on, African Americans, Mexicans, and Puerto Ricans moved into many of the residences of the earlier immigrants. In the early 1950s, the local neighborhoods' business and community leaders organized the interracial Near Westside Planning Board to seek ways to revitalize the area. By the late 1950s, they had procured the approval of federal urban renewal funds to redevelop the Halsted-Harrison area as a moderate-income housing and com-mercial district.

Around the same time, the University of Illinois sought a loca-tion for a permanent Chicago area campus to replace the two-year undergraduate college at Chicago's Navy Pier that had grown out of the GI bill and postwar prosperity. Initially, the university sought a more suburban location because they assumed the campus would cater more to suburban (and, for the time period, consequently White) commuters at the expense of urban students less likely to have their own transportation. When the university shifted its search to possible sites within the city, Mayor Daley's office took the initiative to push for the Harrison-Halsted area already set for demolition and reconstruction funded by federal urban renewal funds.

    The rhetoric of the early Daley administration favored pre-
serving Chicago's "neighborhood character." Yet when Daley and
the University of Illinois sealed the deal for the Near Westside
campus, sweetened by the urban renewal funds originally intended for community reconstruction, they shut out representatives
in these communities from the decision-making process. The
Harrison-Halsted area was also the home of the Hull House organization, founded first as a settlement house by Jane Addams
and other philanthropists in the late 19th century to help out the
first wave of immigrants. By the late 1950s, however, business
leaders from other areas of Chicago now made up the Hull House
board, and they favored a decentralization of Hull House facilities
across Chicago, aided by selling the land to the university. When
the city unilaterally cut the deal with the university, community
residents led by community activist Florence Scala and women of
White, Latino, and African-American backgrounds organized a
campaign of protest that lasted a year before the group's legal
suit lost out in the U.S. Supreme Court.[3]
    It is debatable whether community leaders could have created
and sustained an integrated residential neighborhood with mixed
industrial and commercial uses as they hoped to do. Nevertheless,
the imposition of the university didn't foster relations between
those who stayed on in the remnants of these neighborhoods. As
Mike Royko and Studs Terkel have mentioned, long-time residents view the brick wall that encloses several sides of the campus as the university's fortress meant to keep them out.[4]
    The university's role in the razing of these communities is
emblematic of the school's continual ambivalence toward its
urban, largely immigrant, undergraduate student population. As
an institution, UIC has contesting interests: to serve the community and working-class students, as many in Chicago have argued
should be its "urban mission"; and to establish a national reputation for research. Following the logic of educating a professional
class, the institution saw the necessity of tearing asunder neighborhoods like the ones many of its students would come from so
that it could offer individual opportunity to these communities'
sons and daughters.[5] Partly to counter this contradictory history,
several departments in the university have recently promoted a
"Great Cities Initiative" through academic programs and projects
that seek more interaction with local communities. Nonetheless,
the university's simultaneous need for expansion continue to
threaten neighboring community settings. For instance, the university displaced a 120-year-old populist institution—the Maxwell

Street market, an outdoor market that catered to each new immigrant group over the century—to create a new south campus.

In the mid- to late 1990s, the university remodeled the bleakest aspects of the campus, creating a softer look that some public responses likened to an outdoor suburban mall removed from the surrounding environment of skyscrapers to the east and housing projects and deteriorated neighborhoods to the south and west. Most students would argue the changes were certainly needed to help humanize their experience. Still these architectural changes have occurred simultaneously with the university's courting of a student customer base that could afford other options. Whereas teachers and administrators used to describe UIC students as "urban," the latest university mission statement and publicity material use the term "metropolitan." Unlike the grittier "urban," the language of metropolitan students can encompass two growing student populations at UIC. More international students are choosing UIC as the institution builds its reputation in research. Simultaneously, more suburban families have turned to the cheaper education of UIC for their children when faced with rising tuition costs and a downsized economy.[6] Not surprisingly, the administration has been courting these suburban students, rather than the local Chicago students, for the prestige their better class position—evident in their academic preparation and test scores—lends to the university's changing image.

Only since the mid-1990s has the university begun to publicize its greatest strength as an individual institution—the vitality of its multicultural students. Of the appproximately 16,000 undergraduates in 1990, 40% were of Asian, Latino, or African-American origin.[7] In 1995, the year I observed Rashmi's class, these ethnic groups made up 55% of the first-year students. With these students, largely from urban backgrounds and city high schools, came a wealth of diverse experiences and perspectives in the classrooms that challenged and stimulated all the writing teachers in our program. If the UIC campus was grey, the students brought their own colors, inspiring another of UIC's nicknames among insiders: UN.U.—United Nations University. This is not to suggest that many of the students did not struggle with the university's general ambivalence toward these students' social class status, but rather to indicate the resources they brought to the struggle of their education within these complicated dynamics of history, architectural space, and social expectations.

DEFINING UIC'S STUDENTS

Historically, discussions of UIC have characterized its students
as primarily working class, the first generation in their families to
go to college, and as commuters who often must work more
hours than typical "workstudy" to financially support their education or themselves. Of the commuting majority, 60% come from
the city and another 20% from the suburbs. As indicated earlier,
more recently UIC's public relations has begun to capitalize on its
student diversity of ethnicity and race. With the growing influx of
students from the higher income middle-class suburbs and
recent immigrants whose fathers and possibly mothers have
more professional careers, the student body has diversified more
in terms of social class as well. Most students, however, are often
on a precarious boundary between the working class and lower
middle class in terms of parents' occupations and income.
According to the UIC office of financial aid, in 1996, approximately 75% of students were on some form of financial aid. Of the
7,000 students who claimed status as dependents, about 4,000
came from families whose combined incomes were below
$40,000.[8]

Although these statistics are hardly solid proof of social class
status, they do suggest that these families do not make up the
elite "professional-managerial" class "where the work is often to
define the work of others," to conceptualize and command
(Ehrenreich, 1989, p. 13). According to Barbara Ehrenreich
(1989), this group, whose economic and social status is based on
their education, makes up approximately 20% of the American
population. This is the class, traditionally associated with the
gatekeeping of higher education that most of these students and
their families aspire to economically, if not socially as well. Some
of these parents of UIC students might work in traditionally
working-class jobs or trades that provide an income similar to the
middle-class bracket of professional white-collar work. Yet the
massive loss of well-paying, often unionized, blue-collar jobs due
to corporations' deindustrialization and capital flight has greatly
reduced these opportunities (Weis, 1990).

The majority of UIC first-year students tends to be the traditional age for college, averaging 18 and a half and ranking in the
top 25% of their graduating high school class. Yet the data, and
all the stories UIC composition teachers hear from students and
read in their papers, show that their nontraditional class and/or
ethnic backgrounds often prevent them from graduating from col-

lege in the more traditional timespan of four years. Although these students indicate plans to graduate in four or five years, retention studies show that most students who complete degrees at UIC take at least six years to do so.[9] For most of these students, simple economics is what keeps them from reaching the goal in the time they had originally planned. According to UIC Data Resources, the average number of work hours for first-year students in 1996 is 15 to 20 hours, but by junior and senior year that average rises to 25 to 30 hours per week. One in every five first-year students will leave the school to be readmitted at a later date while others leave for one or more terms to work full time to pay for finishing their degrees. Many UIC students also go through a painful process of switching majors, often because there is no one in the family with college experience to guide their decisions.

Although several of the students I talked with in Rashmi's class had been or were still deeply involved with various nonacademic organized groups, none of the people whom I directly asked about their school experiences referred to any extracurricular activities, good or bad, that took place within the institutional boundaries of their elementary or secondary schools. These circumstances may again be due to their need to work from an early age or because their local cultures valorize the merits of work over organized school or club activities as in many working-class neighborhoods. Yet for many immigrant students, the bonds to their cultural communities and families may hold greater sway over their time outside school. Moreover, these kinds of curricular and extracurricular activities are often more available in middle- and upper class neighborhoods and suburbs. In contrast to this lack of extracurricular involvement, Shirley Brice Heath (1983) characterized the mainstream townspeople in her famous study in the Piedmont Carolinas by their strong socialization to "success in formal institutions and looking beyond the primary networks of family and community" (p. 392).

So given these UIC students' socioeconomic and cultural situations, I define the majority of their backgrounds as *nonmainstream* as one way to understand the positions they take, or conceal, in a critical writing course and the larger university institution. Yet by virtue of their presence in college, these students and their families have also invested, to varying degrees, in mainstream middle-class values of achievement. So the term *nonmainstream* mostly serves to distinguish these students from the dominant White middle-class frame of reference in higher education. However, the term *nonmainstream* does not identify the diversity of the students' perspectives, nor can it help us examine how their socioeconomic situations influence their varied orientations toward school, work, and "critical literacy" as they played out during and after Rashmi's course. Consequently, I use the terms *working class*, *minority*, and *immigrant* throughout this book as critical tools to help analyze the attitudes expressed and discourses employed by my featured participants.

Identifying individuals and small groups by such a broad factor as social class is clearly a complicated business. Socioeconomic groups in late capitalist societies structure class position and status by occupation, income, education, or social practices. Most people remain in their social class because of inequitable reproduction of material and symbolic resources that maintain the truly wealthy. But for the purposes of this book, I simplify these class markers in two ways—first, by income, and second, by the rhetorical term *ethos*, used to refer to roles, values, and behaviors as they make up the various personas one presents to others in multiple contexts (see Goffman, 1973). People can maintain a working-class ethos even as they gain mobility through an income categorized in economic terms as middle class or higher (see Bourdieu, 1984)—just remember comedian Rosanne Barr's working-class image. Similarly, individuals from an economically middle-class background may, to some degree, choose occupations and lifestyles that place them below a middle-class income bracket—as many adjunct teachers choose to work within an increasingly exploitative system. Yet from the perspective of the working class who may not have the economic privilege to choose a lifestyle, this choice is still a middle-class rejection of its own affluence and visible socioeconomic power—as many working-class families viewed the middle-class counterculture of the 1960s and 1970s (Ehrenreich, p. 132). From another view, the parents of many Asian immigrant students have had to take on working-class occupations and incomes in the United States despite their professional backgrounds from their native countries.

As already indicated, these students do not easily fit into a model of pure working class. Like many Americans, most of them identify themselves and/or their backgrounds as middle class, choosing to side with upward mobility. I am not trying to pin them down to a working-class identity or argue that social class determines their ways of knowing, but rather that it can influence their thinking and writing in response to a specific critical writing agenda. I assert that it may often be aspects of an unspoken working-class ethos (shaped also by region, gender, race, and other identity formations) that more middle-class critical writing teachers may misinterpret in these students' discourses and motives.

Although several of the students of color from Rashmi's class were from families with more working-class occupations and incomes, their different feelings of racial identity obviously shaped their orientations toward their situations of social class. Some of the White students I later interviewed identified themselves strongly with their ethnic origins, as in Irish or Greek, but they did not perceive institutions or individuals limiting their opportunities because of their self-proclaimed ethnicity. As Stanley Aronowitz (1992) contends, ". . . while race invariably signifies exclusion, ethnicity signifies subculture. Ethnicity may contain presumptions of structured class inequity, but not a problematic nationality" (p. 53). For this reason, my use of the phrase *working class* in this book primarily refers to influences of various White working-class values and roles. Because different students of color in Rashmi's class were situated in and spoke from different class positions, I find useful John Ogbu's (1987) distinction between involuntary and voluntary minorities. As Ogbu does hereafter, I refer to these two respective categories as *minority* and *immigrant*. In an effort to explain why some minority groups fare better in the educational system despite similar problems with nonmainstream languages and cultures, Ogbu's ethnographic research posits that the crucial difference is sociohistorical. Voluntary immigrants are those cultural groups that have chosen to immigrate to the host country, the classic case being Asian immigrants to the United States. Because they have made the choice to immigrate, Ogbu argues that these groups often accommodate to the implicit demands of dominant society despite the prejudices and socioeconomic discriminations they may encounter. In contrast, Ogbu contends that minority groups situated in caste positions in the dominant culture, such as African Americans and Chicanos in America, have been historically subordinated by the host country through slavery, conquest, or colonization. When these groups encounter or perceive institutional boundaries to upward mobility, they may generate various collective forms of resistance to mainstream achievement.

Among several important corrections to Ogbu's typology (see Gibson, 1997), other anthropologists of education have shown how Ogbu's perspective tends to posit race as a monolithic determinant of opposition or accommodation to the dominant mainstream. Even in the small group of students I write about from Rashmi's class, individuals in each racial or ethnic group had significant variations of social class backgrounds, gender roles, and generational differences that I argue influenced their responses to assumptions of critical pedagogy. As becomes clear in the following chapters, often the students' attitudes complicated the cultural and socioeconomic models that originate from Ogbu's work. Yet the common assumptions in these minority and immigrant communities that Ogbu's models attempt to explain still affected the ways these students thought and wrote about the issues they perceived in Rashmi's class.

RASHMI VARMA AND ENGLISH 102

In the fall of 1994, I sent out a letter to 11 teachers in the UIC writing program whose critical assumptions toward teaching resembled the range of critical pedagogies I mapped out in the previous chapter. In the letter, I contrasted these assumptions to the students we all taught, stating "for some students (primarily African American and Latino) their ways of reading and writing can conflict with and challenge our critical assumptions of multiple perspectives, representation, and construction of the self (to name a few)." I was hoping to strike a chord with other teachers that would interest them to collaborate in my research. Only one other teacher besides Rashmi wasn't White, and Rashmi was the only one from another country. Like myself, Rashmi identified more with a middle-class background, albeit in the city life of Delhi, India, compared to many of the graduate students from working-class backgrounds who were in the department in the late 1980s and early 1990s. A year after my observing Rashmi's class when she and I were writing a proposal for a panel presentation at the Conference on College Composition and Communication, another friend suggested that I tell Rashmi about the "scholars for the dream" scholarship for "minority graduate students." After a semester of discussing teaching issues with Rashmi, I was pretty certain she would not identify with this offer. "I'm not a minority," she informed me when I brought up the scholarship. By this statement, I believe she was calling attention to her class privileges and the inappropriateness of comparing her historical situation to oppressed racial groups in America. Several times in the class she had complicated students' expectations of what socioeconomic groups from the course readings she would identify with. Challenging common presumptions of color and social class, she would argue that sometimes she may find more commonality with the lived experiences of a college-educated middle-class White male than with those of poor minorities.

I asked Rashimi whether she was interested in my project after I read a description of her "research paper" course she was planning to teach:

> *In Our Own Words: Women in the Third World*
>
> This course will be an attempt to gain an historical and theoretical understanding of women in the Third World by looking at ways in which Third World Women have spoken of their own lives and experiences. Historically, women from the Third World have been denied the power and space for self-expression. We shall attempt to seek out *their* voices in contrast to the voices that speak up *for* them. We shall study women's writings and activism as ways in which women represent themselves. There will be a required reading list and films for the first half of the course. In the second half of the course, students will pursue an independent research project related to the course. Two short papers, a long research paper, and class presentations will be the main requirements. (Rashmi's emphasis)[10]

Up to this point, I hadn't had much personal contact with Rashmi, but knew her more for her high reputation as a literature graduate student in the department and for her maintenance of an interdisciplinary postcolonial study group attended by faculty as well as other graduate students. Ironically, Rashmi described her interest in the project through metaphors from ethnography. As a young Indian woman teaching at an American university, she thought of herself "as an outsider in American culture sharing with the ethnographer the sense of being a participant observer" (Varma & Seitz, 1995). She later claimed that many ethnographers of education assume the teacher's voice is one of mainstream authority. It was this sense of being outside mainstream America while holding the teacher's position of authority that she wanted to explore through my participant-observation in her class. "I looked to this project as a way in which I could more directly confront my own assumptions of being a teacher/outsider in the culture of the American university and the larger national culture." So for both of us, the prospects of this research gave us new vantage points to examine how various UIC students may read us as teachers.

Rashmi's class emphasized the politics of representation for women in various situations in Third World countries. The course was also offered in conjunction with a Women's Studies class on women and the Third World for which a few of Rashmi's students enrolled. The women's studies course was structured by geographical region: "If it's week 3, this must be West Africa." Rashmi consciously rejected this structure, arguing to me that it severs the interconnected issues of postcolonialism, global capitalism, and the commonalities of women's struggles. Instead she organized the course thematically by issues such as labor abuses, environment and women's bodies, sexuality and exploitation, nationalism, and activism.

Rashmi's approach to syllabus design was an interventionist strategy that contested American students' general perception of the Third World from the popular news media as geographically isolated incidences of crisis. One of Rashmi's aims for the course was to "somehow directly implicate the students and [herself] in the dynamics through which we produce the Third World woman" as a category of distanced "other" (Varma & Seitz, 1995). In this respect, she wanted the students to become more aware of the politics of their research methods as well as the ideological positions of the readings.

Rashmi described her syllabus to me as a model of her aims for the course—how she wanted to encourage in the students a "more dynamic understanding of what reading and writing research is about." In her syllabus, she saw an overarching theme of investigating world development and labor in Third World situations. In a similar way, she wanted the students "to learn how to generate research within a particular context and examine how it could be viewed in different ways." To this end, the syllabus and evaluative criteria valued complicating these interconnected issues, rather than simplifying them. "I want to force students to think about interconnections, to show them research is not isolated, not a topic in itself. I want them to see how the issues relate to who you are, and how you are implicated, not strictly along gender and race lines, but different global systems within which they are located." At several points, Rashmi told me her strategy was to direct students to the social contradictions embedded in their discourses, such as when a student's paper periodically points to local problems of exploited labor in a given country despite her strong beliefs in the merits of globalization. By pointing out these contradictions, Rashmi hoped to make her students examine local problems in relation to systemic power relations. Virginia Anderson (1997) sees this rooting out of social contradictions as a "tenet central to critical teaching" (p. 207). Criticizing James Berlin's (1996) *Rhetorics, Poetics, and Cultures*, she pointed out that the search for contradictions "is one of the few things Berlin implements by fiat [. . .] Students are admitted into the cadre of productive agents for democracy only if they agree to 'negotiate' or 'resist' prevailing truths. Affirming prevailing views, in fact, is not even an act; it is the passive acquiescence of the willing victim." Although Rashmi's teaching practices were considerably more flexible than Anderson's view of Berlin in her article, later chapters in this study do address Rashmi's students' spoken and tacit responses to this core of critical teaching. Rashmi never explicitly indicated that students taking up political activism should be the response to critical exploration of social contradictions. But she embedded her concern for this goal in the syllabus and sometimes in individual advice to students about developing their papers partly as a way to counter their sense of powerlessness when examining these troubling global issues.

Rashmi's evaluation of students' written work also favored this investigation of social contradictions. In general, Rashmi organized her grading criteria in hierarchical order of complexity of critical positions, organization of arguments, and ability to incorporate academic discourse conventions. I base this hierarchy on her pattern of grading and comments on student papers. Papers that explored complex interrelationships of issues, facts, and social positions, regardless of the student's political leanings, yet lacked a full coherence and articulation of their views tended to fare better in grades than those written more clearly with better organization at the expense of simplifying the issue's situations. The former might receive a low "B," whereas the latter a high "C." By describing these criteria, I do not intend to judge Rashmi's priorities for the class. In fact I found they resembled my own habits of reading and evaluating most genres of academic papers as well as the shop talk of many colleagues. Of course these priorities and language for evaluation were not reflected in several of my student participants' appraisals of their college writing, as the following chapters discuss.

In short, I presumed the content of Rashmi's course and her critical teaching agenda would present several ideological challenges to the students enrolled in the class. At the same time, however, Rashmi's ethnicity and Indian nationality lent her persuasive authority with the majority of women students of color. It is debatable, however, whether Rashmi's persuasive authority was of a more personal nature than her pedagogy of systemic critiques for which she argued. I originally intended to work with a White teacher, assuming I would observe similar issues of teacher–student identities I had encountered in my own classes. In comparison to those writing classes with White teachers, there were only isolated racial and ethnic tensions between student and teacher in Rashmi's class, which I address in later chapters.

To most of her students, Rashmi, who almost always wore casual Western style clothing and spoke with a touch of "received pronunciation," was hardly an "exotic." Even so Rashmi's small nose ring and occasional wearing of Indian-style skirts with ankle bracelets, along with her often formal manner of speech, may have implicitly alerted some of the working-class students to their class difference from her. Most of the class referred to her as a student like themselves, due in part to her younger age compared with teachers in other departments. Nor did Rashmi's teaching methods stray too far from the students' expectations and educational histories. Admittedly drawing from her traditional education in India, she mainly organized the course around whole-class discussion, although sometimes incorporating a "rotating chair" to mitigate her authority in the turn-taking process of talk. The students only met in peer groups three or four times, and they all wrote individually throughout the term.

My research relationship with Rashmi, however, was more collaborative than my situation with the student participants. During the term of her course, we met several times to discuss her views of particular students and the shifting classroom dynamics, and I asked for her viewpoint whenever possible. Before I even knew that Rashmi would be interested in my project, I was alerted to the epistemological dangers of the narrative I was already composing with my research questions. Another teacher whom I had asked early on to participate in the project responded with suspicion underneath her interest: "I don't want my teaching to be your problem." She had already correctly surmised that my project could frame the observed teacher as some kind of villain or dupe to build a stronger story about some of the students. Thomas Newkirk (1996) argues that researchers in education should be up front about the likelihood of reporting "bad news" of the teacher's practices. Rashmi was already savvy to these politics and from the beginning viewed our relationship as a friendly "mutual interrogation."

While I fumbled to build rapport with particular students, Rashmi assumed I was attuned to her students in ways totally unavailable to her. Much later she wrote to me by e-mail: "Funny, I was often filtering events in class through your consciousness (which I was constructing constantly), what I thought your impressions were, and when occasionally you told me what students were talking about, and thinking. Now I realize you were an ethnographer, not an evaluator, but I found it impossible at times to separate the two." Although she found this hyperawareness produced both positive and negative effects for her, on the positive side she feels it helped her realize "how different the outside worlds of these students were." I was surprised by this statement as I often observed her consideration toward the students' outside worlds as she endeavored to integrate them into the issues of the course whenever applicable and ethical. During the term, I often felt she knew more about the students' outside lives than I had learned from them. It appears in the end we each overestimated the other's power.

ENTERING THE CLASS

Rashmi's class met in a windowless room with institutionally gray brick, concrete walls, and oddly shaped sharp angles on Tuesday/Thursday from 9:30 to 10:45, beginning in the dead of January 1995. The students' racial backgrounds were roughly equal thirds African American, Asian of different nationalities and generations (first and second generation), and White of working-class heritage. Out of 22 students, 5 were men. In terms of gender, the class configuration offered a women's "safe house" from the male discourses dominant in other institutional and social spaces of UIC. Mary Louise Pratt (1991) defines *safe houses* as "social and intellectual spaces where groups can constitute themselves as horizontal homogenous, sovereign communities with high degrees of trust, shared understandings, and temporary protection from legacies of oppression" (p. 40). In the case of Rashmi's class, students often expressed differences of opinion, as with issues of global capitalism and the fairness of women's labor (which I describe further in the following chapter), yet they shared a context of women's lived experiences in a variety of male-dominated cultures.[11] Two pregnancies and births during the class term also helped extend these shared contexts, with much well wishing and the signing of cards. Nevertheless, many students simultaneously grouped themselves in class seating by ethnicity, tacitly creating microsafe houses within a multicultural class.

As interesting as these discursive dynamics are, though, I have situated the classroom talk in the background of my study to foreground other domains of particular students' lives that relate to, or conflict with, their responses to the course and assumptions of critical teaching. The more I heard participants express views that contradicted, in different ways, values professed in class, the more necessary it became to view the classroom as only a small part of the picture. In this sense, I am giving the classroom the same amount of attention most of my key participants do.

In the first week and a half of the term, most of the class sat around a conglomerate of several large gray tables that the building maintenance people had pushed together. I first noticed that several students who had not chosen the course were the ones reluctant to come to the table, in particular two men, preferring to remain on the periphery. By the end of the second week, someone had taken away all the tables with no explanations. In comparison to this particular classroom situation, most rooms in other classroom buildings at UIC had the students' seats bolted to the floor in rows, frustrating several composition teachers' efforts to create a less authoritarian ethos for themselves in the eyes of their students. After the tables were mysteriously taken away, Rashmi insisted on everyone making a large circle, sometimes with mixed results, for the rest of the semester. Drawing from her experiences in Women's Studies classes, Rashmi argued, "the way we sit often determines what discussion there is and who participates." Yet the students never arranged the chairs together in a circle as a whole group before Rashmi came in. Occasionally a few early arrivers would begin the process, but the rest never enthusiastically followed it up. In this sense, the circle ironically remained a symbol of academic space and time that the majority of individuals would not acknowledge until they had to. Although Rashmi pushed for a circle, the shape was often more of a horseshoe, with everyone's chairs bordering the walls and Rashmi isolated in the middle or fourth side.

THE LONELY RESEARCHER

Patricia and Peter Adler (1987) argue that qualitative researchers need to establish some form of membership role within the group if they want to understand the world from a group's insider's perspective. In the first week of Rashmi's class, I briefly described myself to students as "kind of like an anthropologist studying the culture that develops in the class." I had presumed that if I portrayed myself as "class researcher," the majority of students would accept and assimilate this role into the class as a whole.[12] Only now do I realize how much I entered the room as another academic, instead of seeking a less institutional role, such as a reporter.

When the class mostly ignored my efforts to assume this public identity, their silence taught me much about their situations in UIC classrooms, as I discuss later. I also assumed I might play a variety of roles with those students who agreed to talk at length with me—possibly tutor, confidante, or reporter, which in some cases I eventually did (I discuss issues of reciprocity with the participants further in Appendix C: Interviewing). Yet when I sought conversation with different students during the first half of the term, I often felt that I was ignored or politely tolerated. The few students who addressed me in the first weeks, all of them White, presumed I was some kind of experimental psychologist. Often in vain I tried to explain the differences between ethnography and experimental research, suggesting that Rashmi's course would be examining these different ways of writing about people. Yet their more clinical image may have fit their schema of academics more clearly because of previous experience as a "test subject," an often inevitable position for the student enrolled in "intro psych." The role they assumed for me suggests that they expected to be a scientific object of study, rather than engage in the dialogue I had hoped for. The majority of students of color withheld comment for the first weeks; none of them spoke to me until I approached them. In part, Rashmi's preference for whole-class discussions over small-group work also made it much more difficult to establish rapport with individual class members.

My institution had indirectly sanctioned my role as researcher, but, not surprisingly, I never felt class members valued that role or imagined it had any connection to their classroom experience. Similarly, I had incorrectly assumed that students would be more willing to talk freely with me because I was not their teacher. I thought because I would have no power over the students' grades, I would have more rapport with these students than those in my own classes. Instead I had less. Some of my field notes read like the lonely kid endlessly hoping someone else in class will become a friend. I felt myself caught up in the fieldworker's issues of seduction and betrayal (Newkirk, 1996), which are unavoidably part of the relationship between researcher and participant. Yet experiencing this sense of isolation showed me that the students could not conveniently find—or in many cases felt no need to find—a role for me within their perceptions of the institutional boundaries between teacher and student in the classroom.

Given their constraints of work, commuting to school, and sometimes multiple family obligations, many of the students viewed their time on campus as investments. Because they had nothing directly invested in me, as they did with Rashmi or other classmates, they generally were not interested in representing themselves to me. Over the course of the term, however, I did gain some students' general interest in my project by repeatedly expressing great interest in them as people. When I did meet for interviews with the students featured in this book, most enjoyed my presence as an avid listener. Some adjusted their speech and discourses based on how they placed me in the university and White mainstream America, which I address when discussing their interviews throughout the book. But generally I was a very low priority in their lives.

I had intended to participate in more extensive interviews with a broader range of students over the semester, but their overloaded schedules often limited the opportunities. Most of the extended interviews took place almost a year after Rashmi's class ended. Consequently, participants were much less likely to speak of Rashmi's course and its critical assumptions out of an immediate pressing concern. However, this lapse of time between the class and in-depth interviews enabled me to see how different people did or did not integrate ideas and values from the course into more immediate areas of their lives once the grades and institutional pressures had little to do with their responses. Only a few qualitative studies in composition have paid close attention to what students had to say about the class or program a year or more later (most notably Herrington & Curtis, 2000; Sternglass, 1997). Perhaps this is because hearing how students do or don't value this small part of their education can often be a humbling experience, as Jeff Smith (1997) rightly claims. Because critical pedagogies aim for social changes beyond the classroom or university, it is important to listen to the ways individuals think about these ideas when they are not acting as students.

THE STUDENT PARTICIPANTS

Initially I chose to follow four students in Rashmi's class who demonstrated behaviors and values that seemed to oppose or resist the critical assumptions of Rashmi's course and main premises in critical pedagogies. I made these first choices on several criteria. First, these individuals were ethnically representative of cultural groups in the class and socioeconomic categories of the working class, minorities, and voluntary immigrants I discussed earlier in this chapter. Mike, a White Irish South-Sider, came from a family of cops (as Mike would put it), a job traditionally associated with the working class in Chicago. Shianta came from Baptist traditions in Black South Side Chicago. Xiao recently came to the United States from Beijing with her husband. Lilia, a Mexican-American Latina, grew up in Logan Square, a mostly Latino neighborhood.

Second, in their thinking and writing for the class, these four students called on discourses and material situations from their backgrounds that could complicate the assumptions of critical theories in the practice of teaching. Although Mike was uncomfortable as a "minority" in this multicultural class of women, he frequently aired his views of the class topics by drawing from a White working-class sensibility. Shianta's reliance on African-American religious discourse in her first response paper had suggested possible conflicts with the coursework's critical expectations. Xiao felt a deep, but complicated need to defend Mainland China's cultural practices against what she saw as Rashmi's Indian prejudices and abuse of the teacher's role. As fascinating as Xiao's perspective was, in the end I did not write about her because I finally determined that these issues of resistance and nationalism for the international student were beyond the scope of this book. By pure chance, I found out that Lilia was involved with a Bible study group. I had been impressed with Lilia's critical articulation and use of a reading's feminist theory in her first response paper, and I wanted to know her views about separating her deeply held religious identity from her school personas in comparison to Shianta's deliberate use of religious discourse in her writing. Over the course of the term, however, Lilia went on to explicitly evoke her religious frames of reference for her critical academic positions, whereas Shianta's use of religious language and arguments became totally implicit. As I discuss in chapter 6, these two students' religious orientations complicate goals of critical pedagogy in ways that few critics, with the strong exception of Amy Goodburn (1998) and Elizabeth Rand (2001), have addressed.

As the class term progressed, I met periodically with these four students who agreed to participate more fully in my study, discussing their writing, views toward the class, and their lives with me through tape-recorded conversations and interviews. Before midterm, I decided these four participants would be the focal points for the issues of critical teaching in composition their views seemed to address for me. And so I imagined other students from the class whom I had talked with serving as background and points of comparison to these students' situations, arguments, and stories. Yet I grew more concerned that I would not be narrating and analyzing the range of responses in the class to the course's critical assumptions. Of these four participants, two—Lilia and Shianta—highly valued the course and its aims, and most of the class shared this enthusiasm at least when there weren't papers due. Still I was concerned that my main participants did not include any of the "successful" students as determined by Rashmi's grades and comments on their papers.[13] As I looked more closely at the comments from students whom I had designated as "background," I discerned valuable similarities and contrasts with the cultural themes I had already begun to sort through in my analyses.

For these reasons, I broadened the group of students I would highlight in the study. Diana, from a Greek-Orthodox background and working-class neighborhood, probably talked more than anyone in the class, earning As for all her work. Yet after meeting with Diana and Mike early that summer, I was surprised how much her views outside the term differed from her classroom talk. Gita, whose family emigrated from India when she was 6, also did well in the class, yet she had insightful criticisms of the cultural politics of English classes. By the end of several interview sessions together, I admired her as a true and articulate "informant" about student practices at UIC. Peter, from an African-American and Puerto-Rican lower middle-class family, offered perspectives that struck me as foils to Mike's White working-class affiliations. Finally, Min Wei, whose family emigrated from Hong Kong in the past 4 years and who had a complicated school friendship with Xiao, the woman from Beijing, offered further support along with Gita for issues of critical teaching and "voluntary immigrants."

Taken together, this larger group of seven students, more than a third of the class, can represent the class in at least two ways because they range across the span of student involvement in the course and academic ability and performance. Nevertheless, I did not choose these students for their typicality within the class, but because I felt their views and situations evoked some of the tensions in our critical teaching practice I think we should be reexamining.[14] In that sense, I may be misrepresenting general aspects of the class as a whole, but that is the danger of any localized qualitative research. I tried to look holistically at these students during my field research. Nonetheless, the ways I have chosen to write about them, in the contexts of specific themes across groups and individuals, clearly give a partial picture of their selves. Out of this range of participants, only Mike appears in each of the following three chapters. Ironically, Mike represents the "other" in classes emphasizing multiculturalism and socioeconomic critique. As Margaret Marshall (1997) and Jennifer Seibel Trainor (2002) eloquently point out, views of students like Mike have often been dismissed in composition studies as ideologically naïve or passed over in favor of more explicitly marginal groups. Yet over the course of the class and my later interviews, I found that Mike's views and social situation in and out of the critical writing classroom challenged assumptions of all three critical terms I emphasize in this work—*instrumentalism*, *difference*, and *resistance*.

Although I would claim these participants can represent the span of interests, academic preparation, and cultures of both Rashmi's class and UIC students, it is more difficult to generalize from their situations and perspectives to urban college students from similar backgrounds and orientations. To make this interpretive leap would be to assume that their cultures and socioeconomic situations are monolithic and not affected by local and individual contingencies (see Clifford, 1988; Crapanzano, 1986). As cultural critics since Edward Said's work on orientalism have asserted, this generalizing tends to portray the "other" culture as inert and passive compared with the dynamic agency of the researcher's readership.

Keeping this political caution in mind, the ethnographic chapters of this book continually shift from describing and analyzing my participants as individual people to viewing them in the contexts of sociocultural groups. My goal is for readers to keep both approaches in mind at the same time. The participants' sociocultural situations, individual lived experiences, and local knowledge reciprocally shape their responses to the critical writing class. In the next two chapters, I situate four of these participant students' responses to critical teachers' indictment of students' instrumentalist approaches to their education.

NOTES

1. In the late 1980s, a group of English graduate students with the assistance of David Jolliffe, then director of Composition, created a unit of readings and assignments on the UIC architecture as social issue for a composition reader at UIC (Jolliffe et al., 1988).

2. The two main features of the original campus were demolished in the remodeling of the mid-1990s. In the same manner of the expressways nearby, several immense concrete and granite upper pedestrian walkways were intended to funnel commuter students through the system of buildings and meet in a massive concrete "forum" meant to be the center of campus. Both were equally inhospitable and impractical. The rough concrete columns that held up the walkway often made the lower pathways wet, dark, and dangerous; the harsh snow or sun rendered the upper spaces uninhabitable. The walkways, designed as a "systems-oriented pedestrian communications network," were meant to accommodate a commuter lifestyle, supposedly allowing students to get anywhere on the campus within 10 minutes without having to deal with other students on the ground.

3. George Rosen's interviews with the protest leaders suggest that some of these wives' husbands were sympathetic to these protests, but were afraid to speak out because many of them were employed by the city or on the city rolls.

4. Rosen's statistical analysis contends that the campus has created an island of higher incomes and land values with a subsequent major reduction in population— a familiar process of gentrification.

5. In his study of professionalization and the waning of the public intellectual, Russel Jacoby (1987) writes, "professionalization leads to privitization or depoliticization, a withdrawal of intellectual energy from a larger domain to a narrower discipline" (p. 147, see also Ohmann, 1990). Carol Severino (1996) notes the correlation between the downsizing and eventual elimination of the more politicized and multiracial Educational Assistance Program at UIC, which sought to serve a specific "urban mission," and the rise of segregated support services organized by particular professional disciplines, such as health sciences, business, and engineering, solely for their at-risk students. Where as early in the century the Hull House organization worked to build more direct ties to these neighborhoods, UIC, like most higher education institutions, mainly offered assistance to Chicago communities in the name of research handed down by disciplined professions.

6. Despite this turn of rhetoric, the university's 1995 mission statement also openly acknowledged those students, like the ones featured in this book, who may come from backgrounds where "a university education is not a long-standing family tradition, and who must surmount economic, social, and educational barriers to

achieve academic success." Clearly this statement seeks to redress rhetorically, if not materially, the contradictory history of the institution's interactions with neighboring communities.

7. The following data on student population comes from the UIC Office of Data Resources and Institutional Analysis in Peverly (1996).

8. This figure does not include students who claimed financially independent status. Approximately 75% of these students with independent status made less than $18,000, although it is uncertain to what degrees individual students are financially separated from their parents. In comparison to these statistics from UIC, the average income for students' families who applied for financial aid at UI–Urbana, the elite state school of Illinois, is $40,000.

9. Out of a cohort of UIC students entering in 1987, 37% graduated in 6 years, whereas another 37% quit the school with poor academic standing. Loeb's (1994) study of students' difficulties in colleges nationwide suggests that more middle-class students are also taking longer to complete their degrees because of the economic downturn or greater fear over their future plans. Yet the average number of years for graduation at the University of Illinois at Champaign-Urbana, the premiere state school, is 4 and a half years, with a graduation rate of 80%. UIC's darker graduation statistics, however, can conceal individuals who may have eventually gone to a different college in Chicago or elsewhere. Nevertheless, the UIC office of Data Resources claims that 70% of all UIC students will be on some form of academic probation during their academic career.

10. Although this description implies that the amount of course reading would drop off in the second half of the course, the syllabus (Appendix A) shows this was not the case in practice. All the students whom I spoke with persuasively contended Rashmi had required too much reading. From their view outside the minutiae of academic disciplines, the readings often seemed to repeat similar points. Although I think there is some validity to this complaint, I also examine its relation to the students' lives outside college; see particularly chaps. 4 and 6.

11. At several points in the term, Mike, whom I introduce later in this chapter, commented on his discomfort as one of only two White men in the class. More important, however, Mike sometimes felt he was verbally attacked for his views typical of working-class men (although Mike would not classify the situation that way). Still Mike displayed an atypical ease with women as peers and friends that may have often hidden a sense of alienation. In later chapters, I discuss Mike's situations and responses to the course in greater detail.

12. Elizabeth Chiseri-Strater (1991) successfully assumed this role in the eyes of the students of Donna Qualley's Prose Writing class at University of New Hampshire in 1987. In that situation, the students were juniors and seniors already more accustomed to acade-

mic ways than the first-year and second-year students in Rashmi's class. In general, Chiseri-Strater portrays these students as valuing her role and readily volunteering themselves for her research of Qualley's workshop-oriented writing class and other classes in their majors. In my case, the situation was more complicated because of the students' lives, how they saw my identities, and, for most, their educational histories. At best, then, Adler and Adler (1987) would categorize my role with the class as a peripheral membership.

13. Rashmi praised Lilia's first papers, deeming her a "strong critical thinker," but not her final research paper project, which I discuss in chap. 6. So while Lilia's critical understandings continued to progress, her written work wasn't reflecting this by end of term.

14. In this respect, I knowingly violate a common rule in most ethnographies of communication and discussions of its research methods. One of the first rules is that the field researcher should focus on the typical and everyday within a chosen cultural group to examine what "communicative competence" is most shared by members of the chosen speech community (see Hymes, 1974; Moss, 1992; Saville-Troike, 1982). My study, however, takes a more narrow focus on reconsidering aspects of critical teaching. I do not intend a full ethnographic description of this class as a community, although I have tried to identify common behaviors and values as context for discussion of particular teaching issues.

Reconsidering Instrumentalist Motives

INSTRUMENTALISM AS TECHNICAL RATIONALITY AND COMMUNICATIVE PRACTICE

"What does thinking critically mean to you?", I asked Peter during one of our interviews. After a short pause, he replied, "I got it. Thinking like, you're given a topic to think about in all different aspects, covering it all." "When do you do it?", "When? When I have to. If I don't have to write a paper, I'm not thinking too critically." To many critical writing teachers, Peter's response might epitomize an instrumentalist view of higher education. An instrumentalist view, as I described it in reference to George's writing in chapter 1, perceives knowledge primarily as a means to an end, rather than a questioning and consequent reconsidering of those ends. From this view, most students do not see disciplinary knowledge in different disciplines as a way to question aspects of everyday life, but only as a rationale of technical know-how—what some social critics refer to as *technical rationality*.[1]

The term *technical rationality* developed from the neo-Marxist cultural theories of the Frankfurt school (e.g., Horkheimer & Adorno, 1972; Marcuse, 1964) in response to the rise of fascism in Germany. To offer one example, the Frankfurt social critics viewed Adolf Eichmann's bureaucratic efficiency transporting Jews to their deaths as the darkest ends of technical rationality.

These critics later argued that contemporary industrial societies, be it under capitalism or Soviet-style communism, reproduce themselves by "mobilizing, organizing, and exploiting the technical, scientific, and mechanical productivity available . . . above and beyond any particular individual or group interests" (Marcuse, 1964, p. 3). In one sense, we see this view today when the executives of multinational corporations believe they need only answer to their shareholders. As I discuss later, composition scholars and other critics in American education have used these critiques of technical rationality to question instrumentalist thinking in students and in the social structures of their students' education that emphasize the rewards and punishments of grades. We can also define instrumentalism as a communicative practice. We speak instrumentally to others when we treat them as objects to be used for our own ends, rather than as living subjects like ourselves. When we do not see ourselves as answerable to the other in our communications, we are acting from an instrumentalist view. Because instrumentalist thinking as technical rationality and communicative practice often overlap, as they do in my research data, I first discuss them separately here to better understand the students' situations I address in this chapter.

    As Paul Loeb's (1994) and Michael Moffatt's (1989) studies of college students in the 1980s and early 1990s reveal, views like Peter's prevail for many middle-class American students. Loeb's 7-year research at 200 campuses nationwide points to the precarious economics of the middle class since the Reagan era, favoring college as a training ground for professionalist ideology (as in training for the business world) rather than a liberal arts education. Regardless of social class, Loeb suggests, many of these students on varied campuses "share a sense of a world increasingly harsh, in which conscience is a luxury" (p. 16).[2] Loeb found that even well-off students at elite colleges believed they must concentrate on a professional business expertise to preserve the upper middle-class comforts of their childhood. Many of these young adults described a self-imposed family obligation to pay back their parents' hard work. Yet in this era of economic survival mentality, they had only considered, or been encouraged to consider, a material reciprocity—paying back with money. Loeb documents how these students—the ones he labels the "adaptors" to the corporate system—insisted on facts and technical knowledge to structure their ethical judgments. Moffatt's ethnography of Rutgers students in the 1980s found many students associated an ideology of professionalism with a necessity to remain an individual. The students' brand of American individualism was their way of coping with the dominance of institutional bureaucracies in the late 20th century.

Loeb's and Moffatt's studies historically situate the students' favoring of technical rationality, whereas Moffatt's study also shows how instrumentalism can be defined in terms of communicative practice. Like many Americans, the Rutgers students assumed a privatized real self separated from a more artificial social self. The social self, which deals with all aspects of institutions and the social encounters that foster individual achievement, requires an instrumentalist approach to communication and learning. For example, George, whom I wrote about in chapter 1, likens his smoothing over customers at the Merry Go Round clothing store to what is necessary for getting ahead at school. In a postmodern culture organized by corporations, many students who talked to both Moffatt and Loeb believed it is often not what one can accomplish that matters, "but how well you can manipulate appearances to those who call the shots or make the deals" (Loeb, 1994, p. 13). In other words, most communication implicitly uses people as a means to an end, "to refine your ability to influence others" (Moffatt, 1989, p. 41).

As I mentioned in chapter 1, Douglas Foley (1990), an anthropologist of education, goes further to argue that people in the middle class tend toward this "alienated communicative labor" because it promotes the display of status and individual prestige. Following from theories of Habermas, by way of Marx, Foley argues that communication is reified within the "fundamental logic of class relationships" when "people unreflectively treat each other as dead objects rather than living subjects, when we treat each other as commodities" (pp. 168–170). Foley compares this theory of commodified talk with Erving Goffman's studies of communication in various institutional settings. Goffman (1973) characterizes language and communication as performances of mutually constructed language games with people frequently deceiving each other and themselves as a way to maintain social order, relying on forms of impression management.

Foley suggests that the corporate and suburban environments associated with the middle class create more anonymous communicative contexts that promote the greater use of strategic instrumental speech—using others for one's promotion within socioeconomic systems. The greater the economic and social mobility, the less likely one will be continually communicating within a small network of people and the more likely one will look to others to promote further mobility and opportunities. In contrast, several aspects of working-class communities contextually constrain the creation of "new variant impressions of the self through instrumental verbal performances" (p. 184). Foley contends that three factors of working-class communities tend to discourage individual impression management. These factors are working-class communities' tendencies toward dense social networks (when people continually look to the same group for multiple resources), their practices of maintaining a more traditional organizational character, and their stronger emphasis on social reciprocity and obligation (largely because they operate in smaller, denser social networks).[3] Foley's analysis of the middle-class Mexicanos in his ethnography of 1980s high school teens in a small Texas town offers an example of this instrumentalist communicative behavior embedded in the context of social class relations. In a town still strained by the White-Mexican race relations from the civil rights era, some of the male teens in the emerging middle-class Mexicano families "did not necessarily abandon their historical ethnic expressive cultural practices." Foley writes,

> By blending instrumental communicative behaviors with emerging Chicano ethnic political symbols, they became mainstream conformists while maintaining an ethnic image among the silent majority of working-class Mexicano "nobodies" [who might otherwise have resented them]. They learned how to work the system, to be clean-cut jocks publically, to get the pretty girls with "straight arrow" reputations, and to con teachers while entertaining their peers. While this is conforming to the system, it is also an ethnic resistance of "beating the gringos at their own game." In contrast, the vatos valorized working class street culture as authentic and practiced verbal confrontations with school authorities. (p. 197)

Scholars in composition studies have long worked against this instrumentalist thinking as indicative of technical rationality and commodified speech. As a major tenet of composition theory, most writing teachers reject the view that writing classes are merely service courses for the university and other disciplines—a view contrary to most other departments in universities. Composition critics have argued against this assumption on historical, political, and ethical grounds (Connors, 1991; Mahalia, 1991; Miller, 1991; Wallace & Ewald, 2000). In the words of Kurt Spellmeyer (1993), these critics often urge that writing classes should offer students a "common ground" between disciplinary expertise and popular understandings. Although Richard Ohmann's political critique of first-year composition was hardly the first, his argument "English 101 and the Military Industrial Complex" specifically traced the discourse expectations in popular writing textbooks of the 1960s to the 1970s to the technical rationality of the Pentagon papers during the Vietnam War. In this way, he demonstrated how much of the reasoning expected in college tended to serve American corporate interests more than promote critical understanding. More recently, composition scholars have looked to poststructuralist critiques of academic and professional disciplines (referred to in chap. 1) to resist the exercise of power through academic disciplinary practices. They argue, as Susan Miller (1991) has, for viewing composition as a limninal site that can interrogate the technical rationality of most academic cultures.

Various teacher scholars in the history of composition studies have also fought against the use of communication alienated from human experience and ethical questioning. Indeed many teachers would likely embrace Habermas' ideal of communicative action. As Foley (1990) summarizes this position, "In free, open trusting dialogic speech lies the ontological basis for uncoerced intersubjectivity, and hence the potential for a rational, truly democratic political culture and society" (p. 171). This ideal certainly encapsulates different expressivist arguments for finding authentic voice as a way to challenge the status quo of commodified talk. However, it could also sum up the goals of more recent postmodern teachers who encourage students to hear a hybrid dialogue of voices, including the constraints of institutions situated in historical time and place. Jeff Smith (1997) labels these "values of open dialogue"—values that resist both bureaucratic "Engfish" and commodified impression management, as our field's pedagogical "Standard Model" today (p. 307). Smith contends that the enforcement of this standard model ironically prevents writing teachers from acknowledging many students' legitimate desires for disciplinary training and upward mobility.

DIFFERENT STUDENT MOTIVES FOR INSTRUMENTALISM AT UIC

For UIC students who take an instrumental view of their education, economic necessity clearly influenced a practical vocationalism. Unlike the traditionally White middle-class students who dominate Loeb's and Moffatt's studies, the UIC students' motives for adopting this stance tended to be more complex depending on their local situations. For some working-class students like Mike and minority students like Peter, they may take this approach to distance themselves from the social capital of mainstream education and forms of institutional identity. In the remainder of this chapter, I discuss Mike's and Peter's views on these issues. For some immigrant students like Min Wei and Gita, an instrumentalist view of their education may be part of a working strategy to sidestep recognized discrimination and limited opportunity in the dominant society. I address this analysis of Min Wei's and Gita's motives in the following chapter. Both perspectives challenge the political efficacy of the writing teacher who organizes her pedagogy around assumptions of social transformation through critical literacy.

Other students in Rashmi's class expressed a strong vocationalist frame of mind as well. Yet over the course of my research, I repeatedly found that Mike, Peter, Min Wei, and Gita—despite their strong differences in cultures and academic abilities—tended to speak and behave in similar ways that critical teachers would identify as instrumentalist. All four also rejected the notion of Rashmi's class as "real work"—a question I had asked all the participants whom I interviewed. I preceded this question with a series of questions about their work or obligations outside of school. In doing so, I intended to elicit from participants a "school's out" ethos for that portion of the interview, which it often did. Mike's response implied that real work requires physical labor. Peter associated real work with the hard sciences to which he aspired. Min Wei, despite her difficulty understanding much of the course readings' complex critical language (that is, when she had done the reading), said Rashmi's course was not like the real math work of her business courses. Finally, Gita claimed Rashmi's class relied too much on emotions to be like the real world of business. As this chapter and the following one will show, these comparative definitions of "real work" reveal much about how the students assessed the critical writing classroom.

I narrowed these perspectives to three common patterns addressed in varying degrees by all four participants. First, more than other participants in my study, they talked about their education as different kinds of social capital. Depending on the participant, they discussed, often implicitly, the need to gain or resist various facets of their education as social capital. Second, they explicitly acknowledged participation in Rashmi's classroom and, to a lesser degree, writing for her class as performances that called for particular behaviors and responses. In one sense, they told me how to perform the politically correct student roles for the leftist teacher, but they also suggested the values embedded in their understandings of performance in the critical writing classroom. These students' understandings should help teachers reevaluate their own assumptions about their critical teaching. Third, unlike the other participants whom I interviewed, all four students claimed that Rashmi's course had no impact on their lives nor predicted it would in their future. In other words, they appeared more openly cynical in private discussions and interviews, seeing their academic labor of critical thinking primarily as exchange value rather than as use in social action.

Both Jeff Smith (1997) and, more recently, Russel Durst (1999) argued persuasively why we must respect students' instrumentalist motives if we hope to gain their trust in the writing classroom. Durst's ethnography of a first-year writing class at the University of Cincinnati demonstrates well how the critical writing teacher loses persuasive authority with students if her agenda ignores their motives for attending college. For these reasons, Durst advocates a pedagogy of "reflective instrumentalism" that works with most students' pragmatic motives for attending college, but seeks to cultivate critical analysis within a framework of students' examining school and career issues through textual and field research.[4] But in both Durst's research and Smith's argument, the majority of students' motives are tied more to conservative middle-class values, not the complex concerns of identity, social capital, and acculturation I found in these UIC students' perspectives. The local situations of these students suggest we cannot assume what these students' motives for instrumentalist behaviors might be. If we make these assumptions, we miss the opportunity for the students and us to examine and perhaps learn from these complex social situations as I hope my ethnographic analysis of Peter, Mike, Min Wei, and Gita makes clear.

BROWNNOSING AND RUBBING IT IN THEIR EYE— MINORITY AND WORKING-CLASS MOTIVES

Peter comes from a lower middle-class family of mixed African-American and Puerto Rican heritage. In the context of Rashmi's class and in conversations with me, however, Peter represented himself as African American.[5] Although he aspires to go to medical school, he imagines this goal as a series of incremental steps between work and further education that will first require him to work as a paramedic and a nurse. Mike, born into a family of cops, is from a South Side Irish working-class background. When I first met Mike, he was considering journalism as a career, because he was working at a newspaper. Now he is talking about becoming a cop like his dad and grandfather before him. As I argue here, despite these vast differences of background, aspirations, and community loyalties, Peter and Mike (both traditional age first-year students) shared a common attitude of instrumentalism to remove themselves from particular forms of school as social capital.

When I asked Peter to describe his school experiences before coming to college, he told me that his high school "made me who I am, as far as school related things, my whole school attitude." Not surprisingly, he did not sing the praises of being opened to challenging ideas. Instead he told me that "I learned when to study, when not to study, when to come to school, when not to come." As teachers we might accept Peter's approach more had he suffered through a poor city high school that did not offer intellectual opportunities, but Peter attended a prestigious magnet school in the Chicago Public School system. In that light, this self-taught lesson in minimalist efficiency reflects the rule of technical rationality. Yet to Peter, his approach serves a deep purpose. Immediately after stating his view, he offered this justification: "I never felt that you had to brownnose as they say, to a teacher or anything."

Peter implied that he maintained his personal integrity by separating himself from an overabsorption in a mainstream institutional identity. "I always thought that if you got it, if you got the knowledge, then it will be rewarding in its own way." His language may echo Mike Rose's (1990) depiction of education's "intrinsic rewards." Yet what Peter said immediately after this also suggested a need to distance himself from the school system, especially as he saw it in college. "I see people trying to get to medical school, they're taking all these *classes*. It's not recommended that you take all these extra classes. They give you set classes that you have to take. If you do well in those, you shouldn't have to fancy up your resume, application to please anybody." Similarly, Peter devalued the unique qualities of his high school, objectifying his learning process. "Everybody thinks Whitney Young is this great smart school. I've been there and I don't think so. They've got good teachers, granted, but if I had gone to this school or that one, I would have the same experience. School is school."

This show of independence toward school authorities extended to the cultural power of grades. He acknowledged and sought the symbolic power they could bestow, remarking that grades "can make you or break you as far as deciding who goes where." But his policy was to make "the best grade possible, the easiest way possible."

Like Peter, Mike also described school's purposes and the value of academic disciplines as divorced from everyday life. School is the place to learn "your basic stuff, reading, writing, chemistry," but he emphasized, "watching TV or hitting on a girl or something is more life than sitting in chemistry and learning phases and period shifts or whatever bullshit they're teaching you. I mean I'm going to learn it, and I've got to get a good grade, but is that all? Well, you're a fool, get a life." Here Mike emphasized the social world outside school more than Peter did (as Peter was more dependent on extended higher education for his goals). But like Peter, Mike resists brownnosing to any institutional authority.

When I asked Mike to describe an educated person to me, he initially spoke of people who tried to impress others with their talk of politics. "I may think certain things about the government suck, but I'm not going to sit there and say, 'Oh yeah, I think Richard Daley is a great mayor or that I think the republican clown would have made a better candidate,' nothing like that." I asked him if this meant he didn't want to be educated in that sense. He replied, "I think you can learn something and still be yourself . . . I mean sure the 'A' looks good, and is going to get you somewhere, but if you get there, and you have no friends, what's the point in your being there? You can have all the money in the world, but if everybody hates you because you're a cocksucker, what can you do about that?" Whether Mike's language indicated a performance for my benefit or an ease with our conversation, I certainly agreed with his life priorities here.

MIKE'S TENSIONS: SOLIDARITY AND PRESTIGE, LANGUAGE AND WRITING

Clearly, Mike implicitly associates acting educated with seeking individual prestige at the expense of working-class solidarity. Several studies of working-class young adults reveal the same loyalties. In Penny Eckert's (1989) study, the mainly working-class "burnouts" in two high schools outside Detroit resented the more middle-class "jocks"—those students who identified with extracurricular roles in the high school institution. In the burnouts' view, the jocks sought social gain through the school's hierarchies as an implicit preparation for corporate life. Eckert points out that the burnouts' parents act similarly in the work world, "avoiding job changes that will put them in superior positions to their peers and separate them from their solidarity peer networks" that have sustained them (p. 138).

Nevertheless, Mike's descriptions of past and present jobs expressed a complicated negotiation between working-class identity and markers of cultural capital, such as college degrees or lines on a resume about professional white-collar work. In this sense, Mike wanted to maintain some working-class values, but hold some middle-class aspirations. For all of his tacit identification with working-class values of community solidarity, he associated two of his earlier jobs working at a supermarket with the dead end of employment. As he advanced from stockboy to working in the meat department "as a kind of apprentice butcher," he separated himself early on from those he saw as the permanent lower working class. "Most of the other stockboys were assholes, real trash. Guys that are going to work there the rest of their whole life. I didn't want to end up working there my whole life. I went there like a month ago, and some people have been there since the store opened, and seven years later are still there."

Working at the newspaper pulling clippings for the reporters, however, Mike sees as a definite marker of higher cultural capital that comes with advanced education. "If I hope to get some of the intellect, a newspaper's perfect, because you can write on a resume that you worked there for four years. Writing you worked in a supermarket, what do they care?" Although Mike told me he enjoyed several aspects of his job at the paper, the way he expressed its benefits toward his future seemed curious. Does his language here imply that intellect is something procured through his work there? Or does it indicate that Mike believes he will be able to claim intellect through the proof of his resume, written evidence of the professional self? Either way it suggests that Mike—whether consciously or not—views intellect as capital (or as a commodity) to be obtained outside his typical domains.

To some extent, Mike associates that middle-class capital with evidence of public writing. When I first talked at length with Mike at the mid-semester of Rashmi's class, he told me he was thinking seriously about a future in journalism, spurred on by the atmosphere and people at his job. Yet when I met with him that following fall, he told me he wanted to be a cop, following in the family tradition of his father and grandfather: "I always grew up, kind of like, cop, you know?" He also claimed police work could act as an ethic of caring: "Even if I just helped one person, then I could say I did something with my life." I asked whether his interest in journalism had changed. He appeared lukewarm on the idea, although not entirely ruling out the possibility. He then referred to his first writing assignment for the newspaper, which he was just given—an album review on the rock group AC-DC. Mike described this opportunity as a deciding factor: "Depends on how I do on it, see how they like it. I guess that's going to decide it almost. If I can write it, maybe I'm cut out for it." Although Mike said he was looking forward to writing the review, his comments also articulated the boundaries of middle-class professional opportunities, as Mike envisioned them through a journalism career, and how those boundaries rely on high competencies in writing (which he may be uncertain he can muster).

Mike claimed there were no connections between his everyday life and the social critiques from Rashmi's course. In stating this claim, he categorized two kinds of school learning. "With some classes, you don't really go back and use it. It's not a knowledge like mathematics where you learn a certain set of logic; I have learned an understanding in this class, of different cultures, that things aren't always right in the world, but not all wrong too." Here Mike doesn't denigrate the value of this understanding compared with knowledge that can be put to use in the world. At the same time, he also treated this understanding of the issues discussed in the course as a commodity. "If I were to travel to another country, I would probably have more understanding. The only place where I would get something out of the knowledge is if I became good friends with someone who is from China, India, or something. I wouldn't be as ignorant to the ways they see it. I may have already learned it from this class." Mike's view here sounds more like a corporate-sponsored cultural diversity training session than the analysis of socioeconomics, labor, and social class that Rashmi fostered. Mike's perspective tends to define culture as static, implying people act that way because that is how they grew up, not because they are continually reshaped by larger systemic forces.[6] He describes this understanding of cultural issues as only useful for smoothing over individual encounters—an example of instrumentalist thinking as communicative practice. Yet his response also emphasizes the importance of social bonds as an end to themselves; cultural knowledge serves to strengthen friendships, not exploit others.

Mike's ambivalences toward gaining social capital in school intertwined with his attitudes toward language use as markers of social class. When Mike told me what he thought made a person educated, he spoke of speech patterns. "I've met people who love saying big words just to impress people, because they know they're smart enough to say them. I know I don't talk correct grammar when I talk. I don't have to. I could speak perfect English and people could hate me because I'm trying to rub it in their eye." Mike's strategy for maintaining community solidarity reflects Gerry Philipsen's (1992) study of Chicago South Side Teamsterville speech in the 1970s. Philipsen analyzes the former Mayor Daley's conscious use of this strategy in public speeches to speak as the White urban working class that supported him.

Mike's concern for maintaining solidarity with his "home culture" may have helped shape his discomfort with other students' discussions of the readings in Rashmi's class. Outside of the class, he commented to Rashmi and me that students were being too critical of everything. Although he did not see himself as wholeheartedly supporting the system, as Rashmi put it, he felt the need to take the middle ground in class discussions of post-colonialist issues. In a mid-semester conference with Rashmi, he commented that he didn't like reading negative things all the time—he felt he had been provided for in life, so he was less prone to make judgments.

With me he referred to a heated debate in class over the corporate exploitation of international labor. "Sure, there is a level of exploitation, but without the job, these people would probably starve. You've got to see the good and the bad. Sometimes people don't want to hear that there are good points to things. They just want to hear that they are being exploited." Mike's language here may smack of free market ideology that underlies instrumental rationality in America today. Yet from Mike's view, there may also be other motivations for this language: (a) to be overly critical is to seek prestige and status in this institutional situation, which goes against his ethics of solidarity; and (b) to reject the value of hard work, perhaps even exploitative labor, is to reject working-class values historically rooted in material necessity.

PETER'S TENSIONS: USING THE SYSTEM AS AN INSTRUMENTAL TOOL

Whereas Mike's view of language values social bonds over the possibility of individual prestige, Peter's responses to language use in different speech settings suggest the difficulties of more divided loyalties. Peter aligned himself with the African-American students from the class who defined "good English" as the difference between getting your point across and speaking "proper" English. After this definition, he immediately denied his conscious use of proper English speech, "no, not me, never the one." But later he also commented that he would never speak to me in the slang of his neighborhood, keeping up a public persona of the educated student (in front of the White Academic Man). Peter claimed he did not associate speaking proper with "speaking White," but more with education. "I've seen some Asian people who spoke properly. I don't think it's White."

Yet when he described how he talked differently in most classes compared with his neighborhood use of slang, he commented, with a bemused air, on his own contradictions. At first he said he uses similar slang at school, but then drew back: "In a way I do, in a way I don't. Then again, if I speak differently, it would also be like fronting in school, so there's a thin line." Peter referred to fronting earlier when I asked him if he compared himself to other students at UIC. He said then that he didn't see himself as "an extreme of anything," contending that other students' extreme roles "just might be a front at school." He offered that "some guys who think they're tough" would not be half as tough on the street without their friends. "I see that a lot," he added, "might not be in terms of acting rough, but acting in a certain way."

Peter's view of fronting also extended to his view of other students' discussion of the readings in Rashmi's class. "In like all the discussions, they always had something to say about everything. I don't think that's *possible*. Sure, know a little about everything. But they seemed to know too much about everything discussed in that class. It seemed fake to me, like b.s." This ambivalence over fronting surfaced again when we discussed the possibility of his using critical talk and thinking as social capital outside the classroom. Mike compared this critical talk for social gains to employing what he saw as objective knowledge in the sciences for economic gain.

In our discussions, he rejected any notion of talking or thinking like a teacher. I asked him whether that kind of language and thought might be important for his future. After dismissing the value of thinking about issues from Rashmi's class in other contexts outside of school, Peter then referred to his own area of study: "Ah man, I don't know. There's medical terminology and the ways you have to use them. Sure I can know the words, what they mean, but blend them into how I talk? All depends on who you ask. I have this distinct view. I'm not here to please anybody. I'm not going to try to do something I'm not comfortable doing." Peter's response suggests that he respects academic talk, but to fold it into his own language could qualify as another form of brownnosing.

Much of Peter's "whole school attitude" suggests that he would not see a college writing course as a place for meaningful articulation of issues from his lived experience. "School can be like a closed system," Peter commented, "not too much happens in school." Yet in his early journal notes and first response paper for Rashmi's course, Peter quickly identified himself with the authors who address the neglect of racism and imperialism in feminist thinking. In this first paper, he briefly referred to experiences with racist police officers and other Whites who feel these police are justified. For these reasons among others, Peter writes that "America will never be the place where I can live . . . happily."

Later in an in-class essay requiring analysis of bell hooks' (1990) essay, "Third World Diva Girls," Peter pointed to hooks' view that some White feminists' racial fear and guilt may prevent them from any critical views of women of color. He drew an analogy between hooks' example and the always positive tone of his classmates' participation in Rashmi's class. Specifically, he wondered whether the White students spoke differently about racial struggles when they went home to their neighborhoods. Nonetheless, when I asked Peter two semesters after the term if he ever thought about any issues from the course, he immediately answered "no." Nor did he see any value for himself in considering these issues outside the class. The self Peter presented to me outside of Rashmi's classroom valued school as economic and cultural capital, but saw no persuasive power in it for social transformation.

In the context of Peter's deep awareness of institutionalized racism, Peter's concerns about fronting and brownnosing resemble the ambivalent loyalties expressed by successful urban African-American high school students in Signithia Fordham's (1988) research. These students must often wrestle between the collective ethos of peer opposition toward mainstream schooling and the individualist ethos of the school's efforts at mainstream acculturation that can serve to justify limited opportunities for their African-American communities. Fordham argues that the successful students in her study adopted varying strategies of "racelessness" to cope with this struggle of forces. Peter clearly did not ignore the issue of race in America and his life. Instead he assumed an instrumental view of his education to cope with these conflicting forces of identity. He used the system as an instrumental tool so he won't be used by the system.

Peter's strategy to deal with these forces helps explain why he valued so highly what he saw as the more objective knowledge in his college studies. As an example of prizing this objective knowledge, he offered up his chemistry class as "real work" compared with the assignments and readings for Rashmi's class. Many students would claim chemistry as harder to study than Third World feminist criticism. Indeed in Moffatt's (1989) study, the majority of Rutgers students claim you can always "bullshit" your way to a good grade in a humanities or social science class. Yet Peter's claim of real work did not center on how hard the work is. Instead he values the science courses for the knowledge that cannot be gained elsewhere. "Chemistry is . . . complex. It's just stuff that I don't know. I see our English class as based on, I guess, your experience in life and just things of how you think about society and the world. Chemistry, physics, any science is like a whole different thing. It's just something you got to study and learn. They'll give it to you right there, can't bring any prior knowledge."

Many critical writing teachers in urban schools design their teaching practices on a process of "defamiliarizing the familiar," making the familiar strange, urging their students to look at experience through sociological or anthropological lenses. This approach can be persuasive especially for urban students who have experienced various forms of sociocultural conflict. Nevertheless, Peter's value system suggests why some of these students may turn off to this strategy if only outside the classroom. At the extreme, students like Peter might see the critical writing pedagogy as endless talk on obvious problems they have learned to cope with, for now, on an everyday basis.

From Peter's perspective, objective knowledge is all that is required to achieve the hoped-for professional identity. In a sense, if the knowledge remains objective, as it is assumed to be in the hard sciences, then it remains somehow separate from the dominant school culture. This strategy may also be why he was willing to engage the social critiques of Rashmi's class, but saw no purpose in carrying them outside the institutional boundaries. To cope with all the conflicts of identity and acculturation, school becomes a process of professionalization, gaining economic and cultural capital, but not critically transforming identity, which would mean acceding to the power of the social capital of the institution.

PETER'S EXCEPTION:
PHILOSOPHY AND ISLAM

Much of Peter's comparisons of his science and humanities courses fit neatly into this social theory of his motivations and guarded psychological investments in mainstream institutions. Still in the course of our last interview, Peter shared with me his piqued engagement in an introductory philosophy course—an interest that in some ways tears open the theoretical box I have fashioned here. In one way, Peter's philosophy course was another form of objective knowledge that could not be acquired outside the institution or outside books produced by academe. He described the course as teaching logical proofs for and against the existence of God from the history of philosophy. The teacher clearly saw no great need to focus on philosophical issues of contemporary society that would more likely be relevant to UIC students (although clearly some students like Peter were motivated by the teacher's logical debates on religious faith). I had heard of this course taught by graduate teaching assistants and had always dismissed its content as alienating and elitist for an urban working population. All of my former students who took the class sounded turned off to explicit philosophical debate because of their experience with the methods and content of this particular course.

For Peter, however, this philosophy course's stance away from social and cultural issues may have appealed to his image of college learning. Peter described it this way: "I thought it was kind of interesting when I said, 'okay, I'm going to take philosophy to be a well-rounded person here.'" In contrast to his view of courses more associated with his political experience, here Peter welcomes the social capital he expects a university philosophy class could bestow on him: the mark of a "well-rounded person" presumably in middle-class circles. Still Peter's language here also shows him pulling back from a deep investment in this image. He describes himself observing the character of Peter the college-goer, "I thought it was kind of interesting when I said," as if he was surprised at himself for getting involved in a class for nonutilitarian purposes. Several graduate student friends who were first-generation students told me that if the courses they took as undergraduates had no utilitarian purpose, like philosophy or Shakespeare, it signified "real college" all the more, with its elitist privilege that some yearned for and struggled against.

Yet Peter also valued the structure of objective logic in the course—its similarity to the "real work" of the hard sciences. When I asked him whether anything he ever wrote for school disturbed his thinking or values, he again referred to the philosophy class. "This God thing. These philosophers come with pretty convincing arguments. With this philosophical stuff, it's very logical. That makes it more persuasive; in philosophy, everything had to come from somewhere. They're putting the something to be God." Peter told me he was brought up Catholic, but later came to "my own decisions," generally dismissing religious faith. "All of a sudden when I had to think about it, this is how I thought. I had more support in believing there isn't one." Perhaps because Peter already agreed with the main political assumptions of Rashmi's course, he granted it little influence over other areas of his life. The philosophy class, however, did challenge his belief, and did so with claims of objectivity that Peter often grants greater persuasive authority. "I don't really think about the third world as much as I do about this religion thing, whether I do believe, do have faith or not. At this time, that's why I am taking it so personal. It could change the way I view things as a whole."

Although Peter spoke favorably of this objectifying of knowledge, he identified in this discourse similar ambivalences he had toward other academic ways of knowing he had encountered. He described the way one should talk and act in this class as "having a philosophy line. It's my first class, so I don't have one yet. It's more of how open you are to what the teacher has to say, what philosophers have to say." Involvement in the course, which Peter sought, required both an openness to the structure of philosophical argument and a disciplined performance of its logics—to give a philosophy line. Although Peter praised the course's logic of argument, he felt this method of debate excluded the personal expression of different students' views.[7] "Our views don't seem to be an issue. It's more like these philosophers stated this."

> Peter: For instance we have three philosophers who proved there's a God. Then you have a group called the Fideles who believed that God exists in faith only. In the paper we have to write, we have to take a philosopher's point of view and argue it with the Fideles' point of view. My TA says, "I don't want any personal views in this paper, just go about it." That's not what I was hoping to do in this class.

> David: So is something lost that way?
>
> Peter: I wouldn't say necessarily lost, but not fully
>   gained out of the class. We have a lot of dif-
>   ferent people with different thoughts. You're
>   not letting them say it, not letting the person
>   express their views in the class, or in the
>   paper. I don't think its going to be a good
>   paper. It's like forcing them to say something
>   along the lines of what you want them to say.

Ironically, in his philosophy class, Peter wanted to relate his and others' experiences to the subject matter, but he psychologically removed himself from Rashmi's class when this approach toward learning was central to the teachers' pedagogy. Peter also expressed this concern for personal communication when he claimed he would have to talk with someone at length to determine whether that person was *truly educated*, which he defined as "knowing a little about many different things." As in many African-American and Latino groups, interpersonal communications can hold as much currency as institutional certificates.

If Peter claimed the issues discussed in Rashmi's class had no influence on his thinking outside school, this was not the case for his philosophy class, which he associated with his recent extracurricular explorations of Muslim faith with an older friend and mentor.[8] Some of the other participants in my study, such as Lilia and Shianta (whom I discuss in chap. 6), traced their responses toward Rashmi's class to their religious beliefs, so I later chose to ask all of them whether they considered themselves religious. This is when Peter first told me about the philosophy course he was taking at the time, weaving his account of the course together with brief comments on Muslim faith and his respect for this friend. Although Peter held on to his agnostic skepticism, he spoke of how both of these teachers' philosophies were leading him to question his disbelief.

> Peter: My friend, he's turned me on to some beliefs
>   of what Muslims think. I agree to what they
>   say to some point. At sometimes I see them
>   contradicting themselves.
>
> David: Where do you see contradictions?

Peter: They believe the Supreme Being is a man
         named Mohammed, came in 1930, taught the
         honorable Elijah. But then again, some
         believe in God as the almighty in heaven.
         Islam means to submit to Allah's will, but if
         Allah is a man, why must you submit to him?
         At sometimes there's a God in the sky and at
         other times, there's a God walking on the
         earth. That's what I don't understand. I think
         they should clear it up for me.

Despite these uncertainties of faith, Peter looked up to his
Muslim teacher, whose name he did not volunteer to me in our
discussion, suggesting all the more how he values his friend's
confidence. When I asked him whether he had any heroes in his
life, he immediately invoked "the guy who turned me on to
Muslim," whom he defined as an educated person. "So far it's
only him. He's taken me in as his own child. I went there when I
got off work this morning. I went to his house at seven o'clock
and he always welcomes you. He teaches me as his own."
     If Peter was having difficulties with the teachings of Muslim
belief, he deeply identified with its political cast of African nationalism. Peter detailed to me the differences between the followers
of Elijah Mohammed's son and those who followed Louis
Farrakhan when he broke away from Elijah Mohammed.
"Mohammed's son believes that black people should go back to
Mecca and have America pay for reparations for slavery while
Farrakhan believes they should stay here." Although Peter did
not linguistically include himself here in his explication of Black
people as Muslim followers, when I asked him whether he would
want to leave the United States if such an exodus did occur, he
answered with an immediate "yes." This is not to say that he
wasn't realistic about this separatist utopia. He did not believe
that this possible exodous would come in his lifetime, if ever, nor
could he imagine leaving America by himself. "So much to be
done that I won't ever have to make that move to go back. I would
have to go with the people."
     These comments indicate that Peter is certainly not apolitical,
although he claimed Rashmi's course had little influence on his
thinking outside school contexts. To be fair, some of Peter's written responses in his journal to Rashmi's question prompts early
in the semester drew in a general way from this African nationalist perspective. Yet in our conversations, Peter never made con-

nections between his growing involvement in this sociopolitical frame of reference outside of school and the arguments entertained in Rashmi's class. Instead he dwelled on the theological connections with his philosophy course and his interests in Muslim nationalism.

Although Peter's and Mike's uses of instrumentalist thinking emerge from different local situations of race and class, they nonetheless share strong motivations to dismiss the college writing class as a catalyst for social change in other areas of their lives. For both individuals, it is the particular symbolic powers that school embodies for them that influence what critical aspects of their learning will or will not carry over to their lives outside college. In the next chapter, I examine how immigrant students and their families invest different symbolic powers in the schools of the dominant culture. Yet ironically these immigrant groups' symbolic associations with mainstream schooling can also promote a rejection of critical pedagogy's main assumptions in the writing class.

NOTES

1. This is not to say that technical thinking is atheoretical. Like other kinds of thinking processes, it requires examining previous assumptions, building hypotheses, and revising them on the basis of experiences. Nevertheless, technical rationality does not assume as a given that hypotheses must be questioned in terms of their social implications and possible effects on the world outside the realm of the specific technical concern. Nor do I mean to imply that people who mainly function in technical worlds do not find themselves considering social consequences. Consider the case of access issues in the design of Web sites. In this case, the problems of access for people with disabilities and less powerful machines led designers to reconsider their assumptions. Still the technical training of these designers did not necessarily lead them to question more systemic issues of the digital divide in the new global economy.

2. Although this view may be generally wide-held, my experience with students in recent years at Wright State University suggests, as always, a possibly more complex picture. We cannot discount the enormous amount of volunteer work that many students do, particularly students who view their religion as central to their identity.

3. Although Foley's explanation tends to make sense, he does not account for traditions of men instrumentally using women in many working-class cultures—a social reality even present in his own data. Nor does he examine impression management and verbal play

as practiced by various subordinated working-class ethnic groups, African-American rhetorics being a prime example, when facing interactions with the dominant White culture. Still his critical approach to speech practices has helped me analyze intersections of social class and race in the speech practices of my participants.

4. Although Durst's pedagogy sounds promising, his book only devotes three pages to specifics of the course assignments. In contrast, Jim Zebroski's (1994) *Thinking Through Theory* lays out a series of critically theorized assignments in which students use field research to investigate the cultures of writing in their majors. In this work, they interrogate the nature of academic disciplines in relation to labor issues and their career interests.

5 . In our interviews, I believe Peter saw me, the White academic guy, as institutionally tied to "the man." Peter shaped much of his discourse with me on this premise, maintaining a polite but distant demeanor, admittedly absent of the street slang he claimed to use to build bonds in his neighborhood. His wary but honest talk with me enacted and reproduced his differentiated investment in school achievements and complicated positioning toward a more stereotypical African-American oppositional identity that I analyze further in this chapter.

6. If we consider William Perry's developmental theories of maturation, Mike's view can also be interpreted as the developmental stage of dualistic thinking Perry claims for many college students (or rather upper middle-class Harvard men if we consider the subjects of his study). Nonetheless, I don't believe this possibility cancels out the importance of working-class values in Mike's responses to the course and our interviews. In chapter 7, I further address Perry's theories in relation to Mike's writing for Rashmi's course.

7. Nick, one of the two University of New Hampshire students featured in Chiseri-Strater's study *Academic Literacies*, expresses the same frustration when he compares the authoritative style of logic and classroom discourse in his upper level philosophy classes to the open dialogic style of Donna Qualley's advanced writing class. Drawing on Nick's comments, Chiseri-Strater makes a persuasive case for a gendered reading of these two classes, where the philosophy course represents the traditionally agonistic male rhetoric and the writing course privileges culturally female connected ways of knowing.

8. We must remember that Peter is talking about his understandings of Islam from the viewpoint of an African American in 1996—years before the events of September 11, 2001.

Immigrants and Instrumentalism

IMMIGRANTS' DUAL FRAME OF REFERENCE

When critical theorists of education apply the term *instrumentalism* to schooling, they always intend a disapproving judgment; instrumentalism is what teachers and students should resist. In contrast, most anthropologists of minority schooling (influenced by John Ogbu's theories) use the term in a descriptive sense to explain how many immigrant communities approach their children's education. In a synthesis of several studies of immigrant attitudes toward schooling, Ogbu and Gibson (1991) concludes that cultural models of beliefs and behaviors for these immigrant groups often lead them to adopt "pragmatic or instrumental attitudes and strategies that are quite conducive to school success" (p. 17). These cultural models serve to organize interpretations of educational situations and guide behaviors in schooling contexts relative to each immigrant group's histories. Unlike involuntary minorities in America, immigrant groups tend to interpret economic, political, and social barriers as temporary problems that can be overcome with hard work and more education for the next generation in a functioning meritocracy. Often they are able to sustain this belief because they have a positive dual frame of reference where they compare their present situation with the disadvantages of their former life or those "back home."

75

Min Wei spoke from this dual frame of reference when she told me her family emigrated from Hong Kong early in her high school years to take advantage of opportunities for higher education and more affordable housing. Like many immigrants to America, neither Min Wei's mother nor her father had attended college; both were now working in the restaurant industry. Min Wei's mother worked full time at her brother's restaurant while her father, who had worked on international ships, had returned to Hong Kong. Nor did Min Wei mention any relatives in white collar jobs, except for her older sister who was presently working in a certified public accountant's office after choosing to leave college. Although Min Wei talked about the advantages of education in America, she spoke more about another dual frame of reference, contrasting the opportunities and quality of living between mainland China and Hong Kong under British rule. It was through this comparison of Asian societies, rather than between Hong Kong and America (or Chicago), that she viewed the advantages of her family's situation in America. Of course the context of Rashmi's course and Min Wei's choice of writing topics likely influenced so much reflection on this comparison in our interviews. Still her comparison of Hong Kong and China suggested to me the ways she values education, what kinds of social capital she expects from it, and how these beliefs may shape her limited investment in critical education.

Gita also identified strongly with a dual frame of reference even though her family had immigrated to Chicago when she was six. Yet this dual perspective emerged more in her understanding of political corruption in India compared with how she perceived the free market economic system, a paradoxical view that both spurred her interest in Rashmi's course and in a way limited its political efficacy for her. Not surprisingly, Gita also valued her American-bred ideal of individual freedoms compared with the gender constraints of her Indian social networks. Her perspective toward these Indian values helped shape her criticisms of Rashmi's classroom and, by association, many critical writing teachers' rhetorical assumptions. Unlike Min Wei's family, however, Gita's grandfather and father had graduated from college, although her father, who works as an environmental chemist, was the only brother of three who finished college in India. Although her father likely makes a middle-class income, Gita stressed that her parents send much money back overseas to support extended family members, suggesting a material necessity similar to working-class families. She added that knowing her parents' expenses has encouraged her to work hard at school so she can later pay her parents back for college.

The very factors of this immigrant cultural model that promote many immigrant children's success in mainstream schooling may also diminish the persuasiveness of the critical writing teachers' agenda for these students. Ogbu and Gibson (1991) wrote that these immigrant groups are "willing and actually do strive to play the classroom game by the rules because they believe so strongly there will be a payoff later" (p. 20). In strong contrast, critical teachers encourage students to dismantle and transform the classroom game as much as possible. When these immigrant groups adopt a strategy of accommodation without assimilation, the parents emphasize the respect of, or sometimes acquiescence to, school authorities regardless of often inferior, overcrowded, understaffed schools. In this view, parents believe their children must make the most of their opportunity, and so they place the burden of responsibility on the child, ignoring systemic perspectives of poor schooling. For example, parents in the rural Californian Sikh community that Margaret Gibson (1988) studied reared their children to treat schoolwork as a job where hard work was to be expected, but presumably not critiqued. Gibson demonstrates how values are enforced through gossip about wayward children in the Sikh community who thus bring dishonor to their families.

Although Min Wei now ascribes to this instrumentalist accommodation to schooling, she initially did not when she attended a Chicago public high school. In her view, the Chicago high school did not move beyond her previous private Catholic school curriculum in Hong Kong. Consequently, she spent three and a half years "doing nothing" but going out with friends in the afternoons, which she felt left her unprepared for the college work of UIC. Her mother was the one who wanted her to get a B.A. Only in the last term or two had Min Wei committed herself more fully to educational goals. Now Min Wei identifies herself as a student role model for her younger sister compared with her older sister, who pursues economic mobility through full-time work. Gita, in contrast, described constant social pressures from extended family in America and Gujarat, India, to excel in school that resemble the constraints of gossip Gibson encountered in the Californian Sikh community. Gita believes she has forged her identity to both conform to and rebel against the ethos of achievement and gender embodied in these social constraints. It is her response to this community ethos that helps lead her to critique the rhetorical practices of Rashmi's classroom in challenging ways.

MIN WEI'S TENSIONS: HONG KONG, CHINA, AND WOMEN'S RIGHTS

After Rashmi's class had discussed Chandra Mohanty's essay, "Cartographies of Struggle: Third World Women and the Politics of Feminism," Rashmi assigned the students to write about their own *politics of location* (a key critical term in Mohanty's essay; for Rashmi's assignment, see Appendix B). In response, Min Wei wrote of the disparity of education in mainland China compared with her native Hong Kong. In this paper, Min Wei suggests that Hong Kong's policy of 9 free years of education have led to "equal rights for men and women" in the colony. By contrast, she argues that mainland China's overpopulation and poverty in relation to other nations compels its people toward short-term goals of survival and quick money often at their own expense through cheap labor. Min Wei's thinking here was undoubtedly influenced by reading Barbara Ehrenreich and Annette Fuentes' (1993) article, "Life on the Global Assembly Line," which provides concrete details of Third World women's exploitation in factories. Rashmi's assignment also required students to respond to another article they had already read in class. At least a third of the class chose Ehrenreich's and Fuentes' piece of investigative reporting. Min Wei writes, "It is because people who are in China don't know how to improve themselves without the help of education. They will care about only the short run of their living without thinking of China future as a whole."

Rashmi's margin comment at this point asks Min Wei to question this dominant belief that lack of education is the sole cause for China's ills: "Or are there other circumstances? Huge population, Scarce resources for example?" In her end comment, she continues this tack. After pointing out that Min Wei could have strengthened her argument about education in Hong Kong with some personal experiences from her life there, Rashmi then counters Min Wei's assumption: "I think the reasons why Hong Kong became more prosperous are wide ranging and deeply embedded in its history." Here near the beginning of the term, Rashmi wanted Min Wei to begin considering the complexity of multiple factors that can account for China's social problems in comparison with Hong Kong's colonialist history. Encouraging a

long-range investigation of these histories, Rashmi finally suggests Min Wei could compare women in Hong Kong and China for
her later research paper.[1]

Regardless of whether it was Rashmi's underlying intention,
the assumptions behind her margin comments resemble Harvey
Graff's (1991) historical analysis of the literacy myth—an analysis
favored by many critical writing teachers (e.g., Cooper &
Holtzman, 1989; Stuckey, 1991; Trimbur, 1991). In other words,
Rashmi's question implicitly challenges Min Wei's faith that education, in and of itself, will necessarily lead to a more just society.
This is not to say that Rashmi discounted education as a crucial
element of self-empowerment for women in various global situations. Whenever students wrote or spoke of education as important to social change, she made a point to agree with them. Min
Wei concludes her response paper,

> After I have read through all of these articles about women
> who are working in the third world as treated as slaves, I feel
> that I am lucky that I was born in Hong Kong and had educa-
> tion over there in order to fight for my own rights. And I
> believe that every woman in the world is capable to do so if
> they have the knowledge. . . . If I were the government the
> first thing I will do to develop the third world is to provide
> education for people.

Rashmi responds, "right on target here." Still the design of
Rashmi's whole course, as evident in her syllabus, spurred students to examine multiple factors, rather than accept education of
the individual as the balm for all social ills of Third World nations.

In one of our interviews the summer after Rashmi's class, I
asked Min Wei how she thought education in Hong Kong led to
equal rights for women as she had stated in this paper. She
replied that when you know more, you know more about jobs,
how to do them, and how to get them. So she believed that the
women gain greater opportunities compared with the Chinese
traditional gender roles where women must stay home and raise
the family. Min Wei's view here reflects a Western mainstream
feminism that privileges women in the workplace. In this sense,
Min Wei believes in collective change for women, a strong change
from the patriarchal history of Chinese cultures, but the change
she articulates here is mainly structured by corporate ideology
(Gordon, 1991). Although she stressed this instrumentalist view
of education, when I asked her what could be the purpose of a

college education if it could not guarantee upward mobility, her answer indicated a stronger political will than her embrace of corporate ideology suggested. Before responding, she paused to consider her answer and carefully chose her words: "If you know things, people can't control you. You can control them." Yet even with Rashmi's class as the contextual background of our discussion, she did not address any ideas from the course about women's education and collective action.

Many feminist readings from Rashmi's class argued against an individualist emphasis on women's careers that neglects the situations of women in the working-class and non-Western nations. But as Min Wei associated her future success with the business world, she concentrated her efforts on those courses and often did the minimum amount of reading in Rashmi's class. Still several class discussions also took up these issues of women and international labor, so she had several chances to consider them during the term. Nevertheless, one reason that she may have tacitly ignored these more radical implications was because the dominant view of women's empowerment through education and rising up the corporate ladder already challenged much of her upbringing in Hong Kong. "You can't easily change your thinking," Min Wei conceded with a deferential smile, after she explained her view of how Chinese women can escape the oppression of traditional gender roles:

> I was raised like this way, you know, women are supposed to stay home, and your husband is supposed to make a lot of money for your family. But when I start going to school, everything starts to change in my mind, but it is still true that even if I am working and so is my future husband, I also expect him to make more money than I do. Otherwise it won't look good, in a Chinese family. People will start saying, "oh how come this woman is looking for a guy at this level, she should look for someone better than her." If I don't have a boyfriend, of course I would look for somebody better than me. But if I already have a boyfriend, I wouldn't expect too much from him.

Although Min Wei was raised with traditional expectations for her gender, the idea of a woman like her having a career is now a given reality.

Min Wei's family situation also encouraged these new expectations of the women gaining financial independence through a professional career. Min Wei is the middle one of three daughters in a family with no sons, and she talked of relieving her mother of this cultural burden by providing financially for her in the future.[2] Since Min Wei's family came to America when she started high school in Chicago, her mother has been the sole parent, working long days in Min Wei's uncle's restaurant. Min Wei also helped out on the weekends in the restaurant and furthered her career working Fridays at the accountants' office where her sister worked. As the possibility of women's independent upward mobility becomes more accepted in Chinese social networks like Min Wei's, the traditional emphasis on a gender hierarchy of domestic and public space has shifted to the symbolic capital aspects of income. So as Min Wei's earlier words attest, the men may not explicitly control the women, but they should make more money. It is in this new realm of competitive income and gender inequality that Min Wei struggles with the shame enforced by community talk. For a woman to make more money than her male mate "won't look good in a Chinese family," and people will start talking to help enforce the norms. Min Wei's comments suggest that the work of negotiating the contradictory pressures of these cultural norms for young immigrant Chinese women is more than enough to handle.

EDUCATION AND POLITENESS

If Rashmi's first assignment and the early course reading led Min Wei to argue for the virtues of Hong Kong society compared with China, this debate continued throughout the term with her classmate Xiao. Xiao was a 27-year old graduate of Bejing University who was pursuing an American business degree with her husband. Although the two women befriended each other because of their commonalities of gender, Asian backgrounds, and difficulties with English, Xiao resented Min Wei's assumptions about mainland China.[3]

In reference to this confrontation with Xiao, I asked Min Wei where her views of Mainland China originated. She answered there wasn't much TV or radio, that she could recall, to give her these impressions, but rather they came from her yearly visits to her grandmother in China when she was young. She described memories of no individual bathrooms, poor water systems, and eating dog meat. Her choice of details implied that her culture shock was also rooted in Hong Kong's national identification with a Western ideology of upward mobility. People from Hong Kong, like her family, would bring their own food to China if they could. She remembered the Chinese treating people from Hong Kong like kings, thinking they were all rich. When they could afford to, people living in Hong Kong would bring over money, TVs, and other luxury items to relatives on the mainland. These experiences, along with the strong Western influence in Hong Kong, led her to view "China as fifty years behind the U.S."

At the same time, Min Wei was open to revising this opinion based on what she knew of the opening of the Chinese economy. She wanted to remind me that China was changing, building industries, and people she knew from Hong Kong were going back to take part in new entrepreneurial enterprises. Min Wei also told me that Xiao had privately convinced her that some of her perceptions of mainland China were inaccurate, particularly her belief that the society did not provide secondary or college education for those desiring further education. This misconception particularly frustrated Xiao because Min Wei had stated it as a fact for her second paper in Rashmi's class. Xiao was also angered when Min Wei chose to pass off as irrefutable fact in this paper her view that mainland Chinese still only desired sons, and that many families practiced female infanticide. Despite Min Wei's willingness to concede these views, she still thought "Hong Kong was better."

When I asked her why she still felt that way, her answer indirectly suggested how she viewed the interrelations of one, Asian cultural codes of politeness, and two, education as social currency:

> Min Wei: Because I know a man, he's about 50 to 60 years old, and he was a teacher in China, and I don't think he's polite at all, even if he is well educated, he's not polite at all. When he's in a rush, he just push people around without saying excuse me. There's difference between well educated and well behaved in China.
>
> David: And so you think people are more well behaved in Hong Kong?
>
> Min Wei: um, not exactly I don't think so, a lot of people say people in Hong Kong don't know manners. Well, I would say they're not educated, lot of women, like 30-40 years old, they stay home and take care of the house

work. If you meet them on a street, even so you say sorry, they still yell at you. This generation, they start going to college, they will be more like, like us, like American people, they're politer than other people.

Clearly Min Wei associates the value of a good education with the strong cultural preference for mutual or hierarchical deference in most Asian societies. As Linda Wei Young (1994) demonstrates, in mainstream Chinese culture, politeness strategies emphasize interdependence of speakers and hearers. Ron Scollon and Susan Wong Scollon (1995) argue that any communicative interaction consists of involvement and independence strategies of face—what they define as "the negotiated public image, mutually granted each other by participants in a communicative event" (p. 35). Asian cultures tend to emphasize the independence of the other speaker, particularly in more formal situations or with unfamiliar people. In comparison, Western cultures tend to rely more on involvement strategies meant to build common solidarity with one's audience. Wei Young argues that the Chinese emphasis on deference and respect of the other's independence originates in the social proprieties and family obligations that were necessary in the long history of a heavily populated agrarian-based society. As Min Wei's reasoning in the prior quote suggests, Min Wei clearly associates these values of propriety and decorum with the social capital of education. The problem with mainland Chinese society, as Min Wei imagines it, is that there is a disjunction between "being well educated and well behaved."

This concern with education and appropriate face behavior surfaced several times in stories she told me of potential renters to whom she showed her family's upstairs apartment. Significantly, when I asked her questions about her attitudes toward spoken language, she recalled one of these incidents to imply her dismay when Americans who have achieved higher education and then work as professionals do not associate that education with these deep values of politeness. I had asked Min Wei if she ever made judgments about people based on how they talk. Would she think differently of them if they didn't speak what she would consider "good English"? She replied that she would think they are not well behaved and well educated. To illustrate, she described a "forty- to fifty-year-old lady" (she did not mention her skin color) who could only complain about everything in the apartment as Min Wei showed her around the rooms.

Although Min Wei recognized that the bathroom wasn't in perfect shape, she held her tongue when this women kept "complaining everywhere in the house." What surprised her most, however, was the woman's liberal use of the "f word," as Min Wei put it, despite her claims of professional status working with computers and clients. "At first I didn't say anything, just let her say whatever, but finally I couldn't stand it anymore." And then I said, "if you are a professional, how can you say the 'f word?'" She said, "Oh, I say that to clients too. They're happy and the boss pays me money!" Min Wei clearly disliked this disjuncture of professional class and impropriety because she also felt the need to explicitly spell out the cultural values at stake here after she related to me the details of her story. "She was saying she's professional, but it's not right that you just say it out like this. I expect you to respect me also. It's not polite at all when you say something—even though you see someone doing something bad. You shouldn't say it out in front of them. You can just talk with somebody else. You shouldn't just in front of them."

Clearly Min Wei describes this woman as rude. Yet the details of her story indicate the woman emphasized involvement strategies, both in terms of topic control and language choice, that assumed an equal or superior power relationship with Min Wei and her business clients. Min Wei characterized this woman justifying her behavior with this utterance, "'Oh, I'm just trying to help you here to improve your apartment.'—But she just keep saying and saying for fifteen minutes." In Scollon and Scollon's (1995) terms, this woman's offering of the conversational topic, rather than deferring to the imposition she was creating on Min Wei and her family, was an involvement strategy. Offering the topic "asserts the speaker's right to advance his or her position on the grounds that the listener will be equally interested in that position and in advancing his or her own position" (p. 85). Similarly, the woman adopts what she assumes is a register of solidarity with her clients and Min Wei through her liberal use of the "f word" through its purposeful breach of professional educated decorum. Min Wei, however believes that the woman's professional status should ensure the use of independence strategies, especially between strangers, which promote mutual respect.

This abiding cultural concern for propriety most likely shaped her main response to Rashmi's class as well. In one of our first talks, when I asked her how she would describe Rashmi's course to her friends and family, she replied after a slight pause, "learn ing about other cultures." When I asked her in the fall semester after Rashmi's course if there was any value in thinking about issues from that class, she returned to this view:

> I think the class that I took we learned mostly different culture of different people. That I will learn something else from other culture. So that when I meet that kind of people, I would keep in mind, oh, they are like this, like middle-east people, they use scarf to cover their face, you know? Then I won't feel weird, and say "how come you cover your face?" I won't act like an ignorant. And, that's about it.

What Min Wei told me she values from the course recalls Mike's comments about "understanding cultures" discussed in the previous chapter. As with Mike, Min Wei does not describe these cultural differences as social issues—sites of ideological struggle as they were addressed in the class. After Min Wei gave this response to my open question, I asked a directed question using more politicized language from the course: "When the class would talk about what are the causes of these cultural problems or causes for women's oppression in different places, do you think that's important to think about outside of school?" Not too surprisingly, this question led to silence.[4]

Unlike most of the students I interviewed, Min Wei did not bring up the issues of women's genital mutilation that had transfixed most of the class members. Of course she may have omitted mention of the genital mutilation as a politeness strategy toward me in our conversations. Instead, as quoted earlier, she recalled a cultural difference, Muslim women's wearing of the veil that could be more easily dismissed as innocuous. However, the class discussed readings and saw an hour-long video that historically situated the practice of wearing the veil as an issue of women's bodies in the context of nationalism (see syllabus in Appendix A). Moreover, throughout the term, Rashmi and other class members repeatedly connected the practice of wearing the veil to other examples of women bearing the brunt of preserving cultural traditions on their bodies, such as genital mutilation, footbinding, and the traditional constraints of Western women's clothing. In fact Rashmi and I agreed that many students were most engaged when the class dealt with particular practices on the body— adornment, rape, prostitution, as they had been with specific descriptions of work conditions. Rashmi took this interest in the particulars as a given and focused on having students build the interconnections between these practices as systems, to teach students "to see between the particular and the general."

So although most other students could recognize these cultural practices on women's bodies as a social issue, Min Wei chose to view them as static differences of other cultures that she should learn so she would not appear ignorant. Yet if Min Wei's values of good education are so entwined with Asian codes of politeness, her emphasis here makes sense. Like most of the other students, Min Wei also understood Rashmi's class best through the particulars. When she spoke about the practice of wearing the veil, she framed it in terms of personal relationships, perhaps even with future expectations of international business relations. If so she implied that she values a deference politeness system for this context compared with the possibilities of social change that could derive from cultural criticism. From Min Wei's view, good education then is to preserve face. Conversely, to critique the cultural practice would be to display disrespect. In this frame of thinking, someone who critically challenges the assumptions of cultural difference would be taking a superior position of power over the other. As Scollon and Scollon might argue, the power situation that occurs when people of different cultures interact often requires more inductive rhetorical strategies that promote independence of the other, rather than a deductive rhetoric of applying critical theory.

MIN WEI AS AN ESL STUDENT IN THE CRITICAL WRITING CLASS

These cultural values of politeness, along with the more instrumentalist mindset of a recent immigrant facing challenges in schooling, may help account for Min Wei's position toward the agenda of Rashmi's course. Nonetheless, we must also recognize the effects of Min Wei' s limited ability with the English language, which consequently restricted her understanding of Western countercultural assumptions embedded in critical theories from the course. According to Gita, most of the class members had rhetorical strategies they could call on to conceal from Rashmi when they hadn't read the assigned articles. "Most people weren't prepared, didn't read, so they didn't want to be embarrassed, or her [Rashmi] getting mad at them . . . so they would just make up anything, just read the title page, might say something to do with this. That's what I did! I'd listen to what people were saying,

I would just say it again, but in a different way, maybe add something else that might not be in the article." Whereas we as critical
teachers might perceive these students' comments in class as
"extending the context and finding personal connections" (what I
recall myself assuming when I participated in Rashmi's classes),
some (or perhaps many) students might view them as finding
strategies to hide their lack of preparation.[5] Min Wei, however,
felt her linguistic ability with English constrained a rhetorical
facility of the good bluff. This is primarily how she measured herself next to other students in the class. "But they're good at
English, they can just say everything, but to me, I don't know
what I should say about the paper [course reading] if I didn't read
about it. And I don't want to say anything wrong that would show
I didn't read the paper—because she [Rashmi] just assigned too
much."

Because of her still limited ability with English-language syntax, Min Wei could not improvise a classroom performance on the
critical topics of the course. Similarly, as a fairly recent immigrant, she is much less likely to be familiar with schemas of
American (or Western) countercultural thinking compared with
the more readily accessible mainstream discourses of the international business world. Regardless of whether some of the other
students agreed with premises of different American counter-
movements (such as environmentalism, feminism, civil rights),
they were familiar with these discourses' general scripts and
could touch on those commonplaces in class discussions to suggest they were making connections with the readings. So Min
Wei's difficulty with the language and discourses of Western
counterculture may also help account for her disinterest in
expressing views on most social issues.

Nevertheless, two other students with similar English-language abilities did make an effort to add to discussions or articulate difficult sociocultural issues in their writings. Like Min Wei,
these women sometimes received mediocre grades due to organization, syntax, and grammar problems, but still they felt more
committed to taking complicated social positions. Sandra McKay
and Sau-Ling Wong (1996) and Stanford Goto (1997) studied
second-language learning among Chinese immigrant adolescents. Both studies argue for viewing second-language learning
in terms of students' psychological investments in multiple identities and discourses. In our interviews, Min Wei expressed her
difficulties with learning English as a whole, which evidently
affected her facility with countercultural discourses in Rashmi's
class, much less the more generic critical language of the social

sciences or humanities. Yet she also told me she expended greater effort on her business writing class she took during the summer after her research writing course. Min Wei was clearly making a calculated investment in the discourses of mainstream business that supported her view of her future self as an upscale professional.

In contrast to this effort for her business writing, Min Wei tended to dismiss the importance of taking critically informed positions in her writing for Rashmi's course. After Min Wei stated as fact in her second paper that most mainland Chinese families wanted sons and that many committed female infanticide, she could not understand why Xiao was so upset at her. "That's just what I write," she told me later. "It's just a paper, you know. I don't want to be mean on that. It's just a paper. I just want to get some ideas out of it. She was thinking that I think that way, just think China is no good just because I'm from Hong Kong and I'm more superior than her. But I didn't mean that. I just wanted to get some idea."

In our last interview, I asked her whether she ever felt as if she were "faking it on papers." In comparison to writing for her first-semester writing course, which required more personal writing, Min Wei sometimes felt she had to "make up some stories" for Rashmi's research paper course, especially when she wrote about birth control in China. I asked her what she meant by "made up stories":

> Its not making up stories, it just what I heard from other people. What I heard according to some Chinese tradition. Like, let's say the Chinese culture [preference for sons] may be long time ago, like two generations before. I really don't know about this time, but I just assume that people in China still prefer son, cause I don't know what's going on in China right now. So maybe that's what I'm making up? Cause I just want to make my point stronger, by using the past history.

Working within the immigrant instrumentalist frame here, Min Wei provides whatever the school task demands without real concern for the implications of its content: "It's just what I write . . . It's just a paper." In terms of face strategies, she defers to what she sees as the authority of the assignment, passing off as present fact what she presumes to be past history. Yet paradoxically, Min Wei doesn't really grant Rashmi's more critical purposes for the paper any credibility, especially in contrast with her concern for the personal face interactions of Xiao misunderstanding her beliefs and intentions.

This paradox seems to indicate how Min Wei will view these different aspects of her college education, at least for now. Working out of her immigrant strategies of accommodation without assimilation, she expects her schoolwork in business to provide her with the cultural capital of the degree and the business knowledge to face possible discriminations in her future workplace. In contrast to this cultural capital for the workplace, I would argue that Min Wei will view courses like Rashmi's as opportunities to gain a particular kind of social capital to help her in interpersonal relations in the international business world. And for Min Wei, what she values in a view of education as social capital is propriety associated with the professional class that calls for emphasizing independent face strategies. As I have demonstrated, this set of beliefs is a view that ultimately is less likely to take up the cultural critique outside the formal writing for the course.

GITA AND RASHMI'S
COURSE AGENDA

Like Min Wei, Gita invested much of her academic identity in the role of future business woman. In fact she was already deeply involved in her family's international marketing consulting business. Unlike Min Wei, Gita has lived in the United States since she was six—a situation that influenced her perceptions of American enterprise, her immigrant Indian community, and her views of social action. Gita was the first student in Rashmi's class who openly admitted to me she would zone out during class discussions that she felt did not directly affect her life or academic progress through the course. Because of her educational focus on business, she knew from the first day of class she wanted to write on women and international labor. "I have to push myself to pay attention, and think about my topic, the final paper. When they are talking about politics and genital mutilation, the environment, they don't interest me, so like my eyes are glazed. I sort of block it out, but as soon as like work, or business, or government comes up, okay now talking about my topic." Teachers of the more traditional research paper class assume that students will devote greater energy to issues that interest them. Indeed that is why many writing teachers assume they should grant stu-

dents full autonomy to choose their own topics at the expense of
more focused group inquiry by the whole class (e.g., Hairston,
1992). Rashmi, however, wanted her students to analyze the
interconnections between seemingly separate issues, such as the
exploitation of both women's labor and the natural environment
in Third World nations.

Two weeks of readings and one video shown in class
addressed theories of ecofeminism from Third World situations
(see syllabus in Appendix A). And several students did, in fact,
take great interest in the issues of environmentalism and indigenous cultures, particularly Rachel, a Latina originally from
Mexico who became Gita's confidant during the class. Rachel
researched the environmental practices of indigenous Indians in
Mexico in comparison with Western development. Also Alla, a
woman and mother who grew up near Chernobyl, examined how
environmental degeneration that often accompanies Third World
development affects women's health. So Gita's concern for maintaining such a narrow focus on business issues led me to believe
that she did not see these interconnections.

> I do care about the environment, but not the way the articles
> brought it out. I'm like, what does this have to do with the
> class? I mean unless she means the environment in which
> women are working, like in the factories or whatever. That
> environment I do care about, but planting trees or something
> like that, that had no interest to me. What does that have to
> do with the third world? I didn't see any connection. Well,
> maybe like the economy and things like that, but not much.

Gita's comments reminded me of other Chicago students who
had trouble thinking about wilderness preservation because their
realms of experience were mostly urban. Rashmi herself
expressed to me her greater identification with urban landscapes,
having lived her whole life in cities. Her concern for urban space
played heavily in her dissertation's postcolonial feminist critique
of postmodern views of women and the city. Still as I believed
Gita not only to be intelligent but very savvy to the discourses
and behaviors of Rashmi's classroom, her confusion here took me
aback.

In our final interview, almost one year later, I asked her to
guess how Rashmi would respond to her complaint that environmental issues had little to do with the rest of the course. Gita's

reconstruction of Rashmi demonstrated that she did understand some of the interconnections that Rashmi hoped would emerge from class discussion:

> Gita: She'd probably laugh first, but then say that it's about time that women notice that they care about the environment in the sense that the ozone layer, plant trees, I guess it shows life, rebirth. I may be closeminded on the subject, but I really don't see why she brought up the green corps, greenpeace movement in the class. She'd probably laugh and try to explain and change my thinking.
>
> David: Why laugh?
>
> Gita: Because she's done research, had experience in that subject.

Gita's capsulation of an ecofeminist stance, "ozone layer, plant trees, life, rebirth" shows she could take on the appropriate discourse and accompanying ecological values. Yet her purposeful shorthand of this social position suggests how quickly she wanted to dismiss its importance for the issues of women's factory labor she wanted to address. In comparison with this presentation of herself as a no-nonsense practical thinker in this imagined dialogue with the teacher, it's intriguing that she portrays Rashmi's pedagogical character through her laughter. Gita may be indicating that Rashmi would recognize the importance of not taking herself too seriously when attempting to persuade her students of other views. At the same time, Gita associates this laughter with knowledge and authority; that is, Rashmi can laugh (at Gita's position or at herself) because she has done the research, and had experience in that subject.

In several other moments in our conversations, Gita showed a similar knack for putting her views in dialogue with an imagined liberal feminist Rashmi. One significant instance emerged as Gita described to me the Chicago neighborhoods in which she had lived after she emigrated from India with her parents at age 6. In her narrative, she asserted that the influx of less educated people into one of these port-of-entry neighborhoods on the Northwest Side fostered more crime, forcing their family to move further north. I asked Gita whether she believed that lack of good education influenced the rise of urban problems in the area—how did she think Rashmi might explain the root causes for the lack of education? "They probably didn't have money to get a college education to become something more. They were like basic nine to five job, trading hours for money. So didn't think much for the future, just surviving on a day to day basis. That's what she'd say."

Because this position didn't appear to contradict any values Gita had espoused up to that point in our talks, I asked her whether this is what she would say as well. Gita's response seemed to anticipate a socioeconomic critique reminiscent of several of the course readings: "Rashmi would say that there was no opportunity for them, so [they were] just thinking from day to day." But Gita's rebuttal in her own voice labels Rashmi's sociocritique as bleeding heart liberalism: "There are lots of opportunities out there, they're not going to come knocking at your door, you're going to have to go out and *look* for them, not expect them on a silver platter." Here Gita clearly speaks from the immigrant frame of reference addressed by anthropologists of minority schooling. Gita attributed this necessity to be independent to the teachings of her grandfather back in India who went to college under British rule and had to make do with less than ideal circumstances. Although Gita did not have to work for moneywhile in college—as Mike, Peter, Min Wei, and many other students at UIC did—she believed her material obligations to her family taught her the necessity of making the most of all opportunities for future economic rewards. She described her usual day as attending school until 4 p.m., picking up her brother from the babysitter, helping him with his homework, doing much of the housecleaning and starting the cooking, doing homework after dinner, and still finding time to assist her parents with the part-time business. "By then, it's almost twelve; same thing over and over again." Gita believed that Rashmi would agree with the then current American welfare system (before federal unemployment was slashed in 1996). Although Gita felt "we should help them out," she insisted the system was "going chaotic."

THE RHETORIC OF SHOWING EMOTION
IN THE CRITICAL WRITING CLASS

Gita believed Rashmi's possible view—that there are few employment opportunties for most people of color in the city—would be "thinking too much through emotion." Gita associated this reliance on emotion with the world of her extended family and Indian community, claiming that when these women discuss "the third world and women subjects" they get "really emotional." "I haven't been there too long to really think like that. I've always been taught if you want something done, you have to go do it yourself." In contrast to what Gita perceived as her extended family's excess of emotion, Gita claimed she tended to rely on "reasoning with the facts."

Indeed Gita argued that the major rhetorical strategies of Rashmi's course were emotional appeals. Significantly, when I asked her whether she felt the reading, writing, and thinking in Rashmi's class was "real work," she quickly replied, "not really," offering a business scenario to make her point. She suggested that in business, people didn't want to hear emotions; she then presented a hypothetical example of working for an environmental company that has been dumping chemicals illegally. "They're not going to want you to write a report to the press that it was wrong and we're sorry. They want you to say something like, we're going to find out who's behind it, even though they know who it really was."[6] From this example, I surmised that "real work" for Gita had no time for what people "felt." I asked her then whether she felt Rashmi's course asked her to take an emotional stance.

> Yes, that particular course, it's basically emotion. I try to stay away from that. Some of the movies we watched, I saw some people that were happy when they walked into the class, when they left they were sort of droopy. It was an emotional class for most of them. But I already know that this existed because I come from a third world society, so I know what's going on there. The class was for people who had no idea what was going on in the rest of the world.

As her comments here imply, Gita recognized the display of sympathetic emotions as a kind of social capital in Rashmi's classroom and, to a lesser extent, in the writing for the course. "In literature, English classes, if you show more emotion, the teacher seems to favor you more."

Unlike some other UIC students who had endured the mechanical instruction of high school literature classes that made little effort to connect with the students' lives, Gita attended an academically strong Chicago magnet school and, for the most part, enjoyed literary discussions in high school English. "It was sophisticated. People did respect other cultures, and we just basically talked like a discussion panel. The reading material was interesting, recent fiction that sort of plays about what is reality, get a feel for what real life is like." This description suggests the influence, if only indirectly, of Louise Rosenblatt's (1938) emphasis on adolescents' experiences and emotional understandings in reader responses emulated by some high school teachers of more student-centered classrooms since the late 1960s.

Yet Gita's simultaneous observation that English teachers tend to reward the proper display of emotion (or the display of the proper emotions conventionally appropriate for one's era and ideological contexts) can be traced back through a long, varied history in English studies. From Hugh Blair's lectures on Rhetoric and Belle Lettres popularized in the 18th and 19th centuries, to the Scrutiny group of F.R. Leavis in early 20th-century Britain and the American New Criticism of Wellek and Warren, English studies have implicitly sought to shape the sensitivity of particular middle-class sensibilities appropriate to the ideological needs of each era's dominant social classes (see Crowley, 1995; Eagleton, 1983; Hertzberg, 1991; Miller, 1997). More recently in the 1970s, as composition studies burgeoned, some writing teacher-scholars like Don Murray and Ken Macrorie responded to the era's questioning of bureaucratic institutions by favoring a view of students finding their own voices—a view that encouraged explorations of students' emotions.

But with the more self-consciously critical turn in composition studies of the late 1980s and 1990s, newer teachers have generally discouraged expression of feelings in favor of questioning social and cultural assumptions embedded within writers' emotional responses to various issues and experiences. For instance, in the teacher's guide for the third edition of *ReReading America*, a popular composition reader on cultural myths of American ideologies, the authors suggest moving polarized class discussions from what people feel about an issue to why they hold these assumptions. These teachers generally believe themselves disinterested in students displaying the proper moral outrage over social injustices.[7] Certainly, Rashmi's comments about her teaching goals, which I addressed in chapter 2, did not indicate any explicit desire for students' display of moral outrage. Gita's perception of this emotional rhetoric within a critical writing classroom, then, suggests two concerns. One, in our view of ourselves as critical writing teachers, we may not recognize situations when we just may have these emotionally rhetorical expectations of students. Or two, what we perceive as drawing out the implications of an issue, articulating its complexities, some students from immigrant or working-class backgrounds may perceive as implicit demands for rhetorical hand wringing, regardless of whether that was our pedagogical intention. Because of these students' historical situations and the values their social groups have formed to cope with them, their sense of integrity and self-worth may lie in the value of "just getting on with your life." From their view, then, they may see little purpose in rooting out the contradictions once you have acknowledged the wrongdoing in the social problem. Gita puts it like this:

> I didn't have a different view from her (Rashmi) throughout [the class], just in the aspects where her overall point of view was, "This is wrong. Something needs to be done about it." I agreed with her, but she, just, went too in depth. I guess that's what teachers are supposed to do but I would say "It's wrong; we should do this because of x, y, and z, but her, she wants x, y, z, a plus b and c, and all that stuff. [Gita's emphasis].

Of course all students, regardless of social background, may complain that their teachers expect an intellectual depth often not required of them in America outside college settings. Indeed Durst (1999) endeavors to show the valuable logic of the University of Cincinnati students' brand of American pragmatism despite their resistance to academic intellectual inquiry. But as I have sought to demonstrate in this chapter and my whole study, this language may have different social meanings for these students compared with more middle-class mainstream students— meanings that critical teachers could better acknowledge and address in their pedagogy. In the following chapter, I lay out my pedagogy with Wright State students in response to the UIC students' social meanings of instrumentalism in their work and education. In chapter 7, I return to this issue of rhetorical hand wringing from the perspective of Mike's writing for final paper in his Rashmi's course. For the remainder of this chapter, I examine how and why Gita held to this perspective of Rashmi's class so that we may better understand its social implications.

When Gita described this dynamic of "showing emotion" in English courses, she offered a moment from class discussion that Mike had also brought up with me (as I discussed in the previous chapter). It was the end of the first month of the term, and class members were discussing their responses to "Life on the Global Assembly Line" (Ehrenreich & Fuentes, 1993). As one of the most concrete writings of the course on one of the most material issues to which all the working students in the class could relate, the article sparked strong sentiments against corporate exploitation of Third World labor. Still a small minority of individual students challenged the ease with which the class majority could denounce these corporations' behavior.

Of this minority, Mike spoke the loudest. Gita told me later she initially thought of Mike as a class clown—an impression Mike certainly fostered for himself. Yet Mike's comments that day made Gita reconsider her judgment: "When he started talking about that, I found that there were other people who actually *thought* like me" (Gita's emphasis). In Gita's mind, she separated the participants in the discussion between those who came from a "business point of view" and those who spoke more from "emotional stuff." She claimed that on that particular day it seemed she and Mike were the only ones coming at the issue "from a rational point of view." In contrast, she characterized the emotional view of the others as solely a matter of ethics; we shouldn't do that because it's wrong. "Why not?" Gita asked, continuing the class debate during our conversation. "If you're talking about economics and business and things like that, you should do that. You save costs and all that stuff, but you should also maintain the environment and the quality of the factory through your production plan or whatever it is. But the other people had no support for saying what they said. Whereas Mike and I had *facts* behind us. Look in the U.S., it could cost ten dollars and up, and in India would cost two dollars. I don't feel like money, money, money, but it plays an important factor."

Like Peter and Mike, Gita questioned the moral authenticity of most students who took the majority position during this discussion and similar ones throughout the term. After several class members registered their disgust toward the corporations' physical and psychological exploitation of women's labor detailed by Ehrenreich and Fuentes, the focus of discussion shifted to the possibility of political action. To my surprise, Mike was the first to suggest boycotting the products of these companies. He offered the boycotting of Coca Cola as a model of local action that could in larger numbers influence global practices. But just as some students agreed with Mike's view, he argued that most people wouldn't be able to give up their pop-drinking habits. In my discussions with Gita, she concurred with Mike: "It doesn't mean much," she stressed, "if you're so concerned, but still go to the

Coke machine and put in your sixty cents." Regardless of whether some of the students thought themselves sincere during this discussion, Gita saw their moral indignation as primarily performances of the appropriate emotional outrage for the benefit of the teacher. "It goes back to what I said before, Rashmi already told us what she was doing, her Ph.D., her dissertation, that that's what she's dealing with, so that's what they did!"[8]

Critical writing teachers could interpret Gita's suspicion of other students' sincerity in this classroom situation as a rationalization of her own lack of social action. Loeb's (1994) study attributes this strategy to several of the "adapters" in various U.S. colleges he profiles, particularly at middle- or upper class institutions. By demanding an often unobtainable purity of motive in those who work for social change, the adapters can avoid any guilty feelings from simply promoting the status quo. But Gita's case is not that easy to theorize away, because she had previously trained as a volunteer for a battered women's shelter despite her parents' disinterest. In other words, Gita acted from two sets of seemingly conflicting convictions. Her socioeconomic situation as part of a first-generation Indian immigrant family shaped her practical views of labor and a free market economy. Yet she did not allow these instrumental convictions to overrule her social concerns for women that had been forged in her clashing situations of culture and gender. Nor, however, would she allow these social concerns to seriously alter her views on business management.

Still Gita also stated several times a strong concern for ethical business practices despite her identification with more instrumental goals of management. In her final paper on women textile workers in India, Gita demonstrated how she can theorize her individual social positioning as an Indian-American woman with business aspirations in comparison with the historical plight of the Indian workers. To do so, she incorporated Maria Mies' writing on Western women's complicity in the new international division of labor and gender. Rashmi focused the class on this reading for two sessions to familiarize everyone with terms used in analyses of Third World development and politics. From a global perspective, Mies argues that when Western women—fashioned as the principle consumers in a gendered economy—look for the best buy they unknowingly underwrite the exploitation of Third World women's labor. Gita told me later Mies' view expressed what she felt about this issue, "but didn't know how to express it till I read it." At several points during our discussions, Gita detailed different examples of bad international work practices with high profit margins from recent TV and print news, such as Nike in Southeast Asia and Calvin Klein in Mexico. "It's like blaming each other rather than taking responsibility. If it's your name on the product, you should be aware to a certain extent what's going on."

In the case of Mike's classroom example of Coca Cola and Pepsi, Gita suggested with a smile that that example did not really affect her because she didn't drink pop and so could not really participate in a boycott. Yet she argued hypothetically that she would stop drinking their products if she found their employees in India and elsewhere "were working under harsh and hazardous conditions." Gita claimed to me that she had stopped buying products in the past if she heard about the company's unfair labor practices, although she could not think of a specific instance. She finally described a conscious effort to look for tags on clothing and other items that say they were produced in the United States as a way to avoid the worst evils of the new international division of labor, although she knows this may not be a guarantee of fair labor for those American workers.[9]

GITA'S TENSIONS: INDIAN FAMILY EXPECTATIONS, GENDER, AND THE MARKET ECONOMY

Although Mike and Peter also believed much of the whole-class discussions were inauthentic performances that they associated with brownnosing or fronting, Gita was the only participant who described these performances in terms of emotion or affect. Perhaps the cultural dissonance some immigrant students encounter between school and home communities tends to promote this awareness. Although Min Wei did not use the same language of affect to describe rhetorical expectations for the class, her Chinese socialization to public discourse certainly made her aware of other class members' different levels of emotion in class discussions that she felt incapable of producing herself. For Gita, however, I believe her tendency to view Rashmi's class through this particular language derives more from tensions in home and community expectations of gender and achievement than cultural dissonance with mainstream schooling. By illuminating these tensions, we may see more clearly the frames of reference that lead to Gita's assessment of critical writing classes, and perhaps then other immigrant students' views in similar social positions to hers.

Gita's choice to major in business management follows the trend of many college students who have opted for more vocational degrees since the early 1980s. Nonetheless, her motives for this choice reveal a more complicated picture that helped shape her view of emotion in Rashmi's class. True to Ogbu's and Gibson's model of the immigrant child, Gita stressed the pressure for monetary success she felt her extended family in America and India imposed on her. As the daughter of the only brother of three who finished college and as a first-generation immigrant who has opportunities unavailable to her female cousins in India, she often feels the burden of obligation to the entire extended family. Yet Gita complained that these family members discounted going into the business world as not lucrative enough compared with the medical professions. "They have this preconceived notion that doctors are going to make money, so everyone in the family, all the teenagers are like I want to be a neurologist, a pediatrician, a surgeon, a pharmacist. When I decided to change my mind and go into business, I became an outcast."

Gita attributed this single-minded goal held by many parents in her extended family to their lack of college degrees. She reasoned that although they are mostly educated, their lack of higher education may prevent them from seeing valuable opportunities aside from the high-status medical professions. Although the parents in the larger family tacitly enforced strong expectations for education in medical fields, Gita's parents entered into their own entrepreneurial venture as many American immigrants have in the past. During Gita's high school years, her parents began a spare-time consulting business to help people in the community get started in international marketing. In part because of this experience, Gita's parents have encouraged her interests in business, including her in the day-to-day work of their consulting despite the objections from the rest of the family.

At the same time, Gita faced mounting pressure from most family members, including her parents, to accept an arranged marriage in her immediate future now that she had turned 18. Not surprisingly, Gita described herself as trapped between two cultures and time periods, contending that the Indian-American community's fear of total American assimilation may have strongly influenced the family's insistence on an arranged marriage. Gita also pointed out that when one of the other daughters in the extended family eloped with a man from a different caste and religion, these family circumstances exacerbated her situation. "Another of the only three girls is going on that track, so that the whole family is up to me. Like, okay what is she going to be doing? Is she going to support the family or is she going to go out of it?"

Gita claimed her family and Indian community implicitly enforced the preservation of these social codes through indirect communication and women's gossip (e.g., Gibson, 1988). Although Gita's parents encourage her independence, she claimed her father often lectures her to "watch what you say in front of other people." Whereas Gita tends toward forthrightness, she believes that the majority of the extended family and Indian culture value "beating around the bush and putting extra softness in the words."[10] "I've gotten into trouble for saying what I think. The gossip travels back really fast to you. In the Indian community, the whole society would know as its like a thousand people; they would eventually know who it is." Gita concluded that her father was beginning to understand her disinterest in getting married soon because he did not rely on the gossip as heavily as her mother. In contrast, her mother denies her view since "she lives in the society where gossip is everything." Significantly, when Gita measured the extent of her own interest in gossip, she used the necessity of work as her yardstick. "I do gossip, but not to where I'm trying to study and someone comes up and goes, 'Do you know this and that?' I don't *care* if it's not going to affect my life! I don't need to know.' Or they say like, 'do you know what Madonna did?' Is Madonna going to come out and help me if I lose my job or something?" Gita was clearly engaging in a great deal of socially aware, high-stakes critical thinking to survive these lived situations. All too often our field's writings on critical pedagogy make it seem like critical thinking only happens, or could happen but doesn't, in the privileged reflection of the classroom.

In her efforts to resist this sway of the traditional Indian women's emotional ethos embodied in the gossip of the community, Gita viewed herself as the family rebel. In our talks, she set her concern for rationality and facts against her mother's love of Indian Bollywood movie melodramas. According to Gita, these melodramas often romanticize the modern conflict of women's autonomy versus the cultural obligations of arranged marriages. These movies, Gita commented, most often reduce women's need for individuality to a quest for authentic love against the will of their families. Despite Gita mother's concern for preserving the tradition of arranged marriages, her mother loves to identify emotionally with the movie's young women who struggle against their outmoded parents. Yet Gita also described her mother's need for practicality and cold business sense, particularly as a working partner of the family's part-time business. Offering her mother as a representative example of other women in the family and culture, Gita delineated these contradictory behaviors of excessive emotions and calculating rationality that she often judged as hypocritical. It is her experience with these contradictory behaviors within her larger family and historical situation that help lead her to see an underlying expectation of an emotional rhetoric in Rashmi's class, where Rashmi did not explicitly recognize this value embedded in her assumptions of critical teaching and writing.

Gita also attributed her skepticism of these behaviors within the extended family to her training for a battered women's shelter. When I asked her how she would describe Rashmi's course to a family member, Gita recalled talks with her father when she took this counseling training:

> Oooh, actually my dad sort of didn't like that I was taking this [Rashmi's] class, I sort of sensed it. He knew that all this stuff already existed in other countries, and it's like, "why do you want to go learn more about that or something of that nature?" Because when I was training for counseling in the shelter, I used to come home and talk, and I think that played a role in my not wanting to get married, because of all the things that were happening and I was listening to. See you doing this, that's what makes you think like that, that's what all guys do, that's what all men do, (softly spoken) beat their wives around. I'm just saying that's something to be considered, but he didn't see it that way.

At the same time, Gita perceived her rebellious urge to speak her mind as a way to preserve the honor she believes she owes to her parents. She remarked that her friends and cousins advise her to sneak out behind her parents' backs and give the family whatever line they want to hear. "But I can't do that. See, I put my parents and my brother first, my relatives next, and then myself. . . . Where I can't dishonor my parents, I can dishonor the *whole society* [Indian-American community] by taking completely opposite views of them."

Gita's need to maintain an autonomy from these varying tensions of the larger family expectations help explain her emphasis on a business perspective compared with the emotional sympathies emphasized in her family's social networks. In our conversations, she framed this autonomy as an entrepreneurial venture: "My priorities are to succeed in starting my own business in five years, so that I won't have to work for anyone." Her pet dream was to eventually live in Australia "because in every other country there is a relative there." Her need for autonomy, then, may have also played out in how she perceived the display of emotions as cultural capital in Rashmi's class, especially when addressing similar sociocultural issues, and promoted her unwillingness to perform this role of moral outrage.

If Gita tended to devalue an underlying emotional rhetoric in Rashmi's class, she acknowledged its importance more readily in two other courses she took around the same time. In the same semester as Rashmi's course, Gita was taking a German literature course in translation that focused on women's hardships in World Wars I and II. Although she found this course also called for emotional responses in a feminist frame of thinking, she found her responses "flowed more easily through a women's connection and a bond to these situations. I saw it more like instinct." She reasoned that because Rashmi's course dealt with business and labor issues, she might have questioned more what she perceived as implicit calls for emotional responses.

Gita also found to her initial surprise that she needed to "show emotion" in her letters for her business writing course she took the semester after Rashmi's class. Several times during our discussion, Gita referred to the difficulties she was having with the demands of this course. She was fast learning her insistence on no-nonsense language did not serve her well when it came to the rhetoric of customer relations.

> We're supposed to write this letter to someone, explain to her that this is not our problem. I just came out and said this is not our problem but if you would like to address it, there's this meeting. And she [the teacher] gave me a C+ for that! I guess even in business when you're writing to other people that aren't involved in the business, you have to be more emotional, have to feel what they are feeling and put that in the letter, so I'm going to have to learn to do that.

Like Min Wei, Gita had more of her future identity invested in the business writing class than in the critical writing Rashmi expected. So she was more willing to develop her facility with rhetorical principles of audiences' pathos and writers' ethos. "You're obviously going to be dealing with people of different backgrounds. They might just be the most emotional person you'd ever meet. To meet their needs, you have to sort of say what they want to hear."

The business writing class explicitly examined the rhetorical usefulness of pathos. In contrast, Rashmi assumed she was emphasizing logos—the exploration of social contradictions and implications through research writing. Similarly, many critical writing teachers want to engage their students in a structured inquiry of moral consequences that leads them to a moral outcome. When immigrant or working-class students' integrity and coping strategies are rooted in an ideology of self-sufficiency, they are much less likely to see the rhetorical usefulness of this academically minded criticism outside the classroom. Instead they may tend to view it as an excess of pathos that has no practicality other than necessary classroom performance.

INFLUENCING THE TEACHER: CONFLICTED VIEWS OF CAPITALISM

Finally, it is this ideology of self-sufficiency in students like Gita, Min Wei, Mike, and Peter that leads them to question the course readings' critical rejection of capitalism as a potential part of the solutions to social injustices. Around midterm, Rashmi and I discussed Gita's first two papers (which led into her thinking for her final paper) and her view expressed in class. Rashmi addressed Gita's perspectives in the context of other students in the class:

> I think a lot of students are struggling with this too. They are learning in a system which affirms capitalism all the time. I'm raising those questions to enable them to see the kind of doubleness of their approach. Many of the students see the contradictions in capitalism, and then they feel it ultimately for the good, that once these women [in developing nations] start earning, accumulated enough, probably there will be better lives for their children. And that's what the top economists say. Costs but in the long run, all will benefit.

Rashmi's comments could certainly refer to the instrumentalist values of work and education expressed by Mike, Min Wei, Gita, and Peter as I have interpreted them. Because of their historical and material situations that have positioned them, in varying respects, on the margins of the dominant professional class, they can locate social contradictions in capitalist formations. Yet it is precisely those situations that also lead them to question many of the critical readings' categorical rejection of capitalism.

Being an attentive teacher, Rashmi proved herself open to these students' situations, or as much as she knew of them from the class discussions and their writings. In fact, at the same time we discussed Gita's writing, Rashmi considered how the students' views were changing her positions. Here, I was referring to how Gita began her second paper, a summary of a historical article about Indian women textile workers. In the beginning of the paper, Gita states her belief in the worth of capitalism, but then spends most of the paper showing the detrimental effects it has on these women's lives when the textile work is industrialized.

> David: So its interesting that you asked Gita in her paper if there is any good coming out of this capitalism if she believes in this.
>
> Rashmi: Yeah, because I'm also revising my positions, and I feel that to take on a totally anti-capitalist position is not going to work in this classroom and also it's perhaps a foolish position on my part.
>
> David: So both revising position toward teaching and activism?
>
> Rashmi: Exactly, and my position toward capitalism. Because I feel there is such a wide spectrum of people who do see some good, and, as some students said, the advancement of science have improved women's lives.

I think both Rashmi and I viewed this moment of the teacher learning from others as an opening for genuine dialogue in the critical writing class—opening ways to critique the theories underlying the readings we may bring into our classroom. As one approach to continuing this dialogue, in the next chapter I detail the process of my work memoir pedagogy in my first-year composition classes at Wright State University and reflect on students' accomplishments with this project.

NOTES

1. Min Wei, however, did not follow this suggestion for her final project. Instead she chose to write on the history of family planning

policies in mainland China. Her final draft was primarily a flowing patchwork of quotations from other sources that summarize the chronology and general impact of these policies. Rashmi's end comments praised the paper as "a good survey of a broad range of state policies," but felt she did not take up a "more concrete argument about women's relationships to state policy." In one respect, Min Wei's writing strategies followed Chinese cultural norms that value the authorities of the past over too quickly analyzing and formulating one's own interpretation. Helen Fox (1994) explains this view of gaining wisdom: "one must repeat the wisdom of the past in order to understand the present" (p. 50). Similarly, Young (1994) might argue that Min Wei's lengthy summaries of China's birth control policies echoes the Confucian concern for presenting the reader with the whole context before addressing a part. Chinese discourses tend to favor the evoking of persuasion through a more holistic understanding, rather than the Western expectations of provoking the reader through deductive analysis. Min Wei also admitted the paper was rushed at the time and far from her first priority, suggesting she fell back on summary as a default structure from her culture or for the necessity of time, disinterest, or lack of confidence as many American students do.

2. Ogbu et al. (1991) found that many immigrant children who persevered through instrumentalist strategies in school held family and/or community goals, rather than individualist aims.

3. Xiao's resentment also directly related to her suspicions about Rashmi's course materials on Chinese female infanticide in relation to birth control policies in mainland China. In particular, Xiao harbored a Chinese nationalist suspicion of an Indian teacher who offered students' critical perspectives of mainland China's cultural inequities and state policies. In several papers, she felt the necessity to defend recent Chinese history, though when I met with her and two friends from Beijing after the term she deeply criticized life in communist China and its restrictions on her education. The mutual friction between Xiao and Rashmi are well worth further commentary. Yet as they relate more to conflicts of nationalism and the issues of international students, rather than the topic areas I have chosen for this study, I include Xiao here only in the context of Min Wei's responses to the class.

4. She launched into another story, however, when I asked her whether there were any times her view conflicted with others. With this prompt, she told of several times when her boyfriend disregarded her opinions. "He believes because he's a man, he's supposed to know more things than me, maybe that makes him uncomfortable, or maybe just the way he is." In other words, in the realm of personal relationships, Min Wei could address cultural gender differences as an issue, but not in her memory of what she valued from the class.

5. Gita also described with amusement how she could detect these rhetorical performances:

> Gita: It might sound funny, but I know by the way their hands move, their gesture, their SPEECH. Their eyes rolling, like going from line to line. I notice those things. I'm not supposed to, but.
>
> David: They're playing out a script?
>
> Gita: Exactly.

6. Later in our discussions, I found out that Gita drew this example from a case study in her course, "Writing for Organizations," which she was taking that fall semester. Ironically, Gita later expressed her frustration with the course's rhetorical expectations for business correspondence. As I discuss later, she ultimately concluded these business genres of writing required a more carefully considered emotional rhetoric than in Rashmi's class.

7. Feminist scholars in composition who reject more masculine rhetorics of rationality prove an exception. Still Susan McLeod's (1997) recent book, *Notes on the Heart: Affective Issues in the Writing Classroom* may be a response to this critical turn away from emotions. She argues that writing teachers often don't pay enough attention to issues of affect and emotion in the writing classroom. Calling on psychological studies, she suggests how teachers can help students manage the flow of emotions and affect in their composing processes, motivations, and interactions. The fact that she felt a need to make this argument indicates many critical teachers' blindness to emotional expectations toward their students.

8. After this particular interview discussion, Gita expressed interest in visiting a class I was teaching. After sitting in on my Writing for Popular Publication class where groups were analyzing movie reviews, she labeled my class more *personal* than *emotional*. Although she claimed she would like the popular critical writing assignments, she would have disliked writing in the personal essay genre from earlier in the course. After the class, she confidently pointed out which groups or individual students she sensed had not done the reading before class and were primarily performing from their knowledge of the particular movies.

9. As my colleague, Nancy Mack, wisely pointed out, ordinary Americans have so few public and popular role models of answerable deeds of activism. Expressing one's political concerns through charity and politically correct shopping are acts of the class.

10. For a discussion of this rhetoric, see Fox (1994).

Making Work Visible

WORKING AT WRIGHT STATE

When I came to Wright State in 1998, I immediately identified several parallels to the history, student population, and initial mission of the University of Illinois at Chicago. First used as a branch campus for both Ohio State and Miami University, Wright State (named after the Wright brothers who worked in their bicycle shop in nearby Dayton) was founded in 1967 just after UIC built its circle campus in 1965. Whereas UIC drew students mainly from Chicago, Wright State draws most of its students from the suburban and rural areas in the four surrounding counties of southwestern Ohio. Although Wright State claims an address in the city of Dayton, Ohio, I find it more accurate to locate it nearby off the interstate. Indeed if UIC's ambivalent history of material space typifies urban issues of gentrification, Wright State's history of physical location evokes recent concerns about suburban sprawl and its problems for farming communities. When Wright State was first built, it faced miles of cornfields; now it lies on a small highway opposite several small shopping centers and a mile away from the local mall.

Like UIC, Wright State was meant to serve a local working-class population of mostly first-generation college students. Until recently, Wright State students were almost entirely from White working-class backgrounds, with most of them working nearly full-time hours to pay for their education or living expenses. Like UIC students, most Wright State students commute to school. Compared with Chicago and UIC, the county doesn't provide adequate public transportation to the school, sadly following the trend in much of suburban and rural America. Lack of parking remains the chief complaint echoed in the student newspaper and first-year students' problem–solution papers.

Yet with the academic and research successes of the university over the past 5 to 10 years, this population has shifted to between 30% and 40% of students living on or near-by campus. Although the majority of the students still work outside of school, I cannot easily assume the students in my classes share common patterns of experience in regard to social class and family backgrounds. Even with this change, the students who come from more middle-class backgrounds tend to identify with working-class values toward work and education. In most cases, the middle-class students' families are only one generation away from more traditionally working-class jobs. Or these students' parents have risen to middle-class incomes and positions through fields that require manual labor such as farming and manufacturing.

Unlike UIC, Wright State's students are 90% White, originating from midwestern or Southern Appalachian heritage. Although the school is only 20 minutes from the African-American neighborhoods of Dayton, many local African Americans spurn what many label "White State" in favor of Wilberforce University and Central State, two nearby historically Black colleges, and Sinclair community college in downtown Dayton. Understandably, the few African-American students who do attend Wright State tend to stick close together and rightly view themselves as an outnumbered racial group on campus. Because of the rich ethnic diversity at UIC, writing teachers there assumed courses organized around generative themes of culture and difference would motivate most of their students' writings and discussion. Culture was the default pedagogy. Perhaps because no group stood out as a racial minority, the UIC students often felt comfortable looking closely at the local practices of their own cultural groups and critiquing the power relations they observed within them.

However, if Wright State University (WSU) students did not share UIC students' more open-minded views of cultural differ-

ence, they did share an emphasis on work identities and a pragmatic orientation toward the intersections of work and education.
During my first year at WSU, I taught an ethnography-based
research writing class; many students opted for their workplace
as the default field site, mostly for their convenience and accessible knowledge. For several of these students who did research
their workplaces, I perceived divided loyalties between their roles
as workers and students. In several cases, students had difficulty
distinguishing ethnographic analysis from reporting on their job
procedures or voicing their work grievances. Although most students introduced to ethnographic analysis toil over the problems
of analyzing as well as reporting, I also began to see what this difficulty might say about many WSU students' views of work. At
WSU, teachers often voice concern that working students value
the security of their jobs over their college studies. Granted,
many UIC students also often identified themselves with a work
ethic before their student roles, but I do not recall them feeling
tied to a particular present job at the expense of school. I believe
now this difference of loyalty to present work identities between
WSU and UIC students has partially to do with the WSU students' more limited job opportunities in a rural and suburban
space away from a major city. WSU students display a greater
loyalty to their jobs, regardless of their satisfaction, because they
believe jobs that pay enough and accommodate their schedule
are hard to find. Perhaps this socioeconomic situation influences
some students' abilities to "step outside" their work roles when
writing about their workplaces.

Regardless of whether the supposition explained this difference between many WSU and UIC students' relationship to work
identity and present job loyalty, the WSU students' deep investments in work identities compelled me to design a first-quarter
composition course on the generative theme of work values.[1] The
UIC students with whom I researched and taught had revealed to
me multiple orientations toward instrumental views of work and
education (as discussed in the previous two chapters). The UIC
students also expressed different priorities toward cultural values
of work depending on their local situations. For instance, some
might emphasize the role of their family in shaping work values;
others might emphasize peers and neighborhood influences,
whereas others might point to tensions of work and values of
success or freedom. I knew my course at WSU needed to provide
spaces for students' own articulation of their multiple values
toward work.

DESIGNING THE
WORK MEMOIR PROJECT

As I initially conceived this quarter-length course, students would develop three projects using three different methods of inquiry as appropriate to the purposes of each project. In the first project, they would explore their life lessons of work through a work memoir. Second, they would analyze community practices of a particular group at work through a work ethnography. Finally, they would examine cultural myths of work they see in particular visual media (a TV show, movie, or Web site) in comparison with the critical insights they would have gained from each other's memoirs and ethnographies of actual work situations. Although the writing genre for this last assignment could have been a media analysis or rhetorical analysis of a Web site, I also imagined students could write media parodies or advocacy letters in response to their analysis. In the end, I did not want to cram the third project in such limited time, and so I limited the course to the work memoir and ethnography. In this chapter, I largely concentrate on the work memoir project.

The participants in my ethnographic research, such as Mike, Peter, Gita, and Min Wei, repeatedly taught me that they could articulate complex understandings of their local cultural and material situations embedded in their use of conventional views about work. For instance, Gita echoed the words of her grandfather that people shouldn't expect opportunities on a silver platter, but, as she articulated her perspectives in chapter 4 embedded in this statement are complex views of the immigrant experience and critical understandings of capitalism and gender exploitation. Through their articulation of lived experiences, these students would persuasively argue for the validity of these common sayings to help them make meaning in their lives in individualized ways that should not be dismissed as merely commonplace. I designed the work memoir project to aid students' articulation of this complexity and validity embedded in their sayings and stories about work. Too often critical writing teachers have tended to write off their students' use of these maxims and narrative tropes as unworthy assimilation to dominant cultural values. As Dawn Skorczewsi (2000) recently reminded us, when teachers encounter a cliché like "hard work will pay off in the end," they habitually challenge the statement's validity with their own clichéd responses in their margin questions.

Typically teachers ask questions intended to push the student to reexamine the appropriate reading from their course, or a contradiction in the students' own paper, that complicates the ideology in their use of the offending statement (as I had done in my responses to George and Kisha). Most of the time when I ask questions like these in students' texts, I realize later my implicit motive was not to learn from others, but to instruct them in what I already believe I know.

My ethnographic research has shown me that when teachers implicitly dismiss the use value of students' commonplace statements, they often do not gain internally persuasive authority with the student writer. So with the work memoir project, I wanted students to demonstrate the use value of their cultural beliefs toward work through their stories of material situations and lived experiences. In the context of Thomas Newkirk's (1997) *The Performance of Self in Student Writing*, this stance toward student writing follows in the best tradition of American pragmatic philosophers such as William James, John Dewey, and Charles Pierce. Like the sophists and postmodernists, the pragmatists did not believe there were foundational truths outside the contingencies of language and changing situations. But unlike the absolute skepticism of these other antifoundationalist perspectives, pragmatism values experience as the arbiter of belief. As Newkirk explains, James would judge the validity of a belief by its consequences—its utility in an individual's or a community's life. Yet the appraisal of a belief can only begin with the willingness to engage in the act of believing. Newkirk offers the example of jumping a ditch: "Suppose I need to jump a big ditch and my ability to do this is in doubt—yet I believe that I can; that belief is a crucial component of the experiment I am attempting. Without it, I cannot make a true test of my ability; or as James ([1896], 1948) writes, 'The desire for a certain form of truth here brings about the special truth's' existence'" (p. 45).

From Newkirk's pragmatist perspective, my work memoir project urged students to ask: "How do we construct our own narrative in a way that empowers, inspires, and sustains us?" (p. 68). Newkirk charges that cultural studies approaches to composition, such as the ones discussed in chapter 1, show "no ethnographic interest in the moral utility of these [students'] commonplaces" (p. 91). Although Newkirk's polemic doesn't account for the whole ethnographic side of cultural studies that does value people's "vernacular theories" of cultural power (see McLaughlin, 1996), he has a point here. Similarly, he rightly contends, "It is paradoxical, if not hypocritical, for compositionists to argue for the centrality of 'class' in our understanding of students, and at the same time advocate a form of skepticism that is antipathetic to the sources of moral and spiritual power in many working-class communities" (p. 101). With the work memoir project, I sought to invest my and the students' ethnographic interest in the moral utility of their pragmatic beliefs toward their lives at work.

I often discuss with students how they must "earn" a statement or claim they make in their writing. To me this remark means they must represent and examine the details embedded in their statements particularly when they appear as clichés like the ones Skorczewski catalogues. When groups in class look at student writing, they look for where they think writers have earned their statements, what paragraphs of greater complexity make the statements credible to us, and why. Yet it's only in the writing of this chapter that I have recognized how apt this metaphor of earning a statement is for these students' pragmatic orientation to school and the theme of this course. They need to work for and earn credibility—to earn respect. More important, a colleague pointed out to me that my subconscious use of this language showed a respect for their language. I also have to earn their credibility.

My ethnographic research had also convinced me that students were more likely to value critical positions in writing through an inductive approach. For students from working-class backgrounds in particular, the material situations of their family's and community's lives lead them to value critical knowledge as something embodied and gained through lived experience more than through abstract thought. In contrast, when students follow a deductive approach in critical writing, they apply a critical theory to their experiences or another text, generally reproducing the blueprint put before them. Therefore, I have come to believe that students are more likely to be internally persuaded: There can be use value in critical writing if they reflect on and analyze their social circumstances on their own without a full-blown theoretical model for them to trace over.

This perspective also suggests teachers should think about critical writing as a process one comes to understand in developmental stages. I use the term *developmental* in reference to Vygotsky's understanding of the continual development of the social self, not as a pejorative notion of an uneducated self as the term is often institutionalized in developmental writing programs. Because deeply committed critical writing teachers are often blinded by pedagogical faith, they tend to forget that anyone's understanding of culture and power comes as a developmental process contingent on the situations he or she encounters. Donna Qualley's (1994) reconsideration of feminism with her undergraduate students provides a compelling example of this developmental process. Qualley came to see that although most current feminist criticism challenges essentialist theories of women and men that ignore the influence of social positions such as race, class, and region, her female students interested in feminist thinking needed to begin with a more essentialist dichotomy (and perhaps not move beyond it in the course of her class or others') that emphasized the necessity of solidarity and larger group cohesion. Without the time for that political development through stages, Qualley argues, these women tended toward a more conservative individualist brand of feminism. Like Qualley, I have come to see the political importance of writing process approaches that recognize people's need to come to new knowledge through developmental stages of inquiry. Thus, if handled carefully, the structures of a writing process approach motivates students to actively engage in interpreting, creating and articulating knowledge in critical writing classes. And that involvement in an inductive approach to inquiry of social contexts, especially as an embodied experience, is more likely to foster students' internally persuasive critical perspectives.[2]

SITUATED PROCESS

To that end, before the class encounters any readings, we begin the work memoir project with a series of prewriting prompts that I would describe as a situated process approach. The prompts are meant to elicit writers' multiple orientations toward cultural values of work through reflection on situated moments of their continually evolving work identity and persuasive influences on work issues in their lives. By encouraging a broad range of concerns or topics within this generative theme, I try to tap into the students' individual motives for analyzing whatever associations they have with values of work from their past. My hope is that in the process they will critically consider the narrative they want to invent for a future self-based on those past experiences, images, and influences. I adapted the prompts from my colleagues Nancy Mack's and Brady Allen's series of writing/thinking activities intended to draw out themes of negotiating identities from multiple angles. In my course, I describe these first activities to the class as mining for stories, playing on this implied metaphor of work and the digging into the calcified rock of memories and associations for the rich vein they might expand on for their memoir writing.[3]

Nancy Mack (1998) argues that in memoir, "the past, present, and future selves can enter into a complex dialogue. . . . Through representation, language gives us the ability to change experience, to rewrite the experience as we decide for it to be. Even memoir involves writing for change, to change the meaningfulness of a past experience." Yet Mack also recognizes that our use of language in memoir "comes charged with the motives of others," sometimes demanding a struggle between conflicting social roles and identities. My prewriting prompts are intended to call forth writers' perceptions of their past, present, and future selves as imagined through the people, places, objects, and institutions that have influenced their present or changing values of work. In the following, I summarize the nature and purpose of each of these writing prompts. These prompts are what I give to the students while I also orally relate some of my own and previous students' specific examples:

1. *Role Models.* Consider those who have been good and bad role models for teaching you about the world of work and possible careers. Thinking about parents, grandparents, neighbors, or even models in the media, whose attitudes about work and discipline (or lack of it) have been influential to how you acted in different jobs and how you want to see yourself in the future world of work.

2. *Places of Work.* Make a list of jobs you have had, whether or not for pay. Which jobs would you want to revisit, which avoid like the plague? From your list, choose one or more to write what you can recall about: (a) personal relationships with coworkers, bosses, customers; and (b) details of place that stand out in your memory.

3. *Objects.* List 10 or more objects from your memory that relate to the subject of work. They can be someone's tool for work or objects that identify their kind of work, such as a metal lunchbox or briefcase, or they might be objects of others that you associated with the kind of work you want to do, such as a computer or particular car. For each object, list what associations

you have with it. Were there any rules (spoken or unspoken) associated with it? What role did they play in how you saw yourself then, what you imagined of yourself for the future?

4. *Career Aspirations.* List careers you are considering. Briefly describe what qualities you would be looking for in a job that you choose to do. For each one, try to list some specific memories that might have inspired these aspirations. You can also try listing your ideas of dream jobs—where did they come from? Or if you associate working with everything drudgery, make notes about moments when you were enthused and energized in a "work activity."

5. *School as Work.* Many students tend to treat their participation in school as a job or as preparation for a future job or work life. With a partner, list ways school experiences are and are not like a job, considering not just classes but social life as well. Now, by yourself choose a positive and negative specific experience from the list and describe the experience to show positive and negative sides of school and work.

Over the course of several class periods, everyone writes lists, notes, and associations from the prompts, each time discussing with a partner the possible topics that emerge from their notes. From these notes, they choose two experiences, or a connected series of events, to expand on for a freewrite that they share in groups to help them choose and develop their ideas for the first draft of their work memoir. In the process, they have generated a storehouse of memories associated with their present work values that they can draw on for their later drafts to enrich and possibly complicate their interpretation of the memoir's main story.

In keeping with my developmental situated process approach to the writing course, the assignment for the first draft calls for an emphasis on self as more than one voice, and the revision requires a situation of self in the social context of others. For the first draft, students concentrate on the self in terms of action and reflection, requiring them to consider their sense of self as a tension between the character participating in the story and an observer reflecting on that participation. Through our readings of published and student model memoir essays, which I address further next, we discuss how the memoir genre requires conflict, complication, and/or growth of self, but not moralizing (admittedly rhetorical moves that help constitute middle-class social distinction as Newkirk [1997] thoroughly demonstrates). The students' goal is to use their story to analyze their views of the working world in their life so far. The revision assignment then extends this sense of self in two ways. First, students compare their work values associated with their memoir drafts to assigned readings that categorize examples of work types and values. Second, students also craft scenes of their experience(s) in their memoir to explore the implications of the social contexts that helped shape their current perspectives. To foster these kinds of complex aims of narrative and analysis, I involve the class in a three-part revision process that is recursive and overlapping over the course of the project. The class reads and discusses models for their work memoirs, they examine theoretical articles on work types and values, and the students develop scenes in their memoirs that dramatize the issues in their represented experiences.

READING AND DISCUSSING WORK

After students have generated and discussed with each other this storehouse of their perspectives, informally noting cultural and socioeconomic patterns, we examine published memoir writings on work experiences and values as possible models for their first draft. Three times I have had students respond to and discuss Ted Kleine's (1994) essay, "Living the Lansing Dream" about his love/hate relationship with his blue-collar town of Lansing, Michigan, and the economic difficulties of finding good work there in the early 1990s after the boon of the postwar period. As a writer in his early twenties recalling his first years out of college, Kleine's situation also approximates the regional values of the midwest largely shared by most Wright State students. Although his father was a middle-class state bureaucrat, Kleine appreciates the working-class cultures of his friends and industrial Lansing's history of previous economic success. Kleine also defines his work values in terms of place (a common view shared by varying working-class communities in the studies of Foley, 1990; Heath, 1983; Lindquist, 2002; Phillipsen, 1992; Stack, 1974). Most important, he pokes fun at himself as a character, never taking himself too seriously despite his sharp analysis of Lansing's historical context, suggesting a model for students' serious play in their writing.

The first time I used this essay, a few students wrote that they could see their friends' struggles with their hometowns in

Kleine's memoir, but I was surprised by many others' public resistance to a class discussion of the essay. Several students refused to believe jobs were that hard to come by for Kleine and his friends in Lansing. They contested he could have tried harder or should have been willing to leave his hometown much sooner. I tried not to argue other than to briefly point to the historical contexts of de-industrialization and effects of globabilization in the early 1990s. By chance, Sandi, one of our teaching assistants, happened to visit my class that day. Sandi grew up in Michigan and knew these hard times from experience—yet these particular students also dismissed Sandi's first-hand account. After all that the students in my research had taught me, I had never intended to challenge students' dreams about individual achievement. Indeed Kleine's conclusion shows he learned his lesson, doing everything possible to get out of Lansing and landing a journalism job in another state. For my part, I wanted us to ask what factors might explain why Kleine stayed as long in Lansing as he did, and how does he convey his views toward work and himself as a character through his details of place. In other words, I wanted to foster an ethnographic inquiry and a focus on writing strategies, rather than provoke an explicit political argument. But the passion of the most vocal class members that early in the quarter prevented the efficacy of this approach that day.

Although I had not intended to contest their ideologies about work, a teacher colleague who comes from a working-class background reminded me later that these students still perceived me as "questioning their religion." By simply directing attention to the problems of the job market, I had touched on a sore point— their fears of finding their place within an ever-changing world of future work.[4] After this blow-up, I looked with trepidation to class members' responses to the next reading I had planned. My fears proved to be correct. Among several short readings, the class read a *New York Times* editorial and its response both written in 1991 during the peak of downsizing in America. Again I did not choose this reading to highlight job anxieties, but to have the students compare the writers' cultural values toward work and social class. In the editorial, Julia Carlisle, a "young urban professional" recently laid off from a network news station, describes the effects of her friends' unemployment and underemployment. In response, Florence Hoff, a working-class mother and clerical worker, chastises the professional's expectations of entitlement, arguing, "we have always taken the jobs you label 'absurd.' . . . We are the people who work Sundays at the mall: the people who

mind your children while you pursue your meaningful careers." I
figured few in the class would sympathize with Carlisle despite
her clear-eyed view of her situation, and I assumed most would
side with Hoff's championing of people whose labor supports the
opportunities for upscale professionals.

I had also chosen to physically arrange all of us in a circle,
where everyone would contribute one statement from their own
response letters during our discussion, rather than have the
strong voices in the small groups take over the classroom dynamic as they had with Kleine's essay. The day before the class,
Linda, who usually kept quiet in class, privately mentioned her
frustration with Carlisle's view and her greater interest in Hoff's
perspective. I encouraged her to speak up in our class the next
day, yet when she did I was again surprised to hear her and several of her classmates lambaste Hoff's view of work and education. Speaking for a working class, Hoff writes, "We left school at
17. There was no money for college; we were not among the bril-
liant few who could win one of the increasingly scarce scholar-
ships. Our parents were short on time themselves." Linda and
others zeroed in on this passage; they objected to Hoff's portrayal
of working people's advancement through educational institutions as a hopeless endeavor. Shrewdly, they offered themselves
as counterexamples: We're here; anyone can find ways to go to
college even if you need to work. Obviously, I hadn't anticipated
how this passage might rub against their faith, their pragmatic
belief, even more than Kleine's essay. For some people in the
class, Hoff's claim was a threat to their future that needed to be
squelched.

Trying to keep quiet for once, I asked if anyone understood
Hoff's position in a different way. After a minute or two, Karen, a
student of racially mixed parentage as she later told me, suggested we needed to consider what kinds of support systems people
have to keep them going in college, especially if they have children. She referred to some friends and distant family members,
arguing they didn't have the money for these support systems
and could not always count on the availability of other people to
help them out. But Josh, who later wrote with knowing humor in
his work memoir about the burden of being a White middle-class
male, skillfully debated all of Karen's examples. Ironically, Josh's
memoir also addressed his deep aspiration to become a lawyer to
defend people whom society had forgotten. Here in our class,
however, Josh marshaled that lawyer acumen he gained from his
father's friends to take apart each of Karen's claims, coercing her

to back down. In a conference a week later, Karen told me she purposely took a devil's advocate position—that she actually agreed more with her class members who resented people's excuses that they could not afford to attend college.

The second time I taught this course, I replaced these two editorial letters by Carlisle and Hoff with Linda's and Josh's work memoirs from the first time I taught the class combined with two articles from *Time* and the *Wall Street Journal* on changing issues of work and family dynamics. Josh's essay examined his view of the changing role of the White middle-class male as well as reflected on the time binds of his dual-income family and his father's decision to leave a high-paying administrative position to spend more time with his family and pursue a Ph.D. Linda's essay analyzed how observing her aunt's caring for her children despite severe cancer influenced Linda's current choice to become a full-time mother in contrast to her parents' sacrifices to their careers for the sake of the family.[5] In a writing response and class discussion, students analyzed and compared the issues and attitudes in the two published articles and how the two student writers represented these social concerns in their memoir writing. My revised emphasis on student models has generally accomplished my goals of the class analyzing issues of work prevalent in most of the students' backgrounds and indirectly demonstrating possible approaches to writing their first draft.

Once students have written their first drafts, they read and respond to two academic analyses of work types and values to better theorize on their work situations and aspirations they are interpreting in their memoir draft. From the field of management sciences in 1989, William Roth categorizes work situations into five types based on a goal of thoughtfully engaging work that he describes as a combination of his top categories—developmental and leisure work. Robert Bellah and his co-writers, a group of sociologists writing in 1985, analyze most people's current work values as a job, a career, and a calling, favoring their final category as the work of the self linked to a larger community. Although both articles argue for a hierarchy of values toward work situations, and so favor particular kinds of work, their writing tends to be more descriptive than prescriptive, using case examples. For this reason, I believe, the students have been receptive to the descriptive, rather than heavy-handed argumentative, qualities of these articles. Many of their written and oral responses express gratitude for the language of these categories, which helps them further articulate their understandings of work experiences and ideologies they have adopted.

In my reading response assignment on the Roth and Bellah et al. readings, the students address what work types and values from the readings their memoir draft most seems to illustrate. I ask them, "Does the work type and value most represented in your draft match your overall values about work—what you hope for in your future? Briefly compare the differences (or similarities) between these values of work for you." They then share their responses in pairs, discussing the differences and comparing each other's memoir drafts. For many students, their previous encounters with work, whether in a job or learning from others' experiences, tend to not measure up to their varied aspirations. The readings' work categories help them examine that distance between work realities and their cultural values. Instead of requiring students to explicitly incorporate their analysis from these categories in their revision, I encourage them to see how their analysis helps them clarify their interpretive focus for the memoir. I ask them how they can convey this analytic focus through their written observations of their past self, their choice of dialogue, sensory details, and the structure of their memoir essay.

CRAFTING SCENES

Along with this process of analysis through reading and writing, students practice crafting scenes to develop the narrative of their memoir and delineate the social contexts that influenced their perspectives and choices toward work in the past. When helping students write in nonfiction genres that encourage narrative, I have come to distinguish between the purposes of developing a dramatic scene as opposed to adding an example. Adding an example primarily helps to support and possibly develop a writer's particular claim or statement, promoting the author's monologic view. Developing a dramatic scene, however, promotes a dialogic view that can serve several functions beyond support and development. I have adapted Susan Wheeler's (1993) key elements and language for crafting dramatic scenes. The students look for these elements in our model memoirs, using color highlighters to make these strategies more visible to their understanding, and practice developing them for their own pieces.

1. Setting the Stage: Place is part of context; it affects and reflects how people think, feel, and behave.

2. Dialogue: to show what people do to each other's feelings.
3. Action and Reaction: what people do, and how they gesture, speak, or listen reveal them.
4. Thoughts, comments, interpretations, feelings (both you as character in the past and you as observer in the present).

Scenes can open up the text to other voices and perspectives in ways that remind me of Kenneth Burke's dramatistic pentad, exploring multiple motives for people's actions and reactions as well as the influence of location. As a dialogical form, scenes can serve three strong purposes for the students' critical writing, which the class discusses using model memoir essays:

1. To let the readers understand your perspective for themselves.
2. To convey the complexity of experiences, the mixed feelings, and responses.
3. To show the influence of these experiences by showing readers the social contexts that helped shape your perspectives.

As the students develop their scene(s) for their memoir revision, they also need to consider the influences of social contexts as appropriate to the focus of their memoir. Our readings of memoir essays offer examples of reflecting on these social contexts when writing scenes of experience. In the revision assignment, I offer these questions (adapted from my colleague Richard Bullock):

- *Place*: Were there any unspoken rules about how to behave in this place? What was appropriate or "normal" behavior? What were normal activities? How much did you follow or resist these rules?
- *People*: What social role or roles did you play in this situation? In relation to others? What behaviors or expectations did those roles involve?
- *Social background*: How did your social background (type of work your parents and others close to you had, your social class, region, ethnicity, religion, etc.) influence your actions and thoughts at the time?

In some of the best writing students have done for this course, their indirect considerations of these questions of social context have led them to a theme I had not really considered—the theme of control over their lives as developing adults.

THE EMERGING THEME
OF TAKING CONTROL

As I look over students' work memoirs from the last 3 years of teaching this course, I now see how many of them deal with issues of control: over their past and future work identities, over tensions between work and family life, over constraints of social class and gender. Often these issues over various kinds of control converge into each other. Janet Bean (2003) also points to this theme of control in her students' stories of work. Following Newkirk's pragmatist view of students' writing, she asserts that "by casting themselves in the role of hero in a narrative of meritocracy, they affirm their ability to control their lives." Bean recognizes what students gain from this rhetorical move, but she also shows how some student writers' emotion over their working-class parents' bodily pains as sacrifice for their children's education disrupts and critiques the main narrative of the narrator's eventual success. In the dominant cultural narrative of success," Bean writes, "parental silence and sacrifice are ethical choices designed to promote the welfare of their children." In the narratives Bean examines, these writers speak their parents' pain, making it salient and present, to honor their parents and critique the system of middle-class achievement that they must still take part in despite emotions of anger, loss, and nostalgia. Students in my classes have often enacted a similar double move in their work memoirs, developing a narrative of self-control while simultaneously detailing the material realities that complicate their story.[6]

These various issues of gaining control in many of my students' work memoirs have helped make me more conscious of another factor necessary for critical writing pedagogy. To be persuasive, the education must be in synch with the developmental issues of the students. This necessary connection between the dynamic development of the social self and the development of critical writing means more than the usual call for relevant topics like current music and media. As Jabari Mahiri (1998) puts it,

New college students are at an age and in a situation that forces them to consider complex issues of identity and family/community connectedness, especially since they have often been distanced from their familiar support systems, and they must determine how they will represent themselves in and to a larger stranger world. (p. 82)

The often wildly uneven transition from adolescence to young adulthood requires continual testing and reassessing of control in all realms of the social self—when should one accommodate, oppose, or resist various forms of power relations in multiple domains of one's life and in what ways given each situation? Compared with scholars of secondary education like Mahiri, teacher-scholars of critical pedagogy at the college level have almost never explicitly addressed these developmental concerns. Yet this necessary connection between the developmental social self and critical writing follows the logic of Friere's view that effective critical teaching must make room for students' individual dreams of freedom within collective work toward social change.

I briefly discuss several students' memoirs to draw out these themes of gaining control in the respective issues of tensions between work and family and in representations of working-class identity. I conclude with an in-depth analysis of the revision processes and critical insights of two female students' work memoir writings.

Not surprisingly, a good number of students in my course choose to examine their control over tensions between work and family life, often reassessing their past history of complicated family life through the lens of their own work situations. For instance, Audrey's Jenning's essay, "I Work Hard for My Money, So Hard for it Honey," opens with Audrey and her father packing clothes, but she is leaving on a trip to Florida and her father is moving out of the family home for good. The core of Audrey's essay chronicles her experiences working a summer in the GM plant where her father climbed from factory worker to a GM executive of labor relations now working outside Ohio and where her brother Roy also works summers to earn money for dental school. Audrey has to negotiate a difficult role as "Rocky Johnson's little girl" when she encounters some workers who are not fond of her father because he sided with management. Through a series of scenes, Audrey demonstrates how the oppressive work atmosphere wears her down and tears at her sense of self-identity. Ultimately the monotony forces her to reconsider her father's and family's situation.

> I always wondered why my father never expressed any feel-
> ings and how he was able to cope and be so strong with all
> that was happening. I then came to a conclusion. I was going
> through a lot of new changes in my life just like my father
> was five years earlier . . . I learned from my father and Roy
> and oddly enough from the assembly line workers, that you
> just have to learn to deal with the cards that you are dealt.

On the surface, Audrey's use of this popular maxim sounds like a
kind of cliché of accommodation to the status quo that critical
teachers tend to abhor. Yet the details of her scenes and analysis
of worker relations in the factory help articulate the complicated
social functions of this statement embedded in her efforts to gain
control over these issues of family and work.

Melissa's essay, "From The Ashes," also opens with family
members moving, this time the mother and children leaving while
the father is away on business. To Melissa, her future work
means self-sufficiency and control over her life and family, the
kind of control she admired in her mother's ability to keep her
family together. Melissa's fashioning of a future working self is
intricately tied to her desire for stable family life unlike the broken promises of her father that she dramatizes in several short
scenes. Building on this theme of control, Melissa also depicts
herself as a girl watching her mother at work:

> I wanted to fill out paper work, go to meetings, and have my
> own desk where I was in charge. Every move she made and
> everything she said was given my full attention. She seemed
> to know it all. Seldom did things go wrong, and if they did my
> mom had the answer. She was in control, unlike the life that I
> had been so accustomed to at home. That type of control and
> unhesitating security is the life I now strive for.

I admire how Melissa's choice of language in this passage moves
from the girl's young, inexperienced understanding of power for a
woman, measuring her mother's control by the outward signs of
her mother's work identity, to the more considered resolve of her
young adult self that now measures control by the possibility of
"unhesitating security."

This theme of family security runs deep in some of my students' writing about their values of, and hopes for, working lives.
Matt's essay, "Like Father, Like Son," follows a familiar but worthy path of a son who wants to work with his father, this time in

the real estate market selling houses locally.[7] Matt's first draft made no mention of these concerns. Instead he had written about the day of his high school graduation, using my writing prompt about school as a job to throw together a conventional compare/contrast paper. When I met with him to discuss the draft, I asked him what he liked about it. I was greatly relieved when he replied, "Nothing. It's all B.S." When I asked why he was in school and what he hoped to do in the future, he spoke about his admiration for his father, who had worked three jobs without a college degree before he passed the real estate exam, and his mother, who lives with multiple sclerosis. Matt and I discussed how he was different from many of his friends who wanted a college education to get far away from their parents. In his final draft, he includes a dialogue with a friend that dramatizes his difference from the common trend of work aspirations.

> "Why do you want to stay close to home and come back here to work?" Joe asked with a tone showing that he was confused with my decision.
>
> "Well Joe, my Mom has gotten really sick lately and I want to be close if anything were to happen, plus I've always wanted to work with my Dad. The funny thing is, you're always the one commenting on how loaded my parents are. Then why wouldn't I want to make the big bucks?" I joked.

Although I know Matt wasn't entirely kidding about his drive for the big bucks, his conscious use of the verb "joked" implies his understanding of what values of success are dominant in the larger culture compared with what situations and values ultimately motivate his efforts at work. In a sense, Matt wrote his essay to speak to his friends like Joe, through scenes of his family's history, his mother's illness, and joking conversations with his dad that belie their fears of the family's future, he wants to lead readers to identify with his choices.

In Russel Durst's (1999) study of University of Cincinnati students' resistance to two critical writing courses, he describes how most students felt their traditions of family were under attack when one course unit focused on critiques of American myths of the model family. What intrigues me about my students' critical reflections on the intersections of family and work is how these concerns emerge largely from the students' own motivations. Perhaps they are more willing to critically analyze these situations when the teacher and course readings do not tacitly intend to squelch the commonsense sayings that motivate and sometimes sustain their families. Indeed in Audrey's, Melissa's, and Matt's memoir essays, those sayings are still there alongside dramatized scenes, descriptive narratives, and reflection that articulate the complex local meanings they attribute to those sayings.

As Janet Bean (2003) demonstrates, students who identify with their immediate working-class family backgrounds often recognize there is much at stake in these issues of control because the family histories of physical labor and pain are so present before them. Like Matt's essay, the final draft of Gwen's essay, "Working Towards My Dream," includes a scene of a father's advice. Although the character of Gwen's father speaks the familiar words that "you can do anything if you put your mind to it," he couches this saying with warnings about how bosses "are usually going to try to make you feel as though you are being watched so that you constantly stay busy." Gwen's first draft narrated an incident where she badly cut her finger in a meat slicer at her deli job. In this draft, the emphasis is on the loss of bodily control. By the end of her revisions, the memoir also examined the theme of social control—of controlling her work identity and her worry of bosses' controlling her life that she saw in her parents' working-class experiences. The writing about the loss of bodily control helped trigger the issues of social control she saw in the physical labor of her parents that she expands on in the revisions. Gwen writes that she knew her father worked harder in a "rundown automotive station than anyone else I knew because every night he came home his hand would be black as night, covered by grease and grime." In comparison, she writes that her mother "had a more clean, business like job" managing a seafood grill. Nevertheless, Gwen describes her mother's job as "very stressful on her because she worked a lot of nights, had to keep control of all the waitresses, and she was always watched by the owner."

Gwen then describes the strains of her different jobs in food service that followed in the work patterns of her mother, first working for her at the seafood grill and then at a local deli. Although both were physically taxing, she emphasizes her relief that in her first job she avoided a real boss by working for her mother and in the second job she mostly worked alone. She describes her father's pleasure that the second job made her feel like she was her "own boss," but she states that he then brought her back to his working-class realities that "one day I was going to have to deal with the boss situation and that the longer I waited the harder it was going to be to adjust." She then adds, "I told him about my dream of becoming my own boss, and he replied by saying that I was going to have to work extremely hard in order to pursue that dream." Surprisingly, the essay doesn't include the anticipated scene of Gwen's oppression under a particular boss. Yet the scenes in her next deli job in another state where she has the accident illustrate the hard work her father foretold, leaving Gwen with no easy conclusion other than a refusal to work in food service any longer, if she is to continue to work toward her dream of full self-control over her work identity, and a reaffirmation of her father's distrust of the bosses class.

Each of these four memoir essays shows why we need to acknowledge the developmental aspects in the range of these themes about control in young adulthood. Yet I have not really concentrated on the process of how these issues of gaining control can emerge from the acts of revision over a succession of drafts, in the deliberate crafting of memories. In several ways, Anna's and Elaine's memoir projects allow me ways to detail that process. In writing about Anna's and Elaine's composing processes, I am wary of including what I believe was my role in the directions they took in their revisions. I do not intend to cast myself as teacher as hero here, diminishing (or entirely assuming knowledge of) their choices and motivations. Nonetheless, I contend that persuasive teaching of critical writing is to various degrees a collaborative effort between teacher and student; at best a Bakhtinian dialogue maintaining what Lad Tobin aptly calls a "productive tension."

PARADOXES OF GAINING CONTROL

In my writing conferences and revision comments, I was clearly guiding some students toward these themes of control. However, I did not know to name this prevalent theme of control until the second time I taught the course when Anna wrote her memoir essay, "Behind the Red Door," about teaching at a day-care center. In her two freewrites based on the prompts detailed earlier, she wrote of two moments from the day-care center. The first was an arrival narrative, chronicling her first day when she stood "behind the red door" hesitant to go into the job interview and the sense of purpose and joy she then found with the children when she did. The second freewrite discussed the problems she had caring for an autistic boy at the center. Before the boy's parents were even aware of his autism, she had struggled to communicate with him. The first story gave her eventual control over her environment and new work identity; the second revealed a moment out of her control. In her first draft, Anna chose to place both stories side by side, stating briefly near the end that she began to make a little progress with the (yet unnamed) boy before she left the job to come to school to become a certified teacher. In our discussion over the draft, in addition to discussing how, why, and where she might develop description, dialogue, and reflection, we talked about the working conditions in the job because the essay implied she was teaching 22 eighteen-month-old children by herself. Anna's revision developed some physical detail of the center's deterioration that to her suggested many of the children's possible home situations.

> Also I began to notice other things such as broken toys and the unsanitary conditions I was now entering. Cars with wheels missing, blocks that were broken, and the dirt and dust that looked as if it had engulfed the whole room. It was just a big shock for me to see because when I was a child everything I had was brand new and sparkling clean. I just couldn't believe these children were playing in such pitiful conditions.

In this revision, Anna made visible the socioeconomic conditions of her labor, and possibly of children in the center, that were also out of her control; it wasn't only the experience of working with an autistic child that threw her. In this sense, Anna took up the purposes of my revision assignment, as I outlined them previously, to examine further the social contexts of the moments they had written about in their first draft.

Anna had also added an introductory scene to the essay that implicitly called my attention as a reader to these issues of control and socioeconomic inequities. Now the essay opened with a flashback to 8-year-old Anna jumping into her grandparents' truck after the school bell only to rush home to play school teaching her imaginary students in her grandfather's office at home—a routine she claims to have kept up for about 6 years. Anna writes, "I was so relieved to see that my classroom was just the way I had left it the day before, the chalkboard clean of chalk dust and my desk was neat and in order." I now wonder whether Anna learned this trope of playing work from another student's essay from the previous year that I offered as a model of a work memoir. Elaine's memoir essay, "Playing Work," which I discuss later, opens with two girls playing secretary in an office. Elaine later contrasts this play with the realities of her temp job and the work situation of her parents. Although I had not specifically suggested others use this same trope of the child playing work, it's likely Anna was influenced by this approach. (Lad Tobin [1993] addresses these dynamics in his chapter on student models for writing, imitation, and peer competition.) In any case, it was the contrast between the child Anna's need to keep her imaginary classroom spotless and the delapidated conditions of the new teacher Anna's day-care center that led me to ask her about this theme of control in my comments.

In the final revision, Anna expands on this scene of play, depicting herself as the 8-year-old child speaking to her imaginary class to emphasize for her readers this need for control.

> "Good Morning class! Let's settle down now and get ready for this busy day we have ahead of us," I screamed. "Now, let's get out our spelling words and read them out loud together." I stood up by the chalkboard with a huge smile on my face knowing that I was in total control over my students. I knew I was able to conduct my class the way I wanted, and not the way of anyone else. My school was the best. It had the best rules that any school has ever had such as: chewing gum, having recess every five minutes, and having parties every day.

By this third revision, Anna is willing to make fun of her child self as a character, both illustrating a child's desire for control denied her as a student and parodying those moments of institutional power.

With this paragraph, she also sets up the theme of control she follows through the memoir when she elaborates on the second draft's association of the broken toys with some of the children she cared for in the center. She contrasts the security of her childhood with their lives of single-parent families, foster families, and biological parents in rehab or jail. "I didn't know if I was going to be able to handle this job. I was getting depressed and downhearted with the stories and surroundings I was now being put into." Anna tries to physically compensate for these social inequities, presumably at her own expense, as many early childhood teachers do. "I knew I had to acquire the perfect environment for these children like the one I once had as a child. In order to do this I had to stay after hours to clean up my classroom. I scraped the hardened dirt that was built up around the edges of the windows and doors. I also went out and bought new toys and games for my kids."

These additions complicate the view in her first draft that the autistic child she later encountered was the only real challenge in her job. Now readers experience a series of complicated situations, some dealing with material conditions and some with developmentally difficult children, over which Anna needs to gain control. Anna used a different font to highlight revision changes in each draft, leaving the different fonts in each new successive draft so readers could see the traces of her revisions. When I used her essay as a model the following year, the class could visibly see the gradual construction of this theme and its complications over the three drafts, making a more persuasive case for revision as a critical process than anything I could have said. Immediately following this passage about the physical changes she attempted in her classroom at the center, Anna indicates through a smart economy of language her gradual regaining of control over time and the new eruption to come. "As art projects, naps, and changing diapers passed by, all I could do was think of the many children's lives I was touching. Suddenly, a mother placed her crying, kicking son Daniel into my arms." She describes how she initially perceived Daniel as another emotionally difficult child she could eventually handle as she had other children. But then she details her observations and reflection over the next few weeks that reveal Daniel's differences from the other children, leaving Anna to wonder if Daniel was deaf. Here in the third revision, Anna again picks up on the theme of control that once more eludes her grasp:

> As an eighteen year old, I didn't know what to do or think about the situation. I began to face reality again. I noticed that the control over my imaginary classroom had now disappeared. . . . The perfect room I once had was tarnished and the perfect kids I once had were now flawed. . . . It seemed things were terribly wrong. . . . All I could do was try my hardest to help Daniel to interact with everyone else along with keeping myself motivated.

Anna illustrates that struggle to stay motivated in one's work, even when one enjoys most of its challenges, when she describes Daniel's mother confiding with her about the tests for autism. "She looked deep into my eyes and when she put him down he ran off into his own world, without even saying goodbye to her. As her eyes shut, she turned and walked out the door, and it was just another day that had to pass at the daycare." In the final draft, Anna creates a short scene with dialogue that illustrates the strenuous small progress she made with Daniel over time, enabling him to "interact a little bit with other children in the class."

Anna concludes the essay reflecting on her broader understanding of realities she must continually face. "On the charming side of reality I noticed that as a person I was able to make positive changes in people's lives. Likewise I found out that the ugly side of reality can be very devastating and hard to get along with. I came to understand that I was not always going to have the total control I wanted over certain aspects in life." In her final portfolio, she included mounted pictures of kids at the center—a gesture that indicates, to me, how much of herself she had invested in this work and her writing about its realities and rewards. Although some writing teachers might dismiss Anna's reflections as a conventional commonplace, they are nonetheless earned by the details that demonstrate the material and emotional complexity of the situations.

Perhaps I admire this essay so much because it is a teacher's story and so, to a degree, our story. And as the husband of a preschool teacher, I know Anna's writing addresses the socioeconomic difficulties of the profession as well as the unexpected pleasures in the gestures of children that keep people teaching. In Anna's writing of her memoir essay, the theme of control was paradoxical. To gain greater control as a critically reflective writer and a more mature image of herself as a future teacher, she needed to examine and rhetorically craft those moments when she could not totally control the conditions and actors in her work world.

CRITICAL PLAY AT WORK: FASHIONING A FUTURE WORK IDENTITY

Elaine's memoir essay reflecting on her past and future work identity did not draw on such dramatic memories as Anna's encounters at the day-care center. Yet her hard look at the everyday grind of her temporary work in a large insurance firm in contrast to her remembered pleasure playing office as a child helped her to examine what perceptions of work her middle-class parents permitted themselves in their family home. Like Anna's and many other students' first drafts, Elaine's first draft employed the trope of the arrival narrative as the place and time of personal change, overly detailing her first day into the world of paying work. As someone who had endured many odd and meaningless temp jobs in his time, I was struck by the drafts' physical details. For instance, Elaine describes assembling pamphlets for a company conference: "The smell of the ink from the various papers began to burn my nose, and the outermost skin on my fingertips felt like it was on fire from shuffling through so many." In most temp jobs, workers often only have these empty details of white-collar detritus in their working day because they rarely have any connected understanding of what the company and its executive employees are doing. In *Clockwatchers*, Jill Sprecher's fictional movie about women temping in a nameless corporation, the four female temp workers and the camera fixate on objects found within the offices. Elaine writes about this first draft in her final portfolio self-assessment letter.

> I was not happy with the scenes describing my actual day at work; I thought they were boring, overwritten, and somewhat pointless. However after talking with group members, I realized these scenes set the stage for the whole purpose of my work memoir—that, truly, work can be boring and simply like a mindless list of tasks barked out by a superior.

Only when I brought Elaine's finished essay into class as a model the following year did I see how the descriptions of her limited movements through different spaces in the company building further illustrated her giving up control to others. These descriptions of space also served to emphasize the theme of work environment she developed in her revision as I discuss further later. In the first setting after she enters the building, she is shown around the maze of all the departments with their "little beehive-like cubicles dividing members of each subdivision." Then she is seated in "a brightly lit corner of the marketing division" to fold the pamphlets. Finally, she is given filing and copying tasks in a much more confined space. "It was kind of lonely and awkward; it was a one-person job, so there was no company, and I actually had to work out of an isolated closet for a while." The spaces of her movement and interaction shrink in size throughout the day until she is working inside a closet.

In Elaine's revision, she added the opening of playing office as a child with her friend, lovingly detailing the items they lay out

on their coffee table desk, such as "startlingly fluorescent while-
you-were-out message memos" and "vibrant yellow legal pads."
Here, at the beginning, these items and play offer symbolic
empowerment:

> and then we got down to business, taking our seats next to
> each other in front of our newly transformed desk and invent-
> ing customers and problems that only we, the model employ-
> ees of a make-believe firm could deal with. This was serious
> work for us, and we never permitted anyone to bother us dur-
> ing the duration of our "office hours."

This revision effectively contrasts the imagined power and pleasure in this scene compared with the often-numbing banality of
Elaine's real office experiences later in the essay. Yet Elaine
doesn't claim the entire temp experience numbed her senses and
intellect; she speaks well of people who would talk and joke with
her even when she was in the closet. Still the inclusion of this
memory of childhood play helped her develop a strong rhetorical
"turn" (as Newkirk terms the reflective shift of realization or
learning in memoir essays) of crafted memory in her essay. After
the descriptions of her first day temping, she writes:

> As a child, I was extremely idealistic and optimistic about
> having a job and the tasks that accompany it. But oddly, I
> immediately noticed that my new office building had no win-
> dows through which to glimpse the outside, sometimes non-
> working world, and a sudden vivid memory came back to me.
> During one of our office games so many years ago, I recalled
> Jessica looking scornfully at me as I shirked my duties to
> dash outside and watch my new neighbors planting a tree.
> And the more I thought about it, the more I realized that
> almost every time we played our game, my attention was
> diverted in some way—I had decided then, often, to read a
> book instead, write a short story about a topic important to
> me, go for a bicycle ride, or just observe a different aspect of
> life through that sunny bay window. I realized that those
> memories held more credence for me than any opinions about
> working.

From this revision of memory, Elaine then reconsiders why
she imagined office work in this "laid back, almost casual, way"
by examining what her parents "both held and revealed" to her

about their jobs when they came home. Her father worked for "a large company in the city," and her mother became a secretary— a job that "filled and reinforced [Elaine's] image of women in the workplace." Although Elaine now recognizes the lack of glamour in their jobs, how often they would work long hours and return home very tired, she remarks how both parents would only bring home the favorable aspects of their jobs. "Basically, our middle-class situation didn't allow for non-working parents. . . . My parents hoped that, by working long and hard and yet not communi-cating it as such to me, they could instill in me a feeling that work was a necessary, but not horrible, area of life."

In her self-assessment letter, Elaine attributes some of her insights here about social class and work values to her written responses to our course readings on work values and types. "In this way, I discovered how exactly I felt about the social concerns and individual convictions that they brought up, and I used my responses to their ideas in my papers." Ultimately, Elaine's reflec-tions on the revision of her memories and their social context give greater credibility to the working self she wants to envision for her future.

> I don't want to feel trapped in an office, slowly suffocating because I can't see the outside world. The things I liked about my job involved the people not the actual duties. . . . Our careers engulf so much of our time and capacities. I would love to set a new example of working in my family by allowing for no separation between what I love to do and my work, to have a job that is rewarding not only for its material results but for its results in my mind, actions, and ethics.

Admittedly, most of my students have not been able to verbal-ize these concerns as eloquently as Elaine has here. Yet many of them identify with her motives, if not her precise cultural values, and so tend to benefit from the opportunity to articulate these concerns as best they can for themselves over the process of the work memoir project. As I have seen these themes of control emerge from the students' writing over the past 3 years, I consid-ered foregrounding the idea of control in the assignment and activities. Fortunately, however, I have also come to recognize that the students' critical articulation of these themes as they relate to cultural values of work remain all the more persuasive to them if they emerge from the students' situations and develop-mental moments rather than be assigned by me as the teacher.

In chapter 6, I examine the situated social meanings of two other cultural themes—individualism and unity—that emerged from some students in Rashmi's class in response to the critical writing teachers' agenda of "difference."

NOTES

1. When I first developed this course, I was not familiar with Jim Zebroski's (1994) writing courses focusing on work that he has taught at Syracuse University (see *Thinking Through Theory*). I would now claim affinity with Zebroski's motives and methods. As I address later in this chapter, I am also indebted to my colleagues Nancy Mack and Brady Allen, for writing process models I have adapted for my course. For another theoretically reflective first year writing course design on issues of work emphasizing the larger theme of social and environmental sustainability, see Derek Owens' *Composition and Sustainability* (2001).

2. See also McComiskey (2000) for another teaching approach that recognizes the critical necessity of understanding process in teaching critical writing. Building on theories from the fields of rhetoric and cultural studies, McComiskey's pedagogy emphasizes the larger social processes of cultural production, consumption, and distribution. In contrast, I am arguing for a situated process approach that allows for the unpredictable developmental moments of the social self if teaching is to achieve internally persuasive authority.

3. The second time I taught the class, I read Seamus Heaney's poem, "Digging" before they began writing from the prompts. Although Heaney's poem doesn't deal directly with mining, it beautifully illustrates this metaphor for writing, work, and memory as he compares his father's farm work digging in the earth to his digging with the pen years later to better understand the values of his father and grandfather's work. Next time, I would also encourage the students' interpretation of the poem before they begin writing.

4. Both Durst (1998) and Wallace and Ewald (2000) describe classroom conflicts over issues of affirmative action. Durst contends that most of the University of Cincinnati students in the classes he observed clung tight to traditional perspectives of family and success in the classroom. If we consider the perspectives of young people whose families have only attained a middle-class income in the previous generation and who now face the unknowns of an ever-shifting job market, it's not surprising that many maintain the necessity of traditions that supported their families in earlier generations. Indeed as I discuss later in this chapter many of my students' writings on work values often lead them to examine concerns of family and control in their future lives. Because Wallace

and Ewald's book also includes a classroom controversy over affirmative action, we need to acknowledge that many current students'
anxieties over future employment will likely complicate the persuasive authority of critical teaching.

5. Linda's scenes of her aunt brings the pain of families' bodies to the
    forefront of her narrative. In Janet Bean's (2003) insightful analysis
    of her working-class students' narratives of work, she argues that
    the students' written representations of their parents' physical pain
    from working class jobs "actually challenge prevailing discourses of
    success that insist on a disembodied view of work," where parents
    silently subsume their bodily pain as sacrifice for the next genera-
    tion. "Expressions of emotion, particularly those of obligation and
    gratitude, become tropes through which children can acknowledge
    their parents' suffering, attribute meaning to bodily pain, and cri-
    tique from within dominant narratives." Although Linda sets up a
    contrast between the unpaid care-giving work of her aunt and the
    paid jobs of her parents, to her credit she also acknowledges the
    bodily exhaustion she often saw in her parents when they were
    home.

6. Most students know that their teachers want "details" in their
    essay, but often teachers' only rationale for this desire is to provide
    more vivid images and to help the reader identify with the writer's
    position. Although I certainly don't discount these reasons, the
    details of material situations are the also the beginnings of social
    critique, what makes the critical analysis possible. In a curious
    way, my view runs counter to Richard Ohmann's groundbreaking
    article, "Use Definite, Specific, Concrete Language" (1979), which
    argued that most textbooks' advice about using details fosters an
    ahistorical and uncritical perspective because it ignores abstract
    inquiry about the historical and material functions of objects repre-
    sented in the writing in favor of a veneer of vivid realism. Although
    I have always admired Ohmann's critique, most writers need to
    start from detailing the reality before they can notice the social
    contradictions and ask questions about them. Both the concrete
    details of situated lives and critical reflection about them are nec-
    essary, but the inquiry is unlikely to come, or be very persuasive to
    students, without the details first. This is why I emphasize the
    crafting of scenes in much of the students' projects because it
    requires students to examine the conflicts of social details in peo-
    ple's lived experience from more than one perspective.

7. As I winnowed down the number of student writings from my class-
    es that dealt in meaningful ways with this theme of gaining control,
    I was uncomfortable with how few of these essays were written by
    men in my classes. I do not mean to imply that these men have not
    produced thoughtful critical writing because some of them have.
    But when I tried categorizing some of the main themes in their
    essays, they seemed to focus on other themes such as discovering
    connections with fathers, regional values of farm work compared

with people in town, finding their joy and identity in aspects of their work situations, or learning about the inhumanity of many working-class jobs and sometimes the humanity of workers they would otherwise have ignored. A woman colleague suggested that most women's cultural and societal positions within family dynamics and work hierarchies may help explain why these particular developmental concerns about control emerge more explicitly in their writing than the men's. Janet Bean's essay, however, offers strong analytical readings of working-class male students' writings about their fathers' labors.

6

Social Meanings of "Difference"

"DIFFERENCE" AND THE CRITICAL AGENDA IN COMPOSITION

One strand of the cultural studies agenda that has grown in American composition classrooms (at least in universities with composition studies graduate programs) is the critical valuing of difference over unity and consensus. Most American students may be receptive to teaching that emphasizes difference(s), compared with cultural studies' critiques of individual success and material consumption, because analyses of difference can more easily accommodate dominant perceptions of individualism. For example, Donna Qualley (1994) argues that a postmodern emphasis on difference for her White middle-class female students can bring out a "radical brand of individualistic feminism as exemplified by such pop icons as Madonna" (p. 32). Since Rashmi's course endeavored to complicate most students' comparisons of Third World and First World women, talk of difference was often prevalent in discussions of cultural relativism.

Composition theorists who have emphasized the term *difference* in their teaching generally define it as a sociopolitical term, useful for developing critical reading and writing. University and business administrators often speak of *diversity*, connoting a level field in which all contributions are equally welcome. In contrast, *difference* as a term among critical academics evokes issues of hierarchies and power relations. Accordingly, when composition theorists have foregrounded a politics of difference in their courses and writing programs, they have generally developed their teaching practice in two ways. In the first approach, the practice may encourage students to explore subject positions, primarily gender, race, and class. In this writing class, difference may be the explicit course content (e.g., Penticoff & Brodkey, 1992), or the course may press students to explore issues of difference in their own lives (e.g., Fox, 1990). In any case, the implicit pedagogy here poses an inquiry into the dominant myth of the American individual divorced from sociocultural and economic factors.

In the second approach toward difference in the writing classroom, the teachers' practice may favor a postmodern valuing of dissensus, believing that efforts toward total consensus (or possibly majority rule) inevitably suppress the voicing of differences within the individual. Similarly, the necessity of consensus or majority rule can inhibit potentially productive conflicts that exist in a social group. Thus, this practice means to challenge the valuing of unity as the basis for group identity and action. Composition theorists have mostly used this critique to rethink classroom collaboration and consensus (e.g., Myers, 1986; Trimbur, 1989), but also as a way to reconsider the social positioning of privilege and power between students as well as with their teachers (see Bizzell, 1991; Jarratt, 1991b). In Rashmi's course, she sought to raise issues of difference and identity politics within a systemic critique of global capitalism. She believes, as do I, that multicultural agendas in American education that do not also address socioeconomic issues in relation to cultural differences can often allow students to maintain a kind of cultural relativism warranted by consumer-based ideologies of individual choice. This relativism lets students off the hook when it comes to developing and taking positions on complex and contentious issue of cultures and power relations.

Lester Faigley (1992) argued that critical postmodern assumptions of difference may be particularly suited for the culturally and economically diverse student population that is fast becoming the norm at many urban universities. In Rashmi's class at UIC, most students displayed appreciation for what they saw as academic recognition of their situations. At the same time, participants in the class rarely if ever used the term *difference* on their own. This chapter focuses on two situated interpretations of difference built around two respective cultural themes from some students in Rashmi's class: the individual and unity. Critical pedagogies routinely interrogate the dominant meanings of these ideological terms, practically tabooing them. Consequently, teachers reading their students' texts (and possibly the students) through these critical assumptions may be more likely to gloss over some students' more local meanings. Yet as Diana's and Mike's positions suggest, these working-class views of individualism have different social meanings and effects than the dominant American ideology. Moreover, Lilia's and Shianta's religious valuing of unity as a way to cope with harsh urban life can challenge postmodern critiques of unity.

DIANA AND MIKE: PERSPECTIVES ON WORKING-CLASS INDIVIDUALISM

Diana is from a staunch Greek orthodox background, a biology major who describes herself as traditional, wanting the role of home mother. Now that her father has passed away, her mother, sister, and Diana teach in and maintain the three Greek schools in the Chicago area founded by Diana's parents. She described the venture as a constant financial risk, especially with the debt from her father's long illness. Diana grew up and lives in Berwyn, one of Chicago's suburbs that is, from the view of Diana, changing demographically from an aging old-world European population to a primarily Latino one. She described neighbors' occupations as "assistants to somebody or secretarial work, blue collar." Diana also remarked she spent most of her time outside school and work with other families and friends in the larger Chicago Greek community. She respects her extended family members who have not gone to college, as her parents did in Greece, because "they put their whole lives into their businesses."

As I described in chapter 3, Mike is Southside Irish from a family of cops. He identifies his neighborhood as the "last good part of Chicago" for cops and firemen who have to live in the city by law. When I first met Mike, he was considering journalism as a career as he does work at a newspaper. A half year after the class, he was talking about becoming a cop like his dad and grandfather. Mike's and Diana's talk displayed different psychological investments in academic acculturation. As discussed in chapter 3, Mike believed school had little impact on or relation to one's life experiences. Diana, however, saw school and experience as more intertwined, leading to an educated understanding of the world. "It's like you learn something and you take it and use it in your outside life. I guess everything is connected to school, everything but morals and stuff—values, ethics." Nevertheless, both of them articulated their positions in relation to common themes of White working-class solidarity regardless of whether they sought social capital through mainstream institutions.

Three months after Rashmi's class ended, I taped a discussion I had with Diana, Mike, and two of Mike's neighborhood friends who also attended UIC. Earlier, near the end of one particular day in Rashmi's class, the White working-class students expressed their differences from the dominant values in their neighborhoods, which they saw as racist. Because I was interested in issues of acculturation and conflict for the students, I asked 3 months later if they would share their neighborhood stories with me. But instead of explaining their separation from the community's values, as their classroom discourse had led me to believe they would, their talk displayed hard class solidarity along traditional lines. They railed on about affirmative action, the ties between race and crime in their neighborhoods, capital punishment, and the general disempowerment of working people. They initiated all these topics in response to my general questions about their schooling and neighborhoods, such as, "What was it like growing up in your neighborhood or going to school?" Never once did they qualify their views in case I might hold a conflicting position. These responses strongly suggest they identified me, the White man, with their race and tenuous socioeconomic position compared with the emerging power of minority groups, as they viewed it from the perspectives of their formerly dominant White working-class communities. Mike's friends also participated in this conversation, one man whose views reflected Mike's and a woman who sought a counterculture stance against the common wisdom of Mike's working-class community. Both of these positions helped provoke Mike's and Diana's performances out of class. In contrast, when I interviewed Diane alone, in my office due to the rain outside and her limited time schedule, she spoke more openly about her intellectual curiosity. This move indicated she wanted to show me, the academic researcher, that she also cared about these pursuits and their role in her future in biology or medicine. Mike, in contrast, maintained an out-of-school persona throughout our conversations, indicating he did not identify or wish to identify with my more middle-class education.

Because Mike and Diana displayed such a discontinuity of positions in and out of the classroom, I asked them about a class discussion on homosexuality in which I thought they did not reveal their felt opinions. The class I asked about was a discussion of Gloria Anzaldua's (1987) "Towards A New Consciousness" that occurred late in the semester. Rashmi included Anzaldua's essay to foster a discussion of Third World women in America— one of the final themes the students explored in the course. Some composition theorists and anthologies have embraced Anzaldua's metaphors of borderlands and the mestiza. Min Zhan Lu (1992), Richard Miller (1994), and others see Anzaldua's images and multivoiced writings as a way for students to explore political and rhetorical positions of identity and language. In these two scenes of talk for Diana and Mike (Rashmi's classroom and my interview/conversation with them 3 months later), how and who gets to define *identity politics* in the public sphere were the implicit issues.

Once after class I overheard Diana proclaim her disgust with homosexuality, claiming it was against God's intent. I wondered then how Diana would talk about Anzaldua's praise of gay identity scheduled later for class reading and discussion. Diana endeavored to speak in every class regardless of whether she had done the reading. Just before this transcript excerpt, several students began to question the role of gay identity in Anzaldua's theories of borderlands, opening a teaching moment for Rashmi (see transcript excerpts 1 and 2).

1) CLASSROOM TALK 4/6/95

Rashmi: How is she using the concept of gayness to understand culture and to understand identity?

Diana: I think that *as homosexuals as something that's different and multicultural as something that's different,* they make a connection between the two because they can relate to something, someone who *knows how it feels to be an outcast, because everywhere homosexuals are considered, you know, "Oh my god, they're so weird."* . . .

2) DISCUSSION AFTER TERM OUTSIDE CLASS 6/8/95 (WITH DIANA, MIKE, AND TWO OF HIS FRIENDS)

Diana: I think it's become a FAD now in the United States. *It's become good to be weird. Everyone wants to be like a freak.* . . . it's become so cool to be bisexual or dress up in drag. *Look at the TV, all the talk*

*shows, all of a sudden there's a great outbreak
because its cool to bring attention to yourself.*

Mike: I don't go and march every year and saying, oh, I'm
heterosexual.

Diana: Yeah! We don't have a heterosexual parade, why
should they do that?

Diana's themes and language in both contexts are similar,
although their social meanings intended for their audiences were
radically different. She correctly reads the theoretical problem
posed by Rashmi's question and responds to that, all the while
maintaining her conservative community's disapproval.[1] Whether
knowingly or not, Diana recasts all that she condemns as linguistic currency for the academic marketplace when in the critical
classroom. The discourse outside class (excerpt 2) mocks issues
of difference as fodder for Geraldo Rivera: "Everyone wants to be
a freak." In the class (excerpt 1), however, Diana's subtle shifts in
language grant Anzaldua privileged cultural knowledge: "someone
who knows how it feels to be an outcast." In class, she positions
the voice of repulsion outside of her subjectivity to a faceless
realm of "everywhere."

When I asked Diana and Mike whether they expressed their
own views during this class discussion, Diana was quick to
respond: "I'm homophobic and I hate them. Not that I hate them
it's just wrong." Her language choice, "homophobic," implies an
awareness of how others who value sexual difference might
define her. She knows their critique and perhaps accepts it as
the authoritative discourse necessary for traveling in some privileged circles. Yet Diana's quick use of the word "hate" and her
belief in the godly origin of AIDS suggest this more critical discourse of homophobia is not internally persuasive. Clearly, these
shifts in her language suggested her ambivalence toward what
she saw as overly liberal academic views of homosexuality compared with the common views in her Greek community. This
same tension surfaced another time outside class when Diana
expressed her disgust with what she saw as America's growing
immorality. She remarked about AIDS, "I don't think they should
find a cure. I think that those people who put themselves in that
position should die. Or not die, but realize what they did.
Because I think there's a reason for everything."

Soon after Diana's first comment in the prior classroom
excerpt, Rashmi synthesized the students' talk of homosexuals

facing gender constraints in American culture into a larger systemic category of "threats to the norm." She suggested there is
also a backlash against immigrants whom others believe threaten
the definition of being American. As a response, Diana then postu-
lated why others may see homosexuals as a threat "because they
are willing to speak for what they want" (see transcript excerpt 3).

3) CLASSROOM TALK CONTINUED 4/6/95

Diana: Uh I mean on t.v. a lot of times when you see people who are homosexual, **they're very outspoken,
they kind of say what they want to say.** They
don't, you know, b.s . . . that's kind of a stereotype
too but, the ones I have heard on TV, or whatever,
or in plays, or whatever, **you always see very
blunt people. And I think that threatens
because they are willing to speak for what
they want.**

Rashmi: So it's become a *political, category,* to be gay—

Diana: *It's become everything.* become all (threatening)—

Rashmi: Okay, any other response to this article?

Here it is unclear whether Diana was still distancing this talk
from the positions she had voiced outside the institutional context with like-minded people and me. Rashmi told me later that
although she recognized Diana's rhetorical turns here, she used
them for her own purposes as the critical teacher. Once Rashmi
has gotten Diana's assent to her metaphor, being gay as a political category, she cuts her off. She believes that Diana took so
many contradictory positions in the class depending on the situation that she admitted to no position.

Nevertheless, Diana's response to Rashmi, "it's become everything," suggests a glimpse of the values and attitudes she
engages when she is with others whom she believes identify with
White working-class concerns. In our discussion after the term
(excerpt 2), Diana's talk reduces homosexuality to a fad along
with other alternative cultures—a point she stressed several
times in this conversation. Yet more important, Diana's talk here
links her view of homosexuality with a resentment of those who
publicly claim difference, those who seek action based on claims
of marginal status. Mike explicitly takes up this view in same
after term discussion: "What I don't like are people who go out

there and make a spectacle of themselves just because they're
gay, they're black . . ." (see also transcript excerpt 4). Perhaps
then Diana's comment in class, "It's become everything," refers to
this larger category of identity politics and difference within the
public sphere. In a later interview, Diana expressed this same
kind of resentment against ethnic groups seeking marginal status when she discussed the demographic changes in her neighborhood and her former elementary school that her brother and
sister were now attending. "What really makes me mad now is
they put everything in English into Spanish. I don't understand
that. I mean this is America. Our language is English. I speak
Greek. I understand pride, but it's like they want to take over, the
stuff they say, like we don't understand them—they are prejudiced toward us."

In my discussion with Mike, Diana, and Mike's friends,
Mike's talk linked this resentment of identity politics to working-
class ethics. He repeatedly stressed to me his neighborhood value
of work to judge the integrity of an individual, the ethic his father
and others had taught him. "I think the big difference between
groups, where culture comes in is that you've got people who are
willing to work for it, and I can respect these people, but not
someone who sits around and complains about how they are
being oppressed . . . sure things are against you, but you have to
work against that."[2]

This view of work and the public domain expressed by Mike
suggests that the individual is on his own. Collective action of
any public nature seems to go against this deep cultural code of
personal integrity historically rooted in material necessity. Yet
Mike's perspective also resembles the peer solidarity network of
White working-class young adults in two other researched communities. Among the group of mainly working-class high school
"burnouts" in the suburban outskirts of Detroit (Eckert, 1989)
and a cohort of more economically successful youth of working-
class "Cityville" on the edge of Boston (Steinitz & Solomon, 1986),
class solidarity is ultimately valued over more middle-class values of individual prestige.[3]

As I summarized Eckert's study in chapter 3, the burnouts
resented the more middle-class jocks' efforts to gain social status
in the high school's various hierarchies as an implicit, and sometimes explicit, preparation for the individual gains of the corporate business world. To reiterate, Eckert points out that the
burnouts' parents make similar choices in the work world,
"avoiding job changes that will put them in superior positions to
their peers and separate them from their solidarity peer net-

works" that have sustained them (p. 138). In this context, Mike's argument that individuals need to prove themselves by their hard work is also a way to speak against those who negotiate for power within more hierarchical social structures. It is an adversarial position against institutional powers that are organized by individual advancement.

Many of the more successful Cityville White working-class young adults in Steinitz's and Solomon's study echo this attitude. They reject their more status-conscious classmates in school who "make sure they serve their own interests first. Being different just for the sake of being different" (p. 31). These students hope to "remain oneself while still becoming somebody" (p. 30). To do this, Steinitz and Solomon argue, they tacitly value and practice family and neighborhood interdependence over individual competition. Individual achievement "may mean remaining tied and committed to community while still doing better financially than their parents" (p. 232). In other words, they seek economic mobility while rejecting or remaining ambivalent to social mobility. Although these working-class students may often implicitly practice an ethics of solidarity in an effort to maintain a community self, they often talk in terms of individualism as "in every man for himself." Ironically, this individualist talk helps give them hope against political cynicism by enforcing an ethical code of it's not who you know—that is, what social capital you can accumulate—but how hard you work. Irvin Peckham (2003) aptly and sadly clarifies the stakes involved in the frequent choice not to pursue social capital: "The working class youth think of that as breaking the rules of the game, but as Bourdieu's survey [in *Distinction*] implies—it *is* the game, or at least a good part of it."[4]

Like the Cityville young adults, Mike sought in our conversations to erase the differences between his college world and nonacademic friends in his neighborhood, even those who Mike views as "racist skinheads":

> Well in my own neighborhood, was I'd go to school, I'd come home, I'd hang out with my buddies, jerk around a little, throw some rocks at some cars, or we'd play baseball. We didn't think of anything, that was our life. Even now what do I do, I go to school, go home, I don't like, go march in rallies, you know? I just have friends, just hang out with them. We don't sit around and talk about, my friends who are racists don't go "I hate niggers," I don't sit around and say "well you're wrong." . . . We don't talk about stuff like that. It's just not brought up, so there's really no influence.

Here Mike demonstrates that he cares more about maintaining long-time social networks regardless of his friends' political stance. Preserving the neighborhood social ties are more important than explicitly practicing a "politically correct" politics that would, among other things, imply an interest in social mobility through a distancing from working-class values and codes of ethics. Mike's developing reluctance to follow career paths that require gaining individual prestige through middle-class institutional mechanisms seems to bear out this view. Like the youth in Eckert's study, he is moving toward jobs organized by clear lines of hierarchical authority, such as the hiring and promotion structures of the public police force (notwithstanding possible corruption of those hiring structures), compared with more middle-class practices of individual negotiations for advancement as he might find if he continued working at the newspaper corporation. At the same time, he complained bitterly to me about the arbitrary authority of the gatekeeping in these jobs—a populist distrust of management, citing his uncle's unfortunate experiences with the test for joining or advancing in the Chicago police as an example of reverse discrimination.

DIANA'S TENSIONS: WOMEN'S SOCIAL MOBILITY AND WORKING-CLASS SOLIDARITY

Although Mike's talk displays this unspoken ambivalence toward social mobility, Diana invests herself differently in these domains of middle-class institutions and informal social networks. Unlike Mike, who saw little connection between school learning and life experiences, Diana defined an educated person as someone who combines their life experiences with their studies. "Not so much hitting the books, but it's both, experiences, your studies, where you've gone, what you've done with your life." As the daughter of two teachers educated in Greece who "came here with nothing," Diana values social mobility through education to help her gain a stronger role in the workplace as a woman. She clearly felt more comfortable with academic trappings than most key participants because she was the only student who suggested we meet for interviews in my school office when her time was too limited to meet elsewhere. As a successful student in the sciences and as a capable writer, she viewed her academic efforts as leading to a professional career that would grant her more autonomy and control in the public world than the traditional female role in her

Greek-Orthodox community. Despite this concern for professional autonomy, she also wished to carry on a traditional female role
in her future home life. Ever since Diana began working at age
15, she has viewed work opportunities from this perspecive of
greater autonomy. Describing working at a local sports and pizza
restaurant, one job among many, she emphasized this freedom:
"So I got to see my friends all the time, and at that point in my
life I was never allowed to go out because my dad was really
strict. I was never allowed to leave the house unless I was doing
something productive. So work was like OUT for me. But with the
job, I was like, wow I can socialize now. That really opened the
door for me after my parents saw I could handle responsibility."
As she spoke of her career choices, it was clear that she valued
the prestige that could come with academic credentials and experience in the field of biology, whether as an MD or a biochemist.
She discussed her worries about competing for medical school
openings with older applicants who have "a stable home and a lot
of stability in their lives," compared with her family's financial
instability.

While in Rashmi's class, Diana often compared women's
inequality in her own Greek-Orthodox culture to the situations
from the course readings and films. During the screening of the
documentary film, "Small Happiness," which depicts the cultural
and economic oppression of women in a remote Chinese village
after the cultural revolution, Diana spoke out in frustration several times when a bride was continually pushed down during the
ceremony by the family around her. While the class was packing
up, she confided to me and several other nearby students that
her grandmother in Greece had purposely drowned her baby son
in retaliation against her arranged marriage just as the bride's
mother-in-law confesses to doing in the film. "All that stuff went
through my family, where the women were looked at in a certain
way, yeah it happens in Africa and Asia, but it really happens
everywhere. And since it was part of my family, it had already
affected my life." Diana's identification with these women's struggles *as universal* ("it really happens everywhere") tended to
ignore, unknowingly or not, Rashmi's emphasis on socioeconomic
and cultural differences of women's situations as they related to
the course's more global analysis.

Yet outside the class scene she stressed to me her values of
traditional women's roles in the family domain: "Cause I think
that I'm not a traditionalist, but I do have a lot of tradition."
Although she saw her future career as the way out of her local

community's limited autonomy for women, she planned to leave the job world as soon as she had children.

> Mothers are nurturers and this and that, and I think we've lost a lot of that in American society, lost it almost completely. . . . And look at all that trouble we have now with kids. I do think it's connected. . . . The reason I want to go to school and get a good job is for my family. Without a family you don't have anything. If I'm alone, what do I have?

When I asked Diana how she would describe Rashmi's course to family and friends, she replied after some consideration, "The woman's place in the world. Her role. Her so-called calling, like what she was here for." Her choice of the qualifier, "so called" indicates her derision of different cultures' patriarchal boundaries. Yet most often in our talks, she used the phrase "a woman's place" in a positive light to describe her traditional stance. I asked her whether she discussed issues from Rashmi's class with anyone outside of school, and she told of talks with her former boyfriend who was also in the Greek community and was "obviously not a feminist." "I would ask him his opinion about what the women's place was, that came up a lot, and usually we would come up to the same thing, but kind of working up to that step." In this way, Diana's language of women's "so called calling" may serve a similar function to her labeling herself "homophobic" when speaking to me. It suggests an ambivalent tension between what she knows are the academically prized criticisms of traditional female roles compared with the values of her Greek-Orthodox community that also echo larger working-class values in America.[5]

Yet neither of these positions Diana expressed in their different contexts of public university classroom and local community are any less authentic for her. Instead she keeps these contexts of women's public roles and their private home roles as separate domains. This separation protects her more middle-class aspirations of women's social mobility within the professional marketplace while maintaining a White working-class solidarity toward concerns in the domains of family and home. In this respect, Diana's seemingly contradictory loyalties concur with the young women in Cityville of Steinitz and Solomon's (1986) study, who tended to practice an ethic of interdependence in the family networks compared with the men's, and Mike's, emphasis on the space of the street and neighborhood. Much of Diana's time and pride were involved in obligations of care for younger siblings and extended family or teaching grade school Greek classes.

Not surprisingly, Diana invested her faith in this family domain as the viable location for social change. Few, if any, of the students in Loeb's (1994) study describe the family as the locus for possible social change as Diana did. Most of the mainly middle-class students Loeb labels as *adapters* to the status quo located agency in individuals who can gain a position of power in corporate institutions—a view that Loeb critiques as either naïve or a rationalization for their present political inactivity. Those students actively involved in various causes valued collective action. Diana's view suggests, then, a different kind of solidarity rooted in traditional working-class values.[6] At one point in our interview, she asked me whether I am ever scared for my children's future. After I replied that I do often think about it, but the yearning for raising a child can help you through that fear, she offered this comment:

> You accept it too. You forget about the world around you and kind of concentrate on your world. Making yourself better, maybe I can't better you and better him, but I can better myself and my family And that's the only way we can make a difference, if we better ourselves in our own way. Our inner selves and our family. Because going out isn't going to do anything because you can't change what people do in their homes. People say you're too young. You think about things that are way ahead of you, but my family is number one.

Diana remains skeptical of those who "go out" and take their politics to the streets through public debates and collective actions as encouraged by most of the readings in Rashmi's class. Although this view is due partially to Diana's valuing self-sufficiency, it may also be caught up in attitudes of social class that resent the display of marginal status for explicitly political purposes.

THE RESENTMENT OF DIFFERENCE AS A FORM OF SOCIAL DISTINCTION

In her study of argument as rhetoric in a working-class bar, Julie Lindquist (2002) contends that working-class Whites often see themselves between a rock and a hard place. Because of their subordinate social class, they do not have much economic or political power. And because of their "race," they cannot claim a marginalized status as an "other." Or most of them tacitly refuse to do so because their racial identification grants their only tie to the dominant American culture.[7] Diana articulated this frustration of the working class in our talk when she lumped O.J. Simpson's treatment in jail with the rich who can buy their way out of corruption. "The people who have the money, those political people or whatever . . . they get treated like kings because they have money, right? There's so many political things, scams going on . . . and they get away with it just because they have a . . . place. Know what I mean?" Diana's comments demonstrate she perceives the conflict principally as a class issue, rather than about race or gender. At another time, she described a class affinity with some of the African-American girls in her 1 year of Catholic high school: "Me and those girls were just getting by . . . we could tell who took the bus because we didn't have cars." Nevertheless, she described feeling alienated from some African-American women in her recent college classes despite her rapport with Jasmine, an African-American woman, and Maria, a Fillipina in Rashmi's class. "Everybody has a slight bit of prejudice in them I think . . . I even see it in my classes, like the Black girls all sit together, and when I go to talk to them, they're just completely ignorant of me."

Much of Diana's and Mike's language play during their discussion with me implies how they think groups with presumed marginalized status might characterize them. Here Mike is explaining why he hid his opinions when he did speak during the class session on Anzaldua (see transcript excerpt 4).

4) DISCUSSION CONTINUED 6/8/95

Mike: What if someone was in there and I go "gays suck."
         I don't want to say all my opinions

         and-

Diana: "I hate 'em all. I want to kill 'em.

Mike: - and hurt someone else. I'm not saying gays suck
         but I mean, *what I don't like are people who go out
         there and make a spectacle of themselves just
         because they're gay, they're Black . . .*

         Its almost like, okay, you're gay. That's just something you are, you can't help it, just like a birth

> mark, I don't go parading, I got a birthmark, I
> wanna be, I want my own parade, because its part
> of me. Or I have blonde hair so I wanna march.

Diana   Do you want to have a blonde parade for all the
             blondes? (laughs)

  Mike: I want to have a blonde parade. That's stupid, you
             know. To have a parade or anything for that matter
             for the fact that-

Diana: I hate blondes.

  Mike: You know-

Diana: I want to kill them all (laughs)

  Mike: I'm not actually blonde. I'm sandy blonde.

Diana parodies her own position—playing the role of rabid bigot. Her humor implicitly criticizes those who would see her as solely intolerant, that would deny her humanity. Yet this play also functions to trivialize more legitimate claims of difference, making it a nonissue, compared with critical teachers wanting to make an issue out of everything.

How then might a composition teacher trained in critical theory read and respond to Diana and Mike in these situations? Although Diana's ability to slip in and out of these roles may imply a postmodern subject shaped by late-capitalist culture, her comparison with a former friend complicates this view. She describes his return from college with white hair, tattoos, and writing on his head: "I understand you can wear whatever you want and do your hair however you want, but they start changing their IDEAS, about everything, about religion, the acceptance of things, just changed completely and I'm like why? Because they don't have the family supporting them, they don't have the right upbringing."[8]

Thus, for students like Diana and Mike, a pedagogy of identity politics may ultimately lack persuasive authority as a means to investigate self and society, reading and writing. Nor can the critical teacher finally theorize their valuing of individualism as "speaking the hegemonic discourse." Mike's and Diana's talk indicates that their understandings of individualism may have more to do with complex issues of White working-class solidarity and resentment than general manipulations of mass culture most often addressed in cultural studies' approaches to the writing class. In the following chapter, I outline the processes and rationales for students' ethnographic research that can lead to students' social critique alongside social affirmation of their cultures and communites—a strategy that can hold greater persuasive authority for students like Mike and Diana.

LILIA: DEFINING THE NECESSITY
OF UNITY FOR URBAN LIFE

Diana's and Mike's frames of reference provoke other ways of seeing White working-class students' discourses of individualism. Similarly, Lilia's and Shianta's social and discursive positions that emerged in their talk with me about Rashmi's course can challenge postmodern critiques of unity.[9] Lilia describes herself as a Latina who rejected the Catholic tradition, although not the Mexican culture, to become a disciple in the Chicago Church of Christ. In this respect, she is clearly not typical of most Latinas who attend urban schools, but neither are her beliefs typical of this fundamentalist church. In conversations with me, she repeatedly associated her beliefs with the ideals of Rashmi's course: feminism, the political power of speaking out, social critique, and activism. At the same time, these positions were often in tension with concerns for unity that some critical theorists might dismiss as "naive."

Unlike most of the students in Rashmi's class, Lilia sought to incorporate into her writings some of the course's most explicitly theoretical positions on difference, race, class, and women's struggles. As mentioned in chapter 4, Rashmi's first response paper required the students to write about their "politics of location" using their discussion of Chandra Mohanty's (1991) essay, "Cartographies of Struggle: Third World Women and the Politics of Feminism." More than half of the students summarized Mohanty's position within their first paragraph and did not return to this reading except in their closing sentences. Understandably uncomfortable with the article's density of postcolonial feminist theory, they often emphasized Mohanty's individual experience as the major source of her views.

In contrast, Lilia used Mohanty's theories of social geography to examine her own heritage as a Mexican Latina and the value of all women gaining, in Lilia's and Mohanty's words, "a voice to fight against 'exploitative structures.'" At one point Lilia writes, "Women [who] are shaped by their culture, and find themselves

in different locations do have a similar struggle that brings them
together despite their differences. The struggle to describe themselves and express themselves freely in society." When Lilia and I
discussed this paper weeks later, she told me she was thinking
about her roles with other women of different colors and ethnici-
ties in her church—what she termed her "sisterhood":

> To have that one purpose, as a Christian, to love God, to be a
> disciple with other women, that really binds us together, that
> really creates incredible unity, despite their opinions even.
> And you do, you get to express yourself a lot.

Throughout our conversations, she stressed women's necessity to have both a spiritual and a political voice, although as a
Christian disciple she values the spiritual life, "your whole eter-
nal being," over the material world. For Lilia, the spiritual and
political came together in her mid-teens, when she dismissed her
family's Catholic traditions for a fundamentalist discipleship,
thus challenging her parents' expected role of the submissive
Mexican daughter. In our interviews, she compared herself with
other Latina women who never become politically involved. "They
are a great part of society but are silenced, in this world, here in
this country. I thought about the many grandmothers and aunts
who are so caught up with their families, their jobs, their home,
that they don't even, are aware of the political world." In her second paper, a required summary of a journal article from outside
the course readings, Lilia refers to the global exploitation of
women's labor in her conclusions. Talking with me, she identified
her religious beliefs with those church organizations who voice
dissent against local governments that condone this exploitation.
Yet she never spoke of her own church taking these kinds of
political actions. Lilia's favoring of a kind of liberation theology,
although she never called it that, is definitely rare for a fundamentalist Christian disciple.
     For her final research paper, Lilia wanted to concentrate on
the prospects for "global feminism" despite the power relations
structured in different women's situations of races and nations.
Her title, "From a Larger Perspective," explicitly seeks unity over
difference and implicitly invokes the language of her religious
faith. One paragraph suggests the frustration she felt reading
articles in Rashmi's class that critique the possibility of a global
"sisterhood." "I believe that's what it strives for [,] that's what
women hope for, but that's not what many articles in English 161

have proven to say." Further on she wrote: "Much 'difference' among one another when there are internalized and extroverted 'differences' crush the spirit of 'sisterhood' and cause discord among women." She expressed similar discomfort with these feminist scholars' "negative critique" in the conclusion of her second paper: "Recognizing the false assumptions and their development is just the beginning of effective research. Soon let's write about research expressing fine productive, edifying results and solutions to the crisis women in the third world countries face today."

Unlike Lilia's previous papers, her final paper reads like a hybrid genre of sermon and editorial calling for unity within women's common struggles, rather than an argumentative researched inquiry into an issue. Lilia clearly rushed this paper more than her earlier course writings. She threw in quotes as examples, including biblical references to Esther and Ruth, but did not develop their implications. Yet her driving concern for speaking out—as she stressed in conversations with me, for directly addressing a positive message of unity tied to her religious beliefs—may have also worked to overpower the expected critically academic discourse.

The critical teacher informed by cultural studies might primarily attribute Lilia's discourses of unity within diversity to the "manipulations of mass culture," as in the "United Colors of Benneton" advertising campaign, or attribute it to a monologic discourse from her church. Yet in our interviews, this view of unity emerged most often when Lilia compared the problems of her west-side neighborhood and early schooling to the haven she found in the local Boys and Girls Club. "When I look back you realize that a lot of your friends are really not involved in a lot of good things, like drugs, gangs, or crime or abuse." By Lilia's account, she now thinks 50% to 65% of her former friends in the larger neighborhood of the school were caught up in gang activity or other dangers. Like many other students from particular Chicago neighborhoods, she could describe to me several incidents of violence that happened to her or her friends. When she moved to a supposedly accelerated high school program near the Cabrini Green housing projects for children of color from several neighborhoods, she witnessed more racially motivated violence. Consequently, much of this schooling dealt with physical discipline, "keeping us down." Fortunately, she was able to transfer to an accelerated school less hampered by these problems.

During these tough periods, Lilia found refuge in the local Boys and Girls Club in Logan Square where she was part of a tumbling troupe:

Lilia: I basically grew up there, going to the classes, volunteering, doing summer work there, very involved until I was like seventeen or so.

David: Do you think the Boys and Girls club took the place of what school might have been otherwise?

Lilia: In a sense, yeah, they always had activities going for kids to nurture them. And their logo or motto, their theme was "we get along." Unity, united, a unit, we're a unit. And even like their Logan Square club tee shirts had like these figures of people holding hands. It made you feel important that you could become someone, you could stay off the streets, you know stay away from the drugs, the strangers, bad company, could stay in here.

Lilia's comments reflect the conclusions of a 5-year ethnographic study of inner-city youth organizations headed up by Shirley Brice Heath and Milbrey McLaughlin (1993). Ninety percent of these organizations judged effective by the teens involved were not organized around ethnic interests. Rather they are built around youth-based projects, often in team athletics or arts troupes, that develop a "a core of personal efficacy achieved as a member of a close and personally collected group" (p. 23). For these youth whose neighborhoods are in socioeconomic turmoil, ethnic and gender tensions could present "one more boundary that could, if flaunted, add to gang, turf, or girl-boy struggles ever ready to erupt into violence" (p. 32). Ethnic and gender identity needed to be embedded in achievement, responsibility, and an immediate support network not often available anymore through their schools or closeby environment.

Although Lilia's situation was not as dire as the youth in Heath's and McLaughlin's research, she clearly speaks for them in relation to her experiences. After we talked about her neighborhood, I asked Lilia what she saw as the cause of these problems. I wondered whether she would provide a systemic critique, as she had in her early papers from Rashmi's class, or a more individualist perspective.

Lot of people say it's the lack of education, lack of money, lack of social-ism? You know family units. Could be a little of everything, you know. I think it needs teamwork, people working together, building that unity, making it—owning it,

making it their territory, making it a right territory, a safe
place to grow up in, for older people to feel safe in . . . You
really also need to let the ones they want to push out, feel
welcome. Because if they did, they wouldn't cause trouble.
They also want to feel part of society and that's the point of
like boys and girls clubs.

Here Lilia does not dismiss the socioeconomic factors, but also
suggests that these critical (more academic) perspectives may be
ineffective at the local level of social change. Or perhaps these
critiques remain too negative for someone who must live within
these problems. Like the organizations Heath and McLaughlin
participated in, Lilia views solutions of team unity in the *doing*,
"rituals, processes, and structures that make room for building
identities" (p. 10), rather than abstract exclamations of collectivi-
ty. In this respect, Lilia's implicit position does resemble a postmodern valuing of power developing from each respective situation. Because Lilia's language sounds so much like a "liberal
hegemonic" critique of the status quo, it might be overlooked by
critical teachers thinking through theory.

Moreover, Lilia believes this unity becomes "even more important when you have a diverse group of people working together"
as in the mixed group of African Americans, Whites, Latino, and
Asian people at her church. This work gains greater significance
when it is not for money or personal ambition, but "because they
like the task at hand and they want to complete it and work as a
team . . . That can mean a lot to someone who may have not had
that before." This talk values difference as the diversity of contributions to the group. For Lilia and others in similar situations,
the problems can come when individuals emphasize difference
over other social values:

Lilia: I think it matters what you use the difference for. I
           think that's the biggest issue, what you do with it.

David: Say a little more about that?

Lilia: Yeah, [it] can do with it [if it] is what happens every
           day, gangbangers hurting one another, because of
           difference, difference. Someone who thinks that
           they're so different, might not want to relate to
           someone else? And might just use it to keep them-
           selves isolated from someone else or from people or
           whatever.

David: Sort of what you were saying earlier about bearing
            a grudge?

Lilia: Holding back.

Lilia's view here indicates that when she encounters academically
critical arguments for valuing difference, she reads them through
these tensions of troubled experience and future hopes.

SHIANTA: THE NECESSITY OF UNITY
AS CONVICTION AND DISCIPLINE

Although Lilia's situation and critical values may be uncommon,
her concerns for unity in her world are not. Shianta, an African-
American working-class student in Rashmi's class who is deeply
committed to her missionary Baptist church, spoke through a
similar language. Both women draw on their church's practices
to articulate these concerns of unity within increasingly tough
environments. But this similar sounding discourse within these
practices holds different motivations in the context of Shianta's
African-American Southside community. From Shianta's position, her church's values of unity offer one way to heal the divisions in her tough world and provide the chance for economic
mobility. In this way, her talk and writing of interracial unity
operate as religious belief and rhetorical strategy within the dominant culture, as I discuss later.

Unlike Peter, who spoke in much more guarded tones about
being African American (although also from Puerto Rican
descent) in America, Shianta did not hold back the boisterous-
ness of her African-American church community that preached a
view of racial integration. Throughout our interviews, she often
threw her head back in laughter and enjoyed the opportunity to
perform for me these stories from her life. She tended to appreciate my interest in the role of a new father and often included me
in her conversation through topics about family issues and care-
giving, rather than viewing me as an academic and another
teacher from her school. Still it was clear she wanted to keep me,
and what I might represent to her, separate from her life and
friends on the far Southside of Chicago. When I asked her
whether I could tape a discussion with her and her friends at a
location of their choice, she got very quiet and said her friends
would probably be too busy. I later asked her if she would be

willing to tape-record a conversation with her friends without me present, which she agreed to, but I perceived her discomfort with this intrusion and so never asked her again. I believe these ambivalences toward me correspond to larger ones about race, unity, and difference in critical writing, which I explore further later.

Whereas Lilia did not refer to her religious views in class talk or formal assignments until late in the term, Shianta couched her concerns for unity within her religious faith in her first response paper—the Mohanty assignment. In her second paragraph, she writes, "Growing up in the city, I've seen poverty. I have lived in this poverty. I have experienced a part of life that no one could help me understand but God. The world needs everyone to come together and to get along to keep it healthy." For most of the assignment, she locates herself, in a very general way, through three contexts: God's unknown plan of a multicultural world, a brief one-paragraph comparison of attending a "mixed" elementary school and an all African-American high school, and the necessity of learning from people's past struggles. She also quoted her reverend in the paper to support her view. The summer after this class, Shianta described her difficulties when she interprets an academic assignment as an opportunity "to be creative."

When I asked her when she felt she had encountered this problem of being overly creative in academic assignments, she referred to this first response paper, which, for several reasons, Rashmi had given a "D." Shianta replied to me, "The first one, that you said you liked, that was being creative, [I] said what I felt without actually saying what I meant."

Although Shianta clearly felt less comfortable with the academic judgment on this paper, her choice of words here—between feeling and meaning—implies an epistemological divide between emphases in traditional African-American religious discourse, focused more on knowing one's world through religious experience, and more logocentric academic assumptions. Indeed, when Rashmi read Shianta's paper, she confessed to me that she was uncertain how to critically respond. Perhaps Rashmi responded that way, as I or many teachers might, because the writing was suffused with generalized religious feeling rather than argument or detailed narrative that might serve purposes of argument. In the end, Rashmi's written comments did not refer to her difficulties with Shianta's religious tone, but to the lack of specific details and inattention to critically assessing one of the course readings as the assignment required.

As Jack Daniel and Geneva Smitherman-Donaldson (1976) point out, cultural practices in the traditional African-American church (such as call and response and individual improvisation) derive from an African worldview that seeks to unite the spiritual and material realms. Community is built through spiritual efficacy circulated through heightened affect and emotion of the group. By Shianta's account, this feeling, compared with academia's explication of meaning, is what she emphasized when told to write of her "location" toward the issues she was learning about in the first weeks of Rashmi's class.

As it happened, this instance was the only time Shianta explicitly referred to her religious beliefs in the context of Rashmi's course. Yet outside of this class, she often called on this religious discourse to express her concerns for unity. Because Rashmi's course had addressed identity politics and the possibilities of collective action, one of the final questions I asked those participants I closely followed was, "What group(s) do you think most need to organize as a group to gain better rights?" (see Appendix C). In class and our conversations, Shianta had often addressed issues of racism. Yet when given this explicit opportunity to speak out for marginal status to challenge racism as a response to my interview questions, she opted for a message of integration forged in religious belief:

> I think that all groups should come together. And instead of trying to be so divided become one. That's how you could put it, because if you just say African-Americans need it, there are poor Whites who need too. What I'm saying is not trying to be greedy and get everything for yourself, there's other people who need also. So peoples is what makes the world go around, and some people, they don't get that message. You know what I'm saying? It takes a lot to get that through their thick skulls that God put em here on the earth. What can you do about it? really nothing. So the major thing is we're all going to have to learn to get along with another.

Here Shianta expresses her concern for unity through a class solidarity: "Because if you say African Americans need it, there are poor Whites too." But she also indicts some African Americans along with many in the dominant White middle-class. Several times in our talks, she criticized other African-Americans' resistance to educational and professional opportunities in mainstream culture. To show how difficult it was to concentrate on learning in the environment of her all African-American high school (despite the racial kinship she felt there), she compared her experiences with a neighborhood friend who went to a successful magnet school on the Northwest side. Although she envied her friend's opportunity, she said the African-American history courses her friend took there "told her all this stuff about hating White people because of what Black people had to suffer."

> What they don't understand is, you can't go around hating people because that's going to make you miss out on something important. What you do is learn from the struggle, they had to struggle to stay in front of the bus, they had to struggle to go to school, but you know what you doing? You wasting your education. Then when it gets taken away, you got to start all over again, you know what I'm saying. So you know, its rough.

She implies that unity can speak for greater socioeconomic opportunity when faced with institutionalized racism. At another point, she made this view explicit: "What a lot of Black people fail to remember is they wouldn't have got that far without those White people who did care about integration, the White people who felt sorry and wanted to help." Shianta's comments hint at her struggles with what Signithia Fordham (1988) calls the "collective ethos" of those African Americans who may resist the individualist ethos of mainstream acculturation. For Shianta, these people are often the ones outside her church.

As discussed in chapter 3, Fordham argues that successful inner-city African-American high school students invest themselves in a raceless persona to cope with the school culture's stigmatizing of "blackness," on the one hand, and the peer culture's practices of an oppositional identity, on the other (see also Ogbu, 1987). To deal with these tensions, these students take on beliefs, to varying degrees, of a color-blind America that will grant worthy individuals upward mobility. Like Peter, Shianta does not adopt this strategy, but her perspective is shaped by the forces Fordham analyzes.

As Shianta's previous talk demonstrates, she doesn't view herself in these terms of racelessness to cope with peer opposition and institutionalized limitations. Nor does she nurture an oppositional identity to mainstream acculturation. Instead she often calls on the discourse of the civil rights movement—the tradition of activism in the African-American church: "they had to struggle to stay in front of the bus, they had to struggle to go to school." Nor does she see herself and her family as apart from the everyday struggles of her community. She described the people in her neighborhood as working class, "because they can make it, but they have to struggle to get where they are . . . most are barely surviving." In comparison, she saw herself as privileged because her higher education would prepare her for "the new world that's ahead."

But she also did not want to disparage those who worked hard yet had, for multiple reasons, rejected possible opportunities for further education. Shianta based her view that "education can be taken away from you" (as she comments before) on two situations: first, girlfriends who lost out on college opportunities because they had children while in high school, and second, her dad who works as a janitor hoping to study for the GED. She described her efforts to council a teen girl to maneuver around "the system" of school funding. She told her to talk to people, "not just in counseling, people who are already in college, who know the ins, how you get around different schools. I was like, 'money ain't the problem, you've just got to get your paperwork in on time.'" In effect, Shianta's view affirms John Ogbu's (1987) position. Like Ogbu, Shianta is concerned that some African American's collective oppositional identity rejects the institutions that could offer opportunity to the greatest number of people, whether these institutions offer individual tokens or actually want to break discriminatory boundaries.[10]

Moreover, Shianta's school experiences have affirmed the value of interracial unity for African Americans to gain economic mobility—the view embedded in the beliefs and practices of her church. In our discussions, she compared the relative order of her culturally mixed elementary school to the chaos she often felt attending a majority African-American high school. Although she acknowledged that her elementary school was smaller and had a principal who could keep control (and, I suspect, had slightly better funding), she emphasized the African-American high school's greater problems of organization and discipline. "There was nothing together, everything was done at the last minute." Shianta also implied that the majority black school faced greater difficulties because the pressures of the neighborhood tended to replicate themselves in the classrooms:

> Going to an all black school, you have to worry about your
> kids coming home safely, because there are shootings and

> stuff up there. I mean it's fun and nice being with your own,
> but a lot of black students don't get the proper care that you
> have—and that makes a difference with a lot of fathers not
> being at home, it depends on circumstances, but it makes a
> difference how a child is raised period, because if parents
> grow up with attitudes, then the children come out ten times
> worse than that. And if you don't bring them up with church
> and have something to fall back on, not saying they all [need
> to be] into God and stuff.

Although she would not dismiss the value of education with
her racial peers, she quickly moves to the problems she encountered in an all African-American high school. Here the acknowledgment of socioeconomic difference is an implicit argument for
interracial unity as well as unity within the African-American
community. That is, these problems are less likely to be com-
pounded in a culturally mixed school or a mainstream one with
better financed opportunities. Of course she may have assumed
that I wanted to hear mostly about problems. Nevertheless, it is
worth noting that she made these comments within a larger context of telling me why she thinks her church and God make a difference in her life. I believe these comments were meant to summarize, and so emphasize, earlier threads of her talk with me.

Significantly, Shianta cites the influence of the African-
American church as the main way to maintain equilibrium and
motivation for mainstream economic mobility when faced with
these socioeconomic circumstances. "When in church, it didn't
matter how bad I did in school. When in church, there was
always a sense of relaxation from stress." She also sees the
church's teachings as a major source of discipline necessary to
endure "the struggles" within the dominant culture and neighborhood. (At one point, she commented to me that strict demands to
attend church, often at nights, could get in the way of completing
her school work, which her father could be more lax about.) This
is why she argues above that African Americans living in situations like hers need a moral order "to fall back on" regardless of
whether they are deeply devoted to worship, "into God and that
stuff." In their research on teen organizations valued by inner-
city youth, Heath and McLaughlin (1993) come to a similar conclusion about the disciplinary value of traditional religions:

> Often youth leaders heard youngsters offering testimony to
> their peers of how their church or their very old-fashioned
> grandmother kept them out of trouble. In many cases, young-

sters able to stay in school and stay out of trouble also
attended strict religious institutions. . . . Young people growing up in the oppressive contexts of depressed urban neighborhoods desperately need a clear coherent value system—a
secure positive belief system in which to cast self and imagine
a future." (pp. 224–226)

In stark contrast, critical pedagogy's aim is to dig up the social
contradictions—to foster a skepticism of dominant ideologies. Yet
for reasons expressed by these teenagers, some students without
economic and cultural privileges may be understandably reluctant to wholly embrace these critical assumptions.

Shianta continually characterized the "positive belief system"
drawn from her Baptist church through metaphors of boundaries. Moral order helps you keep your eyes on the prize: "When
you read the Bible and listen to church, it tells people their role
and that keeps you from overstepping your bounds." Although
this sounds like fundamentalist discourse here, Shianta also
implied she and others like her must keep set boundaries to cope
with the ones imposed by institutionalized racism and its local
effects in her world. "The world expects you to be a certain way,
but as soon as you step outside the boundaries of that, that's
where all the pressure comes from, like the way society has it all
set up for black people." Clearly, she critically reads these situations, but she also needs to live with this critical understanding.
To do that, Shianta seeks to sustain her motivation for achievement through the explicit setting of her own boundaries, drawn
from the moral teachings of her church and its civil rights discourse of unity and community.

Not surprisingly, she is known among her friends as
"Preacher Shianta" for her "different point of view." When I asked
her how she got the name, she referred not only to her state of
mind, but the way she carried herself. "A lot of people went to
church, but I guess it was the way I conducted myself. The way I
conducted myself, they had no other choice." She embodies this
persona to withstand others' rightful but enervating collective
opposition to mainstream achievement. Yet the name came primarily from her self-appointed role with friends as the motiva-
tor—the one who never swerves from this ideology. "I would motivate them to do what they know is right to do. . . . If they felt like
they wanted to work, I reminded them that school came first, and
stuff like that. If we got on the subject of church, I would explain
the Bible, so that's why they call me that." Indeed her various
friends' choice of the label "preacher" may suggest they tacitly

recognized her advice and motivating stories from the Bible as a brand of ideology.

In one of our first interviews, Shianta told how she had to develop this strong motivation for education she found lacking in the community outside her church (and sometimes within it). "Being young, growing up in a kind of society like I did, it was like [for many kids], 'so what? I don't care.' And a lot of our children when [they] start to grow up, start getting that attitude." She began to consider her position when she was unable to attend a superior high school because of low grades. Her father's exasperation got to her as well: "It hurt me because he's been telling me this all the time. One day he said, 'okay, be a nobody, but at least get education for me.' That mean more than all the whoopings I got for bad report cards because he cared, not just for whooping." Clearly making the choice to care about her future through mainstream education and acculturation was not an easy task when faced with the tacit opposition of many in her neighborhood.

When I asked her how she got through this apathetic phase toward school achievement, she spoke of submitting to her duties and a higher sense of her self. "It made life easier, by obeying elders as far as school, work, instead of doin' things my way. They're over me, I don't obey [them], but I submit. It's part of discipline, make the decision to do right. It's your choice." In her occasional comments in Rashmi's class and in our conversations, she drew on this language of submission and boundaries to interpret issues of gender and race raised by the course or her local knowledge. Several times during the term, she referred to the joy women could find as mothers despite the oppressions they faced in patriarchal cultures. At these points, her views often acknowledged the contradictions and injustices of dominant positions. For instance, she saw the main subject of Rashmi's course as control in women's lives: "How women accepted oppression and really couldn't do anything about poverty, how they let other things control them more than their own mind or their own health, or their own importance." Yet she also sought to assuage those more negative critiques through this language of submission to boundaries.

Thus, when she explained to me the importance of religious discipline for motivating her life, she referred to the roles of men and women. Initially she replied from the discourse of feminist critique privileged in Rashmi's class, admitting that "Christianity set up a patriarchal structure." But she then contended that this structure can help sustain a harmony that can benefit all involved when everyone submits their duties to the family and community.

> Whereas man is the head of the household, he is supposed to love his wife as he loves himself, do his duties as the man. Not like the wife oppress him either, [she is] supposed to be his helpmate, carry out, enforce his orders. Nowadays women are more aggressive, but when there are more serious issues, then women will go to the men, talk about it together. So I would say religion has played a big part.

When I consider Shianta's descriptions of fatherless families she has known and the difficulties of maintaining family for poor urban African Americans today, I can understand her concerns for established male and female roles. For she suggests that this traditional structure, possibly as understood by the women of her church, can bind the male to family obligations, maybe morally as well as financially. And part of these obligations requires cooperation—men and women talking out difficult problems together.[11]

Ironically, it is precisely this valuing of the term "unity" in black communities that black academic feminists have resisted. In Marlon Riggs' documentary, *Black Is, Black Ain't* (1995), both bell hooks and Michelle Wallace argue that the use of the term unity in the traditional black church and larger community has worked to exclude women and gays from recognition and power since the tacit goal of this organizing strategy has been to bolster the position of black men within the White male power system. In response, hooks offers the term, "communion" which she contends balances recognitions of difference with the necessity of responsible community. In contrast to these black feminist intellectuals, Shianta's frame of reference as she saw it relating to Rashmi's class, seems entrenched in "patriarchal structures." Yet for Shianta, embracing her church's valorization of unity, despite her acknowledgment of deep troubles rooted in sexism, racism, and socio-economic power, makes for a necessary stability. It is this stability that may then allow for future hopes and the strength to discipline motivations.

As this chapter has shown, situating the views of Shianta, Lilia, Diana, and Mike within the discourses and values of their separate local communities can help us better perceive where the gaps are in theories of difference in critical writing pedagogies.

These gaps reveal that sometimes very different issues are at stake for non-mainstream students than are usually addressed in discussions of students' writing about difference. These individuals' respective language of individualism and unity lead us to questions that are often overlooked when the critical teaching practice implicitly seeks to persuade students to interrogate dominant ideologies of late American capitalism. For instance, which students value college primarily for hopes of economic mobility and which seek social mobility as well? And considering the historical situations of their backgrounds, which students feel they can psychologically afford the practice of negative critique in some areas of their lives?

Both Mike and Diana implicitly express concerns over differences of social and economic mobility, although they tend to speak about these differences using a language of individualism that sounds like the middle-class status quo. Mike hopes for the economic mobility, but remains deeply ambivalent about what kind of social mobility he should buy into. Diana wants to keep the domain of working-class family and community separate from her middle-class professional aspirations. In Mike's case, his community identifies the practice of social critique as rejecting tacit solidarity. In Diana's case, she may reproduce a social critique in the class about the social contradictions between the two domains, but my analysis suggests she will leave that analysis in the classroom.

Shianta's and Lilia's discourses of unity suggest other concerns at stake. Practically every semester I taught at UIC, I encountered one or two African-American or Latina women, often religious, who psychologically invest in messages of racial or inter-racial unity despite their deep understandings of racism toward their community and sexism within it. In some of their writings for my classes, there has been a clash of tones between the critical inquiry of difference I have encouraged and their calls for unity. Perhaps like Shianta, Lilia, and Kisha (the student from my class whom I discussed in chapter 1), they require conviction, rather than critical uncertainty to face the odds against them.

In closing, the situations of all four individuals show that these contexts and values will shape different students' approaches to these calls for critical engagement. In the next chapter, I discuss how we also need to reconsider critical writing teachers' claims of what constitutes their students' acts of resistance.

NOTES

1. Irvin Peckham (2003) also offers an analysis of Diana's performance here in Rashmi's class from the perspective of Bourdieu's
   theories of social class. Peckham developed his Bourdieuan analysis from reading my article (see Seitz, 1998) on which this chapter
   is based. Although I clearly had Bourdieu's typologies of economic,
   cultural, and social capital in mind when I interpreted my data,
   Peckham's deep knowledge of Bourdieu's social research and theory in *Distinction* (1984) and other texts further clarifies some of the
   class issues at stake here.
2. Mike's and Diana's talk clearly drew from anti-welfare discourse
   from the time of 1996 soon after legislative welfare reform, but primarily because it fit their community's values. Both Mike and
   Diana saw themselves as sometimes prejudiced, but not racist
   compared with others they knew.
3. Like the values of any local social group, working-class values are
   going to vary depending on region and historical circumstances.
   Mike's and, to a lesser degree, Diana's community situations bear
   some similarities to these studies' "research sites."
4. Nevertheless, we must again recognize differences of class behaviors in terms of regional cultures. In Philipsen's (1992) study of
   Teamsterville's cultural politics in Chicago, he describes the
   expected seeking of favors from those in the working-class community who have risen in power. As representative examples,
   Philipsen shows community members' loyalties to their alderman
   and the first Richard Daley, suggesting that the reliance on big
   men from the neighborhoods partly derives from old world honor
   codes in Ireland and Italy.
5. Arlie Hochschild and Annie Machung's (1989) study of attitudes
   and practices of work in two-income family households highlights
   this tension over gender roles for many working-class women.
   Hochschild compared attitudes and practices of work in two-
   income families across lines of social class. Although Hochschild's
   observations showed most working-class parents actually shared
   the domestic duties of the "second shift" more equally than middle-
   and upper class parents, their public views about women's roles
   still tended to be more conservative. This is not to deny the empowering force that the necessity of women's employment has had for
   many working-class women, particularly for the daughters. Rather
   this area remains a site of tension among working-class loyalties,
   women's possible solidarity, and ideologies of individual achievement. The teenage girls in Weis' (1990) research express and act
   out these tensions in the postindustrial economy. This socioeconomic situation leaves Weis uncertain whether the majority of
   these women will identify with feminist agendas that challenge
   patriarchy's symbiotic relationship with capitalism in the right's

pro-family rhetoric or side with the "new traditionalist" wing of the women's new right.

6. In a classroom discussion near the end of the term about women's activism in Third World situations, Mike offered a similar view: "In my opinion, you start with the children to treat their sister and mother with respect, and things will change over time. You can't change people's minds." In chapter 7, I explore Mike's discourse of "respect" as his response to the course's feminist critiques and as a major strategy for his final paper.

7. Reading critical pedagogy's emphasis on politics of difference through the lens of Bourdieu's social theories, Irving Peckham (2003) rightly claims "Distinction *is* difference. The struggle for success is primarily a struggle for distinction, which is marked by being different, being *other*, that is trafficking in dissensus. Again Bourdieu's point is that you can afford to focus on dissensus only if you have gained a certain distance from necessity; in fact the assertion of dissensus can be understood as a marker *of* one's distance from necessity."

8. When I was arranging an extended interview with Diana months after my discussion with her and Mike, she warned me that her views change all the time. Yet not only did she repeat similar positions, but also some of the same anecdotes to illustrate them, such as her experience of waiting in the supermarket line behind a woman dressed in a fur coat using food stamps. Diana speculated that this woman got the money for her conspicuous display of wealth by dealing drugs.

9. The purposes of my ethnographic analysis of Lilia's and Shianta's religious discourse share much in common with Amy Goodburn's (1998) "It's a Question of Faith: Discourses of Fundamentalism and Critical Pedagogy in the Writing Classroom" and Lizabeth Rand's (2001) "Enacting Faith: Evangelical Discourse and the Discipline of Composition Studies." Although neither Lilia and Shianta take as strident a moral position as the students Goodburn and Rand discuss, I would agree that close study of devoutly religious students in my research and teaching has made me painfully aware how much critical pedagogy is a faith that also seeks its converts to the right path. My arguments in the rest of this chapter also agree with Rand that these students involve themselves in deep critical thinking every day as they negotiate their resistances to dominant American consumer culture and, as Lilia's comments will show, offer ways for critical writing teachers to engage students' postmodern Christian sensibilities.

10. Ironically, a year and a half after Rashmi's class, Shianta had to transfer to a junior college on the Southside because of a low grade point average (GPA) at UIC. She told me she feels more comfortable with the classes there because "they go more into depth, they don't assume you know the information." Shianta's statement recalled for me Lisa Delpit's (1995) research and arguments in the field of

education examining the different teaching style of "progressive" teachers (primarily White) compared with minority school teachers. Perhaps Shianta felt she gained more from the community college teachers because they taught necessary college skills in a more explicit manner, rather than embedding them in critical pedagogies' greater emphasis on socioeconomic and cultural inequities. For an example of this more explicit "Black" teaching style and its possibilities for different approaches to critical teaching, see Foster (1989). Although Shianta might have found a better place for her learning styles and present needs, in a way she now has experienced first-hand having "your education taken away from you."

11. Shianta's language here echoes the discourse of African-American men's responsibility in the family employed by Louis Farrakhan's "Million Man March," which took place the week of one of our interviews. Shianta told me she and her mother judged Farrakhan in both positive and negative ways that required a "wait and see attitude." Her reverend endorses him only because he is a major figure, but argued that focusing on only one race can be just as bad as White racists—a criticism again founded in her church's concerns for multiracial unity. Although her reverend and Shianta's family agreed with the march's theme of "atonement to do what's right for the Black family," her mother and Shianta were distrustful of Farrakhan's motives for charging all marchers $10. "If the march is so important, then it should be for free"—a view that again sides with needs of poor people.

Reconsidering Resistance

COMPLICATING CLAIMS OF RESISTANCE

When Suzanne Clark and Lisa Ede (1990) asked, "How do we recognize productive resistance when we see it?", they were asking the right question. Clark and Ede took Geoffrey Chase (1988) to task for his simplified labeling of three particular students where Bill accommodates, Kris opposes, and Karen resists the dominant discourses of their disciplines in their university as represented by their senior writing projects. In 1983, Henry Giroux defined *cultural resistance* as oppositional behavior that contains an implicit or explicit critique of domination and fosters opportunities for social reflection. In contrast to the critically productive goals of resistance, Giroux defined *opposition* as unreflective behavior that disrupts or dismisses the dominant authority, and he characterized *accommodation* as acceding to the power of dominant authority. Chase was the first to adapt Giroux's terms to specific concerns of teaching writing and, like any pioneer, cut too broad a path. Clark and Ede argue that Chase's "student examples fall into place with suspicious ease into a hierarchy of three" (p. 280) and that he doesn't fully consider the rhetorical situations of Bill, the student he dismisses as accommodating the discourses of power.

Clark and Ede point out that "Chase's reluctance to credit Bill's interpretation of his experience . . . may represent a dangerous, if unwilling and unconscious, arrogance" (p. 280). My

173

research with the students in Rashmi's class made me more aware of another kind of deep unreflective arrogance by some scholars of critical pedagogy. In discussions of accommodation, opposition, or resistance to teachers' critical agendas, there has been very little thinking so far about whether the student views his or her choices and behaviors in these terms.

Chase wrote about resistance as the hope for students' critical resistance to dominant cultures, discourses, or institutions. Yet in 1991, the collected authors of *Composition and Resistance* began asking why many students tended to resist their own efforts to enact critical teaching.[1] Although some of the authors and discussions in this collection turn the critique on themselves, others—and more important, many critical teacher-scholars who followed in the wake of this book—tend to rely on critical theories to posit a new deficit model—students who lack critical consciousness. As Marguerite Helmers (1994) pointed out several years ago, much of our profession's writings have always represented students as lacking something already possessed by their teacher. Before it was a linguistic deficit; now it's a political one— once again with implications of a moral lack.

To be fair, when Giroux developed his theories of resistance to institutional powers, he implicitly argued for the necessity of ethnographic research to continually inform and reconsider the application of theoretical critique to local situations in schools. Indeed most of his crucial examples in *Theory and Resistance in Education* (1983) came from ethnographic studies of working-class schools. In practice, however, many critical teachers' interpretations of college students' writing and/or the students (as in many of the essays in Fitts and France [1995]) often rely on deductions drawn from critical theories, rather than grappling with the ethics of this necessary dialectic between ethnographic perspectives and critical theories.

In the previous chapters, I examined the participants' local situations and perspectives to argue why particular students' responses, behaviors, and values constituted varied forms of resistance to critical pedagogy. Yet over the course of my research, I became increasingly uncomfortable with my own claims for what finally counted as different students' opposition or resistance. For one thing, college students are already more acculturated to mainstream academic practices than the elementary and secondary students discussed by Giroux and John Ogbu when they speak of resistance to mainstream acculturation. In this chapter, therefore, I examine how difficult it remains to correctly identify and discern resistance (or indeed accommodation or opposition) in some of these students' situations. First, I discuss Shianta's work on her final paper to show the difficulty of separating students' social motives from concerns of material necessity. If some of the students resorted to more instrumentalist approaches to research writing in their final papers (e.g., mostly summarizing sources rather than complicating research assumptions), their strategies may say more about their other work, family, and school obligations than demonstrate an implicit resistance to forms of critical writing and thinking. Second, I refer back to Diana's, Peter's and Gita's rhetorical strategies in and out of Rashmi's classroom to demonstrate that what the teacher may perceive as a student's resistance to dominant cultures may be a domain-specific performance. I also address how these students' complexity of social positions complicates some final statement that they were only acting for the sake of a good grade. Finally, I analyze more thoroughly the discourses that influenced Mike's final paper for Rashmi's class as well as his understandings of that work. Through this closer discourse analysis, I contend that where the teacher might perceive opposition to the expectations of critical writing, sometimes the student may view his actions as meeting the teacher's expectations in a way that also engages his own concerns.

COMPLICATIONS OF SOCIAL MOTIVES AND MATERIAL CONSTRAINTS

As a student interested in a career in public health and nursing, Shianta decided for her final paper to look at the efforts of international women's rights groups to educate women in African and Middle Eastern countries about the medical dangers of female circumcision. In the role of writing tutor, I met with Shianta a few times to help her develop this paper. I took on this role as a form of reciprocation for her help and admittedly as a way to talk more with her outside the classroom. We discussed how she could use her cultural perspectives, particularly her notions of set boundaries and morals, to investigate the traditions of female circumcision. As her tutor, I listened, paraphrased back her thinking, and helped her theorize why educating women to abandon these traditions of circumcision is so complex a task. I knew that Rashmi expected a critical analysis rather than an informational report, so I encouraged her to look for the values in these women's cultures that supported and encouraged circumcision. In doing so,

she could then examine what the health workers trying to educate these women may be overlooking about the values set in
these women's cultural traditions. But what struck me about our
discussions for her paper was the difficulty we had separating
definitions of *customs, culture,* and *tradition.*

This transcript excerpt from a tutoring session shows how I
tried to use Shianta's terms to suggest a cultural analysis she
could shape with her own understandings and the course material. Admittedly, I'm the dominant voice in this patch of dialogue,
and I am pushing her toward an ethnographic perspective
because she often found cultural explanations persuasive in class.

> Shianta: That's why sometimes hard to justify tradition
> without culture because it actually defines
> culture, but sometimes can't untie it. From
> traditional point of view, this woman is going
> to teach her children about circumcision.
>
> David: And that's tradition.
>
> Shianta: Right. So the other is culture. As I said one
> day in class, you can't just actually separate
> the two because tradition defines the culture.
>
> David: So maybe what you want to talk about is this
> interconnection, but part of the reasons these
> women make these choices is because of
> these traditions and culture. . . . Sounds like
> trying to educate people about this [the med-
> ical dangers of female genital mutilation] is
> not a simple thing of just changing cultures
> because culture is related to traditions. And
> traditions are values and morals and set
> orders. Because behind the practice is the
> belief for these women that this is the set
> order of their world.
>
> Shianta: Right.

Shianta then showed me Alice Walker's and Pratibha Pamar's
(1993) book on the topic, *Warrior Marks,* which contained interviews with women caught up in these practices. From this
source, I suggested how she could look at the interviews for
examples of cultural values to analyze in her paper—an idea she
described as looking from "the inside looking out." Shianta was

never able to arrange another time to work on her paper with me after this session. When I asked how the project was going, she told me she was following up on ideas from our discussion.

In the first two to three pages of her final paper, "The Interrelationship of Tradition and Culture," she begins with a cultural analysis drawn from our tutoring discussions, stating that women's practices of female circumcision in some Northern African cultures "help define who they are and what they value as a people." But instead of doing her own analysis of these culture's values to examine why this public health education might sometimes fail to persuade others, she relies on listing ten reasons from one other book and then moves to summarizing factual information of the health problems from the same book. The paper concludes with a page on what methods for educating these women seem effective and then a paragraph returning cursorily to the theme of identity and culture.

When I read Shianta's paper, I initially wondered how much she was resisting my suggested approach of cultural analysis despite her framing of the paper with the ideas of tradition and culture that we had discussed. Did she believe that ultimately it was more important to directly inform others about the health risks than to develop a more indirect analysis? Earlier at midterm of Rashmi's class, Shianta wanted to write on issues of poverty and its influences on public health in West African countries. Later after the term, I asked her what made her switch to the subject of genital mutilation for her final paper. She put it to me this way:

> If you said, "poverty in West Africa" and another headline it said, "genital mutilation," which one would you choose? You're going to choose genital mutilation because you want to know what that is. And especially to black people, don't nobody know genital mutilation. What is that? They want to know. Whereas poverty is like the same old thing, day in and day out. You know it's there and a lot of people, people I know, grew up with poverty, whereas circumcision is something new, something different and it would catch the eye.

Shianta's view of what makes a good topic for research reminds me of Peter's dismissive attitude toward writing classes that want him to reexamine the particulars of his social conditions. That is, everybody knows *that* and we just have to cope with it. Instead write about something unknown and exotic. Yet

Shianta's view also suggests a concern for spreading the word in her community—a rhetoric from her background in the African-American Baptist church and discourses of public health. This motive might partially explain why she leaned on reporting the information in her paper, rather than developing the cultural analysis she had begun to discuss with me. Still when I asked her about the process of writing this paper, she laughed and remarked, "the only thing was I was running out of things to say."

On later reflection, I found it difficult to identify what was the primary cause for Shianta's eventual reliance on the generic forms of a standard research report. I do not see any certain way to separate her motives, limited experience with academic analytical strategies, and the time constraints imposed by work, commuting long distances by bus, neighborhood obligations, and the difficulties of her other classes.

COMPLICATIONS OF
DOMAIN-SPECIFIC PERFORMANCES

In addition to these material realities that constrained some students' efforts to develop sustained critical analysis in their longer papers, some students took different social and discursive positions in and out of the class domain. In the classroom and in the students' writing, the teacher might perceive a student's critical resistance to dominant ideologies, suggesting an alliance with the teacher's critical agenda. Yet in other out-of-school contexts, the same individual might refute or certainly complicate the stance he or she took in class. Out of the seven featured participants in my study, Diana, the Greek-American student, demonstrated this rhetorical practice. Diana consistently took up feminist stances in class discussion, but in conversations with me after the term argued for maintaining traditional roles in the home. All teachers who claim a critical agenda for their classes occasionally face students who mimic the leftist discourse (or often a generic ahistorical approximation) in hopes of a better grade.

Yet as a participant-observer in Rashmi's class, I did not interpret Diana's classroom performances in this way. In the first weeks of class, I imagined she and another White female student in the class wanted to relieve themselves of White Western guilt through their sharp criticism of dominant American myths of international development. In those first weeks, the two women heavily criticized the American government's global policies, whereas most of the students of color initially chose not to speak. Based on Diana's and this other woman's style and content of talk in the first weeks, I wrongly assumed they were from more middle-class backgrounds. From my initial view, I assumed these women were speaking out of an unrecognized entitlement compared with immigrant and minority students in the class, whose motivations for success may be invested in some of these ideologies of American achievement. Other students who privately talked to Rashmi initially referred to Diana as "that girl who talked so much even though she admitted in class she hadn't done the reading." One day early in the semester, Diana prefaced her classroom comments by remarking that although she had not done the reading, she had something to add to the discussion. Diana had no compunction about breaking the students' code of silence on reading preparation for class, suggesting a sense of entitlement after all—possibly attributable to her parents' role as educators.

I later came to believe that Diana argued for a universal feminism, a view shared by other women of different backgrounds in the class, and she felt ashamed of the racism she attributed to members of her Greek-Orthodox community. Thus, I was surprised how strongly she held, outside classroom space and time, to more conservative views that I attribute to White working-class solidarity. Yet as I asserted in chapter 6, we simplify her local situation if we dismiss all of her discursive positions in class as inauthentic. Instead I came to see her reasons for keeping separate these domains of women's public roles in institutions and their private roles in the family and local community (despite the critical teacher's itch to have a student like Diana "problematize" this dichotomy of motives).

Peter, the African-American and Puerto Rican student I discussed in chapter 3, shows another case complicating differences of positions performed in and out of class. Although Peter rarely spoke up in class, his writings for the course, particularly his in-class journal entries, suggested he might be much more invested in the classroom inquiry of race and gender in Third World politics than I later found out he actually was. This is not to say that he did not care deeply about issues of racism, as his interests in Islam suggested he did. Rather he primarily saw further inquiry of the issues in Rashmi's class as perfunctory—a view that was hard to discern solely from his writing for Rashmi's course. Similarly, Gita, who I discussed in chapter 4, valued a resistance to systemic social injustices, as her efforts to boycott particular products and volunteer for a women's shelter demonstrate. But Gita also intuited that Rashmi's course required emotional performances that did not always express her more instrumentalist approach to business and management.

As my "key informant" on students' rhetorical performances in Rashmi's class, Gita forced me to consider another complication of student performances as well. Critical writing teachers take as a tenet of their pedagogy that students strengthen critical consciousness through a dialectic of readings and social experiences. Yet as I discussed in chapter 4, Gita could point out to me many times when her classmates used this teachers' expectation—one that Rashmi and I definitely share—to bluff that they had indeed done the reading. Thus, as all of these complications of domain-specific performances indicate, it may be more difficult to discern what counts as internally persuasive resistance to the status quo in some students' classroom performances than most of the literature on critical pedagogy assumes.

WHEN NO ONE CATEGORY FITS

Finally, I want to suggest that the microdynamics of these students' situations may sometimes be more complex than allowed for by these critical theories of resistance in education. In some instances, students' responses and strategies may not wholly be a case of accommodation, opposition, resistance, or simply a negotiation of positions, but instead a fluctuating interchange of these responses and cultural interpretations depending on the immediate circumstances and contingencies of the rhetorical situations. For example, Ira Shor (1996) analyzes the tendency of some White working-class students to sit as far away from the teacher—the locus of formal power—as possible. By this move, they accommodate the socioeconomic power structure by remaining on the margins of institutionally sanctioned knowledge and authority. Yet Shor contends "Given the outlaw status of their home dialects and community cultures in school, they construct themselves as subordinates who can't escape authority but won't fully cooperate with it either" (pp. 13–14).[2] Thus, according to Shor, these students act out a simultaneous behavior of accommodation and resistance.

In Mike's case, I ultimately found that his responses as a whole could not be slotted into a particular category from theories of resistance. Nor, however, did I feel comfortable finally

labeling his thoughts and actions toward the course as principally *negotiation*—the fourth term taken up by critical teachers. If
this complexity of motives and responses is sometimes the case
in our classes, we should be more cautious in making judgments
based on these theories, even when we situate them with ethnographic stories.

MIKE'S TENSIONS: CULTURAL RELATIVISM
AND CODES OF RIGHT AND WRONG

Throughout Rashmi's course, Mike's responses to the issues
raised by the class alternated between an isolationist brand of
cultural relativism (we can not judge their culture) and an absolutist code of ethics (doing this to women is wrong no matter
what).[3] In most cases, his declarations of cultural relativism side-
stepped a systemic critical analysis of the situation, neglecting
interconnections of gender, labor, and local and global economy
emphasized in the course readings and class discussions. Mike
claimed this rhetorical move was warranted by his ignorance of
Third World cultures. For instance, the first time I met with Mike
outside Rashmi's class, he wanted me to understand his problem
with the expectations of criticism in the course. He referred back
to the documentary film, "Small Happiness," which the class had
viewed several weeks earlier (and that I referred to in the previous
chapters). Like Diana and others, he was physically upset by the
ritual of the wedding family physically pushing down the bride
during the ceremony. But compared with most of the women in
the class, Mike saw himself as ethically unable to critically analyze this practice. "The problem with this class is it's wrong to
accuse a culture of being wrong. In that Chinese film, when they
were pushing a woman down, we may look at it as wrong and she
may not like this, but that's their culture and they've been doing
that for years. Can't expect them to change because our culture
says it's wrong."

   During our talks outside class, he came back to this position
several times, as he did here when I asked him a semester after
Rashmi's course whether the class had changed his thinking in
any ways.

> Not really. If anything it just educated me a little more to
> what might be going on in the third world country. All it did
> was open doors for me. It didn't affect my life. I'm not going to

> change my life. I just can't really do much about what hap-
> pens in China. Second of all, nobody's going to listen to me.
> Who the hell in China gives a shit about what I think? I'm
> just some weird White kid from over in the U.S. I don't even
> understand their culture fully, how can I judge their culture?"

In one sense, Mike's unwillingness to judge other cultures acts out a refreshing humility, atypical of most White American men. Several times he attributed this stance to his discomfort as the "other" in Rashmi's classroom, compared with the class majority of multinational women. Mike confessed to Rashmi and me his discomfort in the classroom situation, sometimes perceiving the women's analysis of issues as one sided—in his words, "just seeing the bad, where there's always good sides to most things." Yet in offhand ways, he acknowledged that this discomfort was productive for expanding his view of the world, as he implies in the earlier statement: "All it did was open doors for me." And unlike many of his male friends, and other studies of men from similar working-class backgrounds, Mike admitted that he found it much harder to chat with guys than girls. He found girls, particularly those whom he had met at college, to be more open-minded.

Still Mike's way of talking about this expansion of his world-view repeatedly diminishes the political efficacy of this teaching for him. In the earlier block quote, he reuses the qualifier "just" twice and the word "all" as a qualifier to undercut the worth of this new understanding: "it just educated me a little more; all it did was open doors for me; I'm just some weird White kid." What is surprising here is the positive strength of Mike's metaphor for education as opening doors if one leaves out the qualifiers "all" and "just". Mike's qualifier indicates that he values this critical education, but it is not enough to persuade him to do more than see himself as ineffectual in the sociopolitical system.[4]

Moreover, Mike's language here implies, in part, an interest in maintaining a stable self tied to the class solidarity of his out-of-school friends, as also seen in his talk from chapters 4 and 6. When I asked him in our general interview a summer after the term if he felt he talked differently in Rashmi's class than in other settings, Mike referred to his cultural relativist view of the class: "No, I just talked the way I did. I can't change that. I really don't know nothing about the Indian culture. I can't pretend like I do. I think that's stupid. Who am I trying to impress? I don't care. I'm not there to impress anyone, you know?" Mike's emphasis here on whether one should make an impression in the set-ting of the critical classroom makes sense with his positions as I interpreted them in the previous chapters. To really enter into a critical dialogue about cultural issues, to entertain the notion of social change and personal transformation in the setting of the college classroom, is also an act of taking on the social capital of the individual academic prestige. It is an act of impressing others with your distinction that Mike's leanings toward working-class solidarity reject. Mike's underlying logic, then, is very different compared with the brand of cultural relativism mouthed by many students—the view that "everyone is entitled to their opinion" most discussed among critical teachers. Faigley (1992) attributes this familiar student phrase to students' consumer-based ideolo-gies of free choice, and Durst (1999) wisely suggests students stick to this language as a rhetorical strategy to evade confronta-tion in the critical writing classroom. For Mike and others stu-dents from similar backgrounds, the responses are a tacit issue of class loyalty.

For some cultural issues from the course, however, Mike felt compelled to evoke a harder code of ethics—to pass judgments of right and wrong that would shut down investigation of sociohis-torical circumstances. For example, when the class discussed and debated the practices of female genital mutilation as prac-ticed in some countries in Africa and the Middle East, Mike's response agreed with some feminists who claim that we can delineate universal human rights.[5] As universal rights feminists might do, Mike boiled the issue down to the unjust use of force. "I am going to think it's wrong because I don't think you should be forced to do anything. I guess it doesn't have to do with cir-cumcision, it has to do with force."[6]

Keeping Mike's alternating positions of cultural relativism and absolutist ethics in mind, it's worth asking why Mike chose the topic he wrote on for his final paper. In choosing a topic, Mike avoided two kinds of issues he had encountered in the class readings and discussions. First, he was able to avoid those cul-tural issues that he did not feel qualified to criticize, such as female genital mutilation. Second, he evaded the more explicitly socioeconomic issues that he viewed as more complicated because he saw benefits along with drawbacks, as with his views of the international exploitation of women's labor, which I dis-cussed in chapter 3. Instead Mike chose an issue that he could speak against in absolutist terms: prostitution in Third World countries. From Mike's perspective, then, he chose a topic that would accommodate what he saw as Rashmi's critical agenda.

THE ETHICS OF BS
AND PERSONAL INTEGRITY

Yet significantly, Mike told me later he did not perceive this approach to his final paper as "BS"ing the teacher—a strategy he could talk about at great length when prompted. As Durst's study indicates, when students believe they are BS'ing the critical teacher, feeding her what they believe is her politically correct line, they are resisting the use value of critical approaches and the possibility of internally persuasive learning for their own purposes. For Mike and Peter, "BS"ing seemed to be both a strategy for handling school assignments and a way of talking about schoolwork that would allow him to separate himself from the schoolwork—to maintain an integrity of self. At one point, Mike put it this way: "Sometimes to get the grade, you have to BS. But even still, seven will be mine, three will be to blow extra air up her [the generic teacher's] ass so she'll give me a better grade." In sharp contrast to this vivid admission of tactics, Mike felt this approach was unnecessary and uncalled for in Rashmi's course: "I told the truth in Rashmi's class, that I didn't know what the hell about anything she was talking about when I first got in there. She told me that it was better to say that. And she said just go with what you know. So I knew I didn't have to bullshit."

Within this environment of trust, Mike also chose to write his final paper in a more personal genre of research writing that Rashmi, influenced by postmodern feminist theories of discourse and more autobiographical styles of academic writing, offered to the class as an alternative approach.[7] By taking up the genre of explicitly situated research, as Rashmi or I might call it, Mike believed he could evade the need to "BS" and elude what he saw as the false authority of the research paper genre. Mike clearly resented demands of academic discourse exemplified by the genre of the research paper as he perceived it. Whenever I asked him questions about his college writing, he invariably went on the defensive against teachers who rejected his use of personal experiences to find an entry into more academic topics. "Well, that's my life. I'm not going to sit here and say (mimicking the deep-toned authoritative voice of a filmstrip narrator), 'the flight path of a monsoon bird' or some bullshit like that. I'm going to say how it relates to my life a little more. Not my life was like affected by this bird, but more . . . (with a resigned tone) I'm not real good at research papers." Mike clearly recognizes that he cannot ignore the forms of discourse he knows are expected in institutional writing fields, even as he parodies and challenges their authority in language.

Commenting on his problems with the school "system," as he put it, Mike claimed that he had never had to write a paper before this first year of college. Because Mike went to a Catholic boys' school, I found this rather surprising and presumed he meant write an official research paper, that sad high school experience many students had related to me where the teaching of nitpicking proper form eclipses any motivated inquiry. Still it seemed unlikely that he could wholly escape that high school rite of passage. "You've got to be aware of that," he told me. "Not everyone learns how to write a paper in school." Mike's statements on teaching writing implied his sense of good writing as cultural capital that had eluded him. "They say it's good to use adjectives, but wait, don't use so many. They don't tell you how many is too many. You're supposed to be assumed to know that."

But instead of seeing first-year writing classes as a chance to examine these rhetorical choices of style, Mike had already decided writing could not be taught and viewed teachers' evaluations of writing as subjective. "How can you judge how someone writes? You can judge if I use the wrong verb or spelled something wrong, grammar, but who are you to judge what I write about or how I write about it as long as my points come across." Significantly, these remarks on the subjectivity of writing evaluation emerged out of Mike's rejection of speaking "perfect English" because it would be "trying to rub it in their eye." My interview question, "Is there such a thing as 'good English'?", elicited from Mike these associations between rejecting English as cultural capital and his sense of the inability to teach writing.

Coming from this view of himself as a writer in college, Mike immediately took up Rashmi's offer that the students' final paper could be a "creative project" that incorporated personal voice and experience. "Anyone can write a bullshit research paper," Mike argued at midterm, "take a book, reread it and rewrite that, but it takes more to sit there and think about something. I actually work on those things." He saw this invitation for creativity as a chance to write about his "impressions" of the issues the course had raised for him, including his situation as a White guy in Rashmi's classroom. Mike's paper begins with his brand of cultural relativism, but the language soon shifts to a code of dualism. On page two, Mike writes, "I am not educated in the ways and customs of third world nations. I have never been there and probably never will. But that doesn't mean that I don't have an opinion on what is wrong and right."

THE CODE OF HONOR AND RESPECT

Mike's paper, entitled for readers' titillation, "Turn on the Red
Light: A Look Into the Red Light Districts of Third World Nations,"
stresses his moral judgment against prostitution in Third World
countries, with specific reference to Thailand and the Phillipines.[8]
He opens the paper examining his confusing position as the male
other in Rashmi's class. Although he feels out of place, he agrees
more with his female classmates than his friends outside school,
who argue "minorities are under us" and "women are there for
people to screw around on." From this point in the introduction
of his paper, however, Mike's paper relies on a discourse of
respect and, to a lesser extent, a code of honor for its major warrants. This code of respect and honor is reminiscent of White
working-class Teamsterville communicative practices demonstrated in Gerry Philipsen's (1992) study. Through ethnographic
research, Philipsen contends that Teamsterville men believe it is
their role to protect the reputation of the family's wives and
mothers, in the form of respect, as part of an implicit cultural
system that maintains the men's personal and family honor.

Mike also called on this language of respect whenever he
sought to justify to me his views of race as "color blind." In our
conversations, he would evoke the necessity of respect taught by
his parents, particularly his father: "I was taught to respect people, not to judge people by what they look like. If someone shows
me disrespect, I'm not going to care who the hell they are." In his
nine-page paper, Mike combines a four- to five-page recounting of
the nature and effects of Third World prostitution (drawing from
three articles, one thoroughly discussed in class) with two incidents in his life about respecting women. In the first incident, he
describes his sense of shame when he continuously cheated on a
girlfriend because he followed the advice of buddies. In the second incident, he points to when he stuck to his principle of
respecting women even though he believes she was not worthy of
that respect.

In one sense, I interpret Mike's use of this local discourse of
respect and honor as his negotiation with the critical discourses
of Rashmi's class. By drawing on local values, he finds personal
justification for the critical view of Third World sexual exploitation shared by many class members. Nevertheless, the ways he
shapes this justification through this discourse of respect also
suggest a resistance to the course's favored ways of developing
critical positions, as becomes apparent further later.

After summarizing his position as a White male in a class dominated by women from many cultural backgrounds, Mike writes, "I believe that women should be respected. That is why when I discovered what this class was about I stayed. I figured why not?" Following this code of ethics, Mike claims by analogy that forcing women into prostitution is "the ultimate form of disrespect." Not surprisingly, Rashmi's margin comment here urges Mike to question the purposes of this language: "Could that be a position of condescension? Why not just fight for women's rights?" Indeed Mike's conclusion to his paper appears to confirm Rashmi's suspicions that men's honor may be the primary subject of this discourse.

> In my opinion, I think it takes more of a man to treat a woman with respect than to take advantage of them. There is no excuse for prostitution on both accounts. Any man who has to resort to either paying or forcing a woman for sex isn't much of a man at all. And it doesn't matter what culture— you're wrong, it's universally wrong.

Philipsen's study locates this kind of talk among Teamsterville men in an old world code of honor, where "his reputation, and thus his sense of well-being, is constituted by the public perception of females linked to him by blood or marriage. . . . The status of a woman is directly linked to his own status" (p. 110).

Clearly Mike did not wholly side with this old world male privilege. Yet when pressed to rationalize his position in his paper, Mike tends to fall back on the discourse that shapes much of his world outside school, rather than examine the complexities of his topic. Rashmi's final comments summarized this problem as a critical paper: "Not very well researched. Interesting insights, but a very complex issue has been treated somewhat simplistically." At several points in the paper, her margin comments endeavor to show how Mike could have developed a more systemic analysis, rather than trapping himself in a one-sided argument. At the bottom of his first page, Mike states that he wishes to "establish, according to different sources" the exploitation of Third World women through various forms of prostitution. Next to this, Rashmi implies why this is not a suitable thesis for a final paper: "So what? Will you be examining a *particular* practice or proposing a theory?" She challenges his list of reasons and types of Third World prostitution (which mixes up possible causes with effects), pointing out that "each one belongs to a different category." And when Mike seeks to conclude the paper, throwing up his hands and exclaiming he still can't understand why so many men in these countries will exploit women, Rashmi reminds him, "What about economic exploitation? International economy? These issues need to connect."

IT'S NOT COMPLICATED

A summer after the course, I asked Mike how he interpreted Rashmi's comments on this final paper:

David: She says here she thinks a very complicated issue has been treated somewhat simplistically, do you think that's?

Mike: I don't think there's anything so complex about being forced into slavery. It's wrong, plain and simple. How can you go any farther saying its wrong, unless you have common sense. Any person with common sense knows it's demeaning, it promotes a lot of diseases, there's nothing good about it. I just think its wrong to make it seem so much more complicated because its not complicated.

David: Do you think by trying to make it more complicated?

Mike: It might have hurt my paper.

David: When you tried to make it--

Mike: In U.S. people do it because they're good at it or they like the sex or they want the money, but there there's almost always other reasons. Women are more forced into it over there. So it's a little more complicated in that sense for me, but it doesn't change my point.

David: Do you think by making it more complicated, it cuts down what people need to hear or know?

Mike: Problem is, somewhere along the line the point might be lost if you keep on padding it.

Although Rashmi and other critical academics understand the complexity of these issues as requiring analysis of social and economic systems (as suggested by her comments on Mike's paper), Mike understands complexity here as a moral question. In response to Third World prostitution, he states, "I just think it's wrong to make it seem so much more complicated because it's not complicated." In contrast, recall his views of the international exploitation of women's labor: "Our culture just looks at everything the wrong way, just seeing the bad, where [there are] always good sides to most things." To Mike, a complex problem means there is some good and some bad; it's shades of gray, which at best, if one has time, should be sorted out.[9]

He gave me some examples of this reasoning when I asked him what topics or issues he remembered several months after the class. What's also important here is the overall context in which he framed these examples:

> I don't know. I guess the only thing I learned is that (pause) no matter where you are, things suck. It doesn't matter who you are, cultures have their things, they suck. Sure, there's lot of good things about cultures, some stuff that we didn't get into. Examples would be the forced circumcision, okay. That definitely sucks, but I'm sure that there's also good things about the culture, but you can't just knock off the culture. It's almost like propaganda, like saying, "I had to hate all Germans because some Germans were nazis." Or living here in the U.S., we have plenty of freedoms, the right to bear arms, but we also have a hell of a lot of guns. Always going to have a dark side to every freedom.
>
> Or with communism, if you have everything at the same price, you don't get ripped off; if everyone makes the same amount, everyone can afford to eat, so that's good. Crime is down because everyone can afford to eat, so that's cool. But then you're forced to live almost like a slave. So there's good and bad. If there's a way to figure out for everyone to always have money. But you can't. Look at Bosnia. There's problems everywhere. Things suck all over.

Although I had asked Mike what he remembered, in one sense he used the opportunity to perform for another teacher, to rephrase the question as, "What did you learn in school today?" (although we were having breakfast in a decidedly working-class diner nearby UIC). I later came to associate Mike's view here—that "things suck all over"—with Gita's objections to rhetorical hand-wringing that I discussed in chapter 4. Mike and Gita came to their worldviews from contrasting working-class and immigrant backgrounds. But they both imply a need to "do what you got to do" (as Mike would put it). From this view, material necessity requires that one dismiss the longer deliberations and analysis of sustained critical writing.

For Mike, questions of American freedoms and communist states are complex because the moral understanding of these issues is not self-evident. Forced prostitution, however, is not complicated because everyone agrees its wrong. To claim it is a complicated issue, to address a more systemic analysis, then requires "BS"ing the teacher (what Gita might have described as putting in more emotion). But because Mike trusted Rashmi's interest in students' views, he wished to avoid this strategy: "Somewhere along the line the point might be lost if you keep on padding it." So paradoxically, by resisting the more analytical critique that Rashmi argues for, Mike stays true to what he believes are the purposes of the course.

Furthermore, by choosing to speak from his local discourse of respect and honor as a way to forge personal connections with a global issue, Mike exacerbates the problem posed by his practical views of moral complexities. Philipsen's observations and interviews in his Teamsterville study demonstrate that under the community's working-class code of honor, the appropriate male response toward affronts to women should be nonverbal, usually physical in nature. You don't talk it out; you hit 'em. So Mike's reliance on this discourse and its tacit assumptions against verbal deliberation with others may have promoted the premature exhaustion of what little academically sanctioned analysis he provides in the paper. From this view, once you have stated your position for respecting women, anything else you could say is padding.

Mike's paper was certainly not a shining example of the work other students accomplished in Rashmi's class. As in most classes, several students did write advanced papers that incorporated the students' own understandings with critical perspectives they had gained from course readings, discussions, and their own research. I chose to focus here on Mike, however, because long consideration of his contexts for writing in Rashmi's class left me dissatisfied with the ways we critical teachers tend to talk about resistance in our writing courses.

In the end, I don't think Mike's situation or those of the other students I discussed in the previous section wholly discount the theories of resistance in education. In fact I have relied on those assumptions for the premise of my research. Yet these students' situations and perspectives do indicate that we may tend to apply the terms deductively before we have made a concerted effort to understand the students' local situations and interpretations of their education. In the last two chapters, I examine and demonstrate the benefits of internally persuasive authority that I see in pedagogies that require more inductive theorizing from the students and the teacher. In chapter 8, I address how and why the teaching of ethnographic research writing can offer a more persuasive version of cultural studies' aims in composition.

NOTES

1. One of the difficulties with the premises of *Composition and Resistance* was that the authors used the term *resistance* to describe what they encountered from their students. From Giroux's frame, however, these descriptions refer more to his idea of opposition than his view of resistance as social productive action. Recently, Elizabeth Flynn (2001) articulated terms that account for these complications in the case of the critical writing teacher's classroom. Flynn redefines Giroux's idea of resistance as *strategic resistance*, the "planned and positive action in opposition to oppression." In contrast to the activist stance of strategic resistance, she defines *counterstrategic resistance* as resistance that "deliberately disrupts liberatory practices" and *reactive resistance* as a "spontaneous and emotional reaction that can have multiple and conflicting motivations and effects" (p. 18).

   Although in Flynn's taxonomy the naming of what beliefs and actions constitute "liberatory practices" in a given situation still generally seems to be the teacher's purview, Flynn's term of reactive resistance allows much more for the complexity of students' and teachers' actual responses to each other that she argues can sometimes lead to productive change, as she demonstrates with examples from her feminist-oriented classroom. She also shows how these three categories can blur and overlap as students' "identities also shift from context to context," a view similar to my own in this chapter, especially in regard to Mike's writing for his final paper as I address further later.

2. Shor names this particular practice as "the Siberian syndrome," implying these students "have learned socially to construct themselves as intellectual exiles" (p. 12). Most teachers would verify these behaviors and possibly Shor's interpretation. Shor is careful to differentiate degrees of these practices, discussing those working-class students who do choose a seat up front and in showing

ways that many of these students are intellectually curious outside the classroom contexts. Moreover, his book chronicles a growing understanding of these people in his classroom as they reach for mutual negotiation of the course curriculum over the course of the semester. Still I am uncomfortable with his choice of a term that implies neuroses and a backwoods lack of sophistication.

3. Educational theorists might easily interpret Mike's alternating positions of absolutist ethics and cultural relativism as only stages of his intellectual development. This view would follow William Perry's (1970) model of college learning, assuming that Mike is on the cusp of the less mature dualism and the more enlightened cultural relativism and may someday reach the pinnacle of committed relativism. From this view, Mike's age may be more important than his socioeconomic background. Of course contextual studies of education over the last 20 years have challenged the universalist assumptions of Perry's study of White Harvard men. As an opening move for the social turn in Composition Studies, in 1984 Patricia Bizzell offered a clearer reading of Perry's conclusions, asserting what they show us is the cultural influence of educational institutions, not a universal path of cognitive development.

    Five years later, Marilyn Cooper (1989) justifiably maintained that cognitive and social development are always complimentary. More important, in her reading of *Women's Ways of Knowing: The Development of Self, Voice, and Mind,* Cooper examines the socioeconomic situations of the women interviewed by Belenky et al. (1986) and the implicit hierarchy of epistemological positions the authors attribute to them. Through this social analysis, she contends that "so called cognitive stages are rather ways of thinking developed in response to particular situations and circumstances, determined by a variety of complex factors, including dominantly gender and socioeconomic class" (p. 152). Seen this way, intellectual development and maturity do not follow a linear path, but are "contextually triggered." In the rest of this chapter, I also assert that much of Mike's responses are contextually triggered and in part rooted in his working-class experiences and sense of self-identity.

4. Mike's sense of powerlessness here also suggests the potential advantages of student research writing projects beginning with the local situation of the students' cultures, where a student like Mike is more likely to perceive a sense of agency. In the following chapter on student's ethnographic projects, I elaborate on the theory and practice of beginning with students' affirmation of cultures as a more persuasive means to social critique.

5. As I mentioned in chapter 4, the majority of the participants I interviewed remembered this issue more than any other. At the time of the course, most members of the class were viscerally shocked by these practices. Both Diana and Shianta, in addition to two other students, wrote on the topic for their final paper, while

Peter included it as a section in his final paper. Rashmi also used this issue for the only occasion of role playing in class discussion, splitting the class up into four groups to debate the issue: universal human rights advocates, ethnocentric Westerners, cultural relativists, and indigenous African women. Although each group had to brainstorm arguments for their position, after 10 minutes or so people tacitly chose to abandon their group roles and argue their views. Although Mike was in the ethnocentric group, with me and Diana among others, he soon spoke from the position of universal human rights once the role playing deteriorated.

6. Mike also categorically condemned issues of Third World sexual exploitation—a position that might have then prevented him from examining their multiple causes and effects. When it came to writing his paper on an aspect of this issue, however, his warrants emerged more from working-class codes of respect and honor than essentialist arguments of human rights.

7. Few students took up an alternative structure, presumably sensing that to accomplish that task well would require more work than the standard research paper. Although Rashmi spoke for these alternatives, she was concerned about a few students in her classes who needed to gain some distance between their research and themselves. She offered Xiao, who I referred to in chapter 4, as an example. Rashmi saw this concern about students' objective distance as a teaching problem for her as her theoretical background persuaded her all research was "kind of tainted," but she still saw the need for "some semblance of objectivity" in the students' work. She reasoned that if these students only read to confirm their own experiences, this confirmation was not going to teach them much about research, which was her main goal for the course.

8. Mike deliberately took his title from "Roxanne," a song by the 1980s rock group, The Police, which has the chorus refrain, "put on the red light," referring to prostitution. Just before the last day of class when students would turn in their final papers, Mike mimicked Sting's high falsetto voice singing this line over and over as other students and I were discussing their "allnighters."

9. Mike's position here could also be compared with the students in Durst's research who tended to resist intellectual complexity in their research-writing course. Durst attributes that resistance to populist strains of American pragmatism. But I think it's important to also see Mike's view as part of a working-class focus on necessity (as Bourdieu might put it) in contrast to the perceived luxury of intellectual speculation (what Lindquist [2002] characterizes as the working-class rejection of the academic play of "what if?")

8

Social Affirmation
Alongside Social Critique

RETURNING TO TEACHING

As I began to analyze the themes I found in the interviews and fieldnotes from Rashmi's class, I felt a gap widening between my roles as researcher and teacher in my own classes at UIC. As a researcher, I grew ever more aware of the problems for critical writing pedagogy implied in the views of Mike, Peter, Gita, and others whom I have discussed in the earlier chapters. But when I tried to imagine pedagogical responses to these varied issues of persuasive authority, I drew blanks. For a period of 2 years or so, I had to reconcile myself to the contradictions. I had to go on teaching for my living regardless of whether I had cooked up the "answers" to the troubling questions raised by my research.

At the same time I found myself experiencing this gap between researcher and teacher, I had already begun teaching at UIC a version of English 102 as a course in ethnography— "Writing Culture: An Introduction to Community Research."[1] Strangely enough, it took several years to realize that my teaching of ethnography was one of my strongest theoretical and practical responses to the issues of persuasive authority I learned about from these students in Rashmi's class. It took even longer to articulate how teaching ethnography can also help foster the necessary humility for the critical writing teacher. Of course I began teaching research writing as students' ethnographic research of their cultures because it corresponded well with my research interests and fascination with local Chicago communities. I also understood that the ethnographic research offered a vital bridge between academic and local ways of making knowledge. Only with time and more experience have I been able to more fully draw the connections between my motives for this teaching approach in light of my own research and a theoretical understanding of what "makes it work" for me, if not others.

Teaching students critical writing through their own ethnographic research can offer a more persuasive version of cultural studies' aims in teaching. Writing teachers who draw on theories of cultural studies generally want their students to analyze the effects of social and institutional discourses and examine the possibilities for (agency) within the intersection of these discourses and material situations. Unlike most cultural studies approaches, however, ethnographic research encourages an affirmation of students' local situations before or alongside social critique of the cultural situation. It is this process of social affirmation that I have found motivates students toward a more internally persuasive social critique of local cultural groups and often their larger social contexts. Moreover, ethnographic methodology calls for the deferment of critique and the ethnographer's inductive building of theories about the local situation. This deferment of critique and inductive approach to theorizing helps create the space for the social affirmation of students' local knowledge.

Ethnographic methodology can promote students' social affirmation of local values on several levels—of situated place, embodied cognition, and material realities of people's everyday lives. If we consider a continuum of cultural practices and tacit values, these three areas of study would be more on the side of working-class values than the side of those in academia and the more socially and economically mobile members of the middle class. These forms of social affirmation tend to emerge from specific kinds of participant-observation, as I show next, creating a comfort zone that can allow for more self-motivated social critique, often more from the insiders' perspective.

In contrast to the emergence of affirmation from the forms of participant-observation, the more internally persuasive aspects of students' social critique tend to emerge more from the inductive processes of ethnographic methodology. In my teaching of students' ethnographic research, I have identified three particular processes that tend to promote self-motivated critical analysis. First, some students encounter contradictions between their observations and interviews—a situation my sequence of assignments tends to encourage. Second, because they mostly build their own theories from the cultural patterns they interpret from their data, they are more likely to be persuaded when they see connections between their local theories and discussion of power relations and social structures in model student projects and published readings for the course (as well as classes they may have in the future). Third, when students have to mediate cultural interpretations of material situations in their field sites, they often find themselves concerned with issues of power in their process of representing these cultures in their writing.

Of course when and if these aspects of affirmation and critique do occur, they emerge more in fits and starts from the recursive processes of students' inquiry than in any neat linear fashion. In the following sections, I lay out the general processes of inductive theorizing that underlie the design of my teaching ethnographic research and examine some of the difficulties and teaching philosophy that arise from this approach.

INDUCTIVE THEORIZING AND COURSE DESIGN

As Bruce McComiskey (2000) argues, when writing teachers want their students to engage critical theories in their writing, they tend to present theory as a content or subject matter to be applied to students' experiences or other texts. I contend this teaching strategy tends to favor a deductive approach to theory. In the university, the theory as content matter comes first. Yet the students in Rashmi's class repeatedly argued for the value of practice (what you actually do) over theory (how to think about what you do). I am not claiming that they rejected the importance of theorizing, but that the practical immediate stuff is what makes theory possible. It cannot start from the abstract.

The everyday lives of many working-class, minority, and immigrant families often require practical applications of knowledge for economic advancement. To better their families and communities, they may also require practice as improvised tactics to maneuver within the larger social system (see DeCerteau, 1984). In contrast, our social system tends to materially reward the professional managerial class for their theorizing (those who conceptualize in their jobs), including self-proclaimed critical teachers, although we certainly aren't rewarded with the big money.

Invariably most students, particularly from working-class back-grounds, are more persuaded to reconsider their assumptions when they compare their experiences and values with each other rather than when we offer an explicitly theoretical lens. At our most honest moments as teachers, we admit the hierarchy of internally persuasive authority for our students in the classroom: first it's their peers, then it's a toss up between the teacher or the text, both often considered suspect repositories of knowledge.

Moreover, the students in Rashmi's class repeatedly taught me that the application of established critical theories rarely allow for the complex variations of locally defined perspectives such as theirs. As I discussed in chapter 5, the participants in my study persuaded me that they needed to develop critical arguments inductively, building theories from analyzing local under-standings, if they were to ever see anything internally persuasive about those discursive positions. They need to do it themselves to see anything persuasive about it. What's at stake is who is developing the critical theory: the students or the teacher? If the method of critical research and writing is primarily deductive (the application of theory) or assumes specific critical ends, then the teacher resides over most of the theory building. The issue here is not one of avoiding coercive power because my research suggests that we teachers often have far less persuasive influence than that. Rather, when students build their own critical theories of a local situation from an insider's view, they tend to see more purpose to the social analysis and sometimes its critical use value in their lives.

In the inductive approach, theory is an activity, or rather it emerges from activity, instead of a specific content to be applied. Theorizing in ethnography builds slowly from gathering social practices and developing patterns and schemas based on local knowledge. Adhering thoughtfully to a general ethnographic methodology, rather than relying on critical theories, helps ensure that the students mostly create theory rather than consume it.

Although I see great worth in Chiseri-Strater's and Sunstein's (2002) emphasis in *FieldWorking* on ethnographic portfolios, at Wright State, I have to teach in a 10-week academic quarter. So I have come to organize the students' research as three papers that follow through the research process of observations, interviews, and a final synthesis of analysis in earlier papers that also incorporates secondary research. In ethnographic courses, the assignment sequences and discussions begin more slowly with students collecting and comparing "practices" (ways of doing particular things) from their communities before trying to critically analyze how these ways of behaving and talking are also interpretations of their world. When as a class we rely on the demands of an inductive methodology, we focus more on the heuristics of research instead of pre-formed theories to be tested out. We get students to look closely at particular instances of cultural space, language, social structures, membership roles, and so forth. In the class, we talk about looking for power relations within the field site, but we don't assume that we know beforehand what those relations might be.

When students observe and analyze within these premises, they often encounter social contradictions or issues of power relations between what groups say and what they do (just as I did when UIC students in my research would perform different roles in and out of the classroom). They particularly encounter these contradictions when they move from observations to interviews, as I discuss more fully later in this chapter. This juxtaposition of studying a local group's practices (through observation) and their theories of those practices (through interviews) is the core of the course that ideally leads to a more critical analysis, particularly as they begin to compare these local theories and practices with issues in the larger society in preparation for the final synthesis paper.

In their final paper, the students need to examine how a comparison of their observation paper and interview paper, along with secondary research, may raise new questions for their final paper. They also need to consider how their analysis in the earlier papers and the process of their interpretations over time in the fieldsite should help structure the organization of the final paper. To help them develop the organization of this final synthesis, students draw inferences of purpose and form by analyzing and discussing two kinds of model student final papers. In one model, the ethnographer organizes the paper by claims, each supported by examples and analysis from both observations and interviews. In the other model, the ethnographer demonstrates how her understanding of the group or fieldsite changed over time. Often this approach emphasizes the differences between what the ethnographer initially assumed from her observations and the understanding she gained from the interviews. In terms of Van Mannen's (1988) tales of the field, the first organizational approach emphasizes the realist tale, building an argument of cultural interpretation, and the second approach the confessional tale, highlighting the different ways of making knowledge between ethnographer and research participants.

PLACE, EMBODIED COGNITION, MATERIAL REALITIES

When the students begin observations in their fieldsite, I hand out this set of heuristics, which corresponds with selected writing activities from *FieldWorking* and our discussions of ethnographic readings and student ethnographic writing from previous classes.[2]

Beginning Your Observations—What to Generally Look For:

talk

What is said, who says it, when, and in what contexts?

What communications are openly stated and what are unspoken?

What patterns of language use can you see?

behaviors

How do people act and react to each other?

Do members act out any "rituals" of expected behavior?

What values might be associated with these behaviors?

What might they be saying to each other through their dress, manner, and so on?

power relations

How might people be showing solidarity and/or status through their talk and behaviors?

How might talk and behaviors relate to different social roles within the group and culture; do they relate to gender or social class or other social positions?

location

How do people relate to the setting(s) they are in?

What does it suggest about the values and attitudes of the culture and the individuals in it?

How does setting influence behaviors and talk?

Reflection Notes:

After each observation, write reflection notes. To make sense of your experience and help generate your interview questions, write about any of the following that you can relate to your observation notes. Clearly, these questions are interrelated:

• Patterns of behavior you witnessed?

- Any contradictions in behavior?
- What you think are the reasons for the behavior?
- The insiders' view of what they do and think?
- Ideas for what to focus on in next observation?
- Questions about what you don't understand?
- Your own cultural assumptions about these observations?

Although we spend much time discussing the concepts of participant-observation, I describe this beginning field work in their assignment as observations because I cannot assume the degree to which the student will or can participate in some membership role within the chosen fieldsite. Yet the word "observation" implies the ethnographer's body is removed from the scene—that she is all eye and perhaps a hand scribbling away. In practice, however, the act of ethnographic observation and reflection tends to privilege embodied cognition and its relationship to spatial schemas and the often unspoken material realities of lived experiences. Students can clearly understand power relations in the form of their bodily responses to a situation, if only in terms of degrees of comfort or discomfort within a particular social space and human interaction. In most cases, we all know in our bodies when we walk into a room whether we are welcome. Both the methodology and concerns of ethnographic analysis, as loosely interpreted in these beginning heuristics for participant-observation, help students critically articulate these bodily experiences.

Ethnography's focus on fieldsites helps many students tap into their cultural knowledge of local places that make up their lives and particular spatial schemas attached to these places. As Julie Lindquist (Seitz & Lindquist, in press) points out, many ethnographic studies of American working-class communities attest to their importance of a common place to affirm values and ways of understanding their world (see, for example, Eckert, 1989; Heath, 1983; Lindquist, 2002; Phillipsen, 1992; Stack, 1974). Traditionally, many working-class communities have relied on dense social networks, turning to the same people for different kinds of needs and resources, compared with the loose social networks of middle-class individuals (Milroy, 1992). Thus, a local sense of place becomes all the more important if most of the people in your social networks for needed resources inhabit the same local space. As Lindquist (in press) writes, "people who inhabit these communities are not only geographically less mobile than their middle-class counterparts, but their habits of inquiry and critical understanding are also frequently tied to local experiences and interests."

Tracy's ethnographic project when she took my class at Wright State (WSU) illustrates well a group's critical understanding through identification with local space. Tracy researched the "deli girls" (women who were actually in their 30s–40s) at her job in a small independently owned market in a medium-size rural town. Among Tracy's conclusions, she found how important the culture and atmosphere of this 40-year-old store were for these women who worked there full time. The women compared their interactions with each other and their regular customers to the commercialized impersonality of the supermarket chains that have taken away most of the local store's business.

Although students from working-class backgrounds likely seek economic mobility, not all desire social mobility, as my ethnographic study of Mike's views from Irish Southside Chicago have suggested. In America, this social mobility is often tied to physical mobility, the ability and willingness to dislocate from place as jobs require it. Derek Owens (2001) argues that in contrast to many working-class cultures, the practices and mobility of academic cultures tend to profoundly dislocate themselves from an embodied understanding of local place.[3] Lindquist asserts that some working-class students can be rightly suspicious of "the motives of middle-class teachers who try to get them to 'leave home' in the interests of becoming more experientially and intellectually mobile." In contrast to more disembodied forms of academic inquiry, such as purely textual research, ethnographic methodology begins with an affirmation of the researcher's and participants' embodied understandings of place.

Yet methods of ethnographic research cannot only affirm values of local places, they also affirm the embodied cognition of spatial schemas—our mental maps that form through bodily activity of repeatedly moving through spaces and interacting physically with others. As students examine the interactions of communication, identity, and location in their field sites, they draw maps of the physical space. On these maps, they sketch in how people negotiate their movements within it, claim ownership of it, and mark it with cultural meanings understood, or not, by other members of the group. For instance, one of my students recognized how people of different social classes congregated in particular sections of a suburban bar. Another examined the workers' use of spaces in a local Wendy's restaurant, noting how they would frequently retreat to the space next to the drive-thru window to hide from a particular manager's gaze.

Although people's cultural maps of place is one form of embodied cognition, students conducting ethnographic research often have to ask what have they come to know through the repeated enactment and unspoken memory of physical actions. Heath's study of how children learn in Roadville and Trackton suggests how central this form of embodied knowledge may be for some working-class cultures. Heath asserts that Roadville parents tend to teach their children culturally valued activities like mechanics or cooking by silent demonstration and generalized encouragement. "Adults say, 'do it this way,'" without detailing the steps or components of 'this way'" (p. 229). For Roadville children, the parents' nonverbal approach to these activities also teaches them to value working-class common sense as learned through the body over a more middle-class approach of explicit verbalization. From a slightly different angle, Trackton parents tend to avoid verbalizing the proper way to manage a physical activity because they implicitly recognize that their children need to learn to improvise to face future power struggles caused by various forms of institutionalized racism. As Trackton's Annie Mae said, "They gotta know what works and what don't [. . .] Whatcha *call* it ain't so important as what you *do* with it. That's what things 'n people are for, ain't it?" (p. 112).

Julie Cheville (2001) further explicates these complexities of embodied cognition through her ethnographic study of an Iowa women's basketball team. As Cheville makes clear, athletes mainly rely on their embodied cognition, often at a subconscious level, to know how, when, and why to act immediately in a given play of a game. The players' minds must learn and know in deep coordination with the active doing of their bodies in their bounded physical spaces of their expected roles on the court, which must be in synchronous play with the bodies and minds of their team mates. Cheville's analysis of the team's "systemic balance" shows how each player must spatially know, understand, and anticipate the playing styles of each team mate coordinated as a dynamic unit if the athletes are to play well as a team. The team goal, which can only be achieved through processes of learning by embodied cognition, is *intersubjectivity*, which Cheville defines for this situation as "that capacity to move beyond introspection to reflexive understanding of oneself through the activity of others" (p. 71).

Last, ethnography's emphasis on participant-observation and insiders' perspectives also allows students a chance to examine how people they know cope with difficult material realities of jobs and various inequities of social class. In my classes at WSU, many students from working-class backgrounds who have cho-

sen field sites related to their social backgrounds—like a local
tavern in a rural county known for its drinking per capita, mom's
bowling league, or dad's roofing company—were more willing to
identify with their working-class informants and examine issues
of social class than most UIC students from similar class backgrounds. I believe the greater racial homogeneity of WSU students made it easier for some to identify class tensions as influential factors in their field sites.

In individual conferences, these students seemed grateful to
have their lives affirmed by an ethnographic approach. Although I
assumed all along that Nate was writing about a working-class
bar and a critical validation of that community, he didn't internally realize it until I asked him what kind of people don't regu-
larly go there. After he responded, "there's a particular class of
people you would never see in there," he realized his role of advocate, writing about people far from his school world.

At the same time, these students' willingness to address concerns of social class allowed them to also challenge more conventional critical views of economic and social mobility. Nick's interviews with a blue-collar foreman and white-collar estimator in his
father's roofing company amply showed how factors of social
class can influence attitudes of work in this company. Yet when I
asked him whether he wanted to develop this aspect for his final
paper, he stated with a grin that the foreman was actually from
an upper class family who had chosen the blue-collar life.

For Dominique, the inductive nature of participant-observation helped her better understand her friend's motives for stick-
ing with a Mary Kay Cosmetics sales group that Dominique also
critiqued as exploitative of women in the socioeconomic position
of her friend, a single African-American mother with a full-time
job. Dominique, also a single African-American mom, had already
harbored suspicion of the company's recruiting practices based
on her experiences with family friends. She recalled attending
one of the big sales meetings with friends a few years earlier, noting the bad acting on the sales video, the main speaker's "too
wide for comfort smile," and the line of "pink Cadillacs that
aligned the parking lot hotel"—corporate symbols of the big
recruiters' achievements.

Yet when Dominique attended local meetings of her friend's
sales unit at a small storefront building in Dayton, she described
the meetings as an African-American women's support group,
complete with affirmations and gospel-style testimonials to the
swaying and clapping beat of taped songs like "Independent
Woman." Despite this support, she also viewed the discourse of

the group as so deeply invested in an exclusive identity of professional women that its leader and members ignored any material or emotional concerns of the women's lives. Nevertheless, experiencing the physical energy of the local meetings convinced Dominique of their affective value for women like her friend. Dominique writes in the conclusion of her observation paper, "This group emphasizes that once one believes in him or herself, the sky is the limit regardless of what success is for them. [. . .] The monetary possibilities with this business is a small part of it and the rest is the group's very positive attitude which makes everyone want to be around them."

Once Dominique recognized the value of this affective support, she was able to draw a more complex picture of her friend's psychological investments in the Mary Kay success stories. From the interview paper to the final paper (aptly entitled, "Tailgating a Pink Cadillac"), Dominique contrasted the everyday material realities of her friend with two successful Mary Kay saleswomen featured at the city-wide breakfast meeting. One was retired and the other was a homemaker with a willing husband. Dominique writes, "It appears that finding thirty hours each week to work the business is the key to having a chance at the Cadillac. When you are a single working parent, thirty extra hours doesn't exist, unless you sacrifice sleep." In her conclusions, she addresses both the psychological value for women like her friend that she experienced through participant-observation at the local level and the larger socioeconomic contexts of material conditions she examined more closely in her interviews. "Even though the mental support is mentally beneficial, I think physical support supplementing this would allow single mother consultants to best capitalize on their investment with this company and truly give them an equal shot at that success which the videos so proudly proclaim. I think a motivational speech from a pink Cadillac driving single mother is in order."

WORKING THROUGH THE AMBIGUITIES AND ANXIETIES

Because students must figure out inductively what their ethnographic research is about, many encounter an early period of frustration, often during the first draft of the observation paper.[4] Most ask after the first two observations, "What am I looking for?" or "What do you want me to look for?" As my colleague Deborah

Crusan suggested to me, the many unknowns of ethnographic research may intensify the ambiguities, and thus the students' anxieties, that underlie any critical writing assignment from the students' perspective. From the students' view, any writing assignment involves an instrumental ambiguity expressed by the question, "What am I doing this for?" They rightly wonder what ends this work will serve for their immediate and long-term goals. Ethnographic research, with its deferral of conclusions until later in the process of field research and writing, can escalate this instrumental ambiguity and the anxieties that accompany it.

In terms of critical writing assignments (those that deal with interventions into the composing of the status quo as discussed in chap. 1), a critical ambiguity arises, which, from the students' view, could be expressed as, "What can this show me about my life?" For some students, such as Peter from Rashmi's class, this question may be meant as a challenge to the purpose of the course. For others, this question may reveal a motivated interest in the assignment, yet one still fraught with anxieties. Either way the extended deferral of social critique while students continue seeking out "patterns" among actual people using their bodies as well as their intellect can also serve to exacerbate anxieties underlying this critical ambiguity. These instrumental and critical ambiguities continually grate on each other like tectonic plates, with one or the other repeatedly breaking through the surface in forms of anxiety or frustration.

Once the students have written some field and reflection notes, they need to orally process and articulate what patterns from their fieldsite they are coming to know. When students share their data in a small group, hearing the response of others to the cultural patterns they have begun to notice helps relieve some of their anxiety over these built-up ambiguities. To a large degree, the students as ethnographers have so far concentrated their observations and reflections on the "being here" (as Clifford Geertz [1987] would put it)—being attentive to the ongoing moments of their observations and how various insiders might perceive them. The small-group discussions of possible cultural patterns help students move from this relative immersion in the moments of "being here" to the more analytical textual space of "being there"—recognizing what patterns and details outsiders find significant and worthy of analysis (at least from the teachers' point of view). Using Chiseri-Strater and Sunstein's language of *unity* (the common patterns) and *tensions* (people's complications of these patterns) helps students invent the coherence of what first appears as random observations. Near the due date for the draft of the observation paper, the students discuss in small groups and write notes based on this prompt:

Identifying Cultural Themes by Looking for Unity and Tensions in Your Fieldsite or Social Group:

First, take out all your field notes and, using the questions below, mark or highlight notes that refer to these areas. You are looking for patterns and coding your notes.

Now, as a group, discuss each project using the time to test your hunches about cultural themes and to learn from group members' questions (write them down!).

1. What common patterns of behaviors have you noticed?
2. How might they relate to social structure and/or social networks of the group?
3. To people's use of space?
4. To spoken and unspoken meanings of language there?
5. What tensions have you noticed? If there seem to be no tensions, what factors might account for that?

During this small-group time, I walk around, eavesdrop, field individual questions, and ask them when appropriate.

As Jim Zebroski (1994) explains, if students have done their field research well, they can be anxious about having too much material to choose from, rather than the usual too little. They worry about what to emphasize and what to leave behind. For this reason, I agree with Zebroski that it helps to have someone else impose filters, and thus also blinders, on the patterns they are beginning to interpret from their notes. So as soon as the energy of the small-group discussions come to a rest and off-task talk takes over, I get them to freewrite using either of these organizational heuristics (the first one adapted from Zebroski's set of possible thesis statements).

Now Write:

Based on this analysis of your data, what might be a theme or thesis to help organize your draft?

If stuck, consider these two models:

Most people would think _____ about (your social group or
fieldsite), but what they don't understand about (this group)
is _____.
Or
Write about the *kinds of knowledge you think are necessary to
be considered an insider.* Do some display that knowledge to
show others their solidarity or status within the group?
Describe some examples from your observations.

After this discussion and writing activity with their peers,
most students have identified general cultural patterns and can
point to some concrete details from their observations that show
these patterns. What's more difficult for most is naming and analyzing a selection of those patterns to develop a coherent cultural
analysis—in other words, to build a theory of social interactions
in this local situation that also accounts for various insiders' perspectives. Here is where I see the role of my conferences with students doing ethnographic projects. Over time I have to come to
take a twofold approach in conferences that moves between
ethnographic interviewing and theoretical scaffolding. Although I
believe other effective teachers of ethnographic writing make similar rhetorical moves in student conferences, it is important to
articulate what exactly we are doing here and what makes it persuasive to most students. In part when I do it well, our collaborative conceptualizing of the student's data and project help allay
current anxieties and motivate interest in developing the analysis
because, from the student's perspective, it provides answers to
the general instrumental and critical ambiguities I discussed earlier. In writing about conferencing with students, particularly
those conferences that motivate students' ethnographic theory
building, it's difficult to avoid accusations of portraying the
teacher as a hero. Yet by describing these conferences as theoretical scaffolding, I am claiming that teachers doing ethnographic
projects need to take a more assertive role in conferences than we
usually advise to new teachers—a role that requires us to draw
on our sociological imagination and theoretical tools as needed
for each given project and student. (By this statement, I am also
asserting that teachers who have knowledge of basic sociological
frameworks and have dealt with problems of ethnographic methods in their own projects will be far more prepared for the "teaching moments" of ethnographic research when they emerge in talk
with students.) Yet the potential hubris of this role must be tempered by the simultaneous role of the ethnographic interviewer

who recognizes she is more often wrong than right in her assumptions of others' cultural knowledge.

Often when students tell me in conference that they don't know what to focus on, I ask, "What do you find interesting?" This benign question acknowledges the inevitability of the individual motives of the field researcher to shape the cultural interpretation. The question also confers to them the authority for the knowledge of patterns and anomalies they interpret from their fieldsite; in that regard, they do know more than I do. In terms of ethnographic interviewing, it's also an open question that calls for an informant's selected interpretation of observed reality. From this question on, the process requires rhetorical listening, helping them test out hunches: "Could it be this, or maybe this?" As with ethnographic interviewing, it all works best when I can be deeply attentive to the responses of the student as an informant of the group she is studying. Often students will say, "No, that's not it. It's not like that."

For example, after some initial difficulty, Rob chose to study his brothers' 11- to 12-year-old male friends. In his first observations, he watched them play basketball and was surprised how uncompetitive they were with each other. They would choose games that would not embarrass the less competent players, and the better players continually retrieved the ball and performed various courtesies for the good of all. Yet he grew frustrated when the boys chose to watch TV instead when he could next take fieldnotes. In conference, I first asked him how the boys interacted with each other when they watched TV, but he dismissed the possibility of any patterns like the ones he saw with the basketball games. After I attempted a few more questions, he noted that what struck him most was what his brothers did as soon as he walked into the room. From another room, he had been observing them watching Pokemon, but as soon as he entered, his brothers changed the channel to MTV. I suggested the significance of their performing identity, which echoed a previous students' paper we read in class about teenage girls shopping and the formations of identity. These connections led Rob to discuss how his brothers saw him as a role model. We then articulated together how Pokemon and MTV could be seen as markers of middle childhood and later adolescence. Once Rob could name this situation he participated in, he began to draw out inferences from his fieldnotes. The boy who had been the weakest basketball player knew endless details about the Pokemon characters, and the others granted full authority to his comments during the show, suggesting again their noncompetitive values in the group. But when

Rob's brothers switched to MTV, this boy lost the floor to another who displayed his knowledge of all the bands that he gained from his older brothers. As Rob relayed to me the details of this pattern, I realized he had named a limninal moment when these boys were in between these stages of social development as they identified them with products of mainstream commercial culture.

Sometimes the role of ethnographic interviewer may take longer to pay off, but those moments can demonstrate the necessity of patience and trust in the process. As a devout lover of motorcycles, Paul was researching the culture of a biker bar he had frequented and had easily noted the connections between each group's more visible cultural values and the brands of motorcycles they drove. From Paul's view, the working-class "dirty bikers" who drove Harleys acted as if they owned the bar, followed next by the "businessmen bikers," who often had more expensive bikes (although some of those were Harleys too) than the dirty bikers and were more willing to talk to other biker groups in the bar. The dirty bikers claimed status by naming the next group, based on the lower cultural status of this group's bikes, as the "rice burners"—a pejorative term for Asian-made bikes that reveals much about nationalist values in many working-class biker cultures. Although Paul commented that the groups generally kept to themselves with some minor tensions between the dirty bikers and the rice burners, he also observed how all bikers would receive a nod when they first stepped in the bar as a show of unity that draws the line between "riders and non-riders."

In our conversation about his observation paper, Paul continually referred to the themes of freedom and being an individual among the bikers and for himself as a biker (who jokingly admitted he fell in the rice burner group from lack of money to buy a Harley). I agreed that these themes might be shared values across groups, but Paul could not find a way to examine them in terms of observed behaviors and talk. Paul chose to interview one of the businessmen because they were more in the middle and more approachable. When I received his first draft of the interview paper, however, I was frustrated by the continued technical details about each bike, such as their cubic centimeters, that his informant had owned. This tendency reminded me of other male students who prefer to write in a technical style more appropriate for *Popular Mechanics*. As a writing teacher, I felt that Paul was missing the focus on cultural behaviors and values, but as an ethnographer, I knew I was missing something—a cultural value that Paul, a relative insider, was implicitly practicing.

I also wondered why, although some of the businessmen bikers owned Harleys that cost more than the ones owed by the dirty bikers, Paul believed the dirty bikers still enjoyed the highest status in a cultural hierarchy based on bike ownership. I had presumed it was because the dirty bikers maintained the authenticity of the cultural role (or some might view as cultural stereotype) that grounds the larger biker culture, and that their actions represented the greatest depth of freedom valued by all the biker groups. From Paul's view of the insider researcher, I was only partially right, if at all.

In our conference about his interview draft, I asked him whether he could clear up my confusion over the higher status of dirty bikers despite their sometimes less expensive bikes. After a few minutes, Paul explained to me the importance of customizing your bike. The dirty bikers tended to do the most or only customizing compared with the other groups, devoting the greatest amount of time, effort, and ingenuity into remaking their bikes, and so earning the respect of the other groups. Once Paul explained this connection to me, he realized for himself that the action of customizing symbolized the values of individuality and freedom he had been trying to show in his papers. As Paul writes in his revision,

> The only way to get the title of individuality is by having something rare and unique. Anybody can go to the showroom floor and buy a bike and drive it home the same day [. . .] The key to customizing is making the bike yours, one of a kind, and letting your personality show from the special modifications that were made to the bike.

Although Paul may have had difficulty reaching this insight because he was so immersed in the culture (and I would guess its working-class appreciation of technical know how), I couldn't see what he was trying to show me because my academically oriented middle-class upbringing did not include any mechanics or their necessary ingenuity.

TRIGGERING SOCIAL CRITIQUE

Although students' social affirmation of local values and ways of making knowledge may emerge from the participant-observation, the inductive processes of ethnographic methods tend to foster the students' self-motivated social critique. As many of my student examples throughout this chapter attest, one internally persuasive aspect in the process is the building and testing of their own cultural theories. Here I want to discuss two other recursive moments in the ethnographic process that promote students' social critique: first, the complications between observations and interviews; and second, the ethical difficulties mediating between the fieldsite and one's written representations. In identifying these three processes, I don't mean to claim that most students will develop critical insight from all three. Nor can I predict which one it will be or when it will trigger social critique that is meaningful to the student or if any of these processes will have this persuasive effect.

Many students find complications between what they observe people do in their fieldsite and what people say about what they do there. More often than not, students gain critical insight about the social dynamics or larger social contexts of their group when they have to analyze more closely the possible reasons for these contradictions or their initial misreadings of the situation. My stated goal for the interview paper assignment makes room for the possible revision of the student's analysis as appropriate for each given field situation, stating that "this paper should either complement, supplement, or call into question the previous conclusions you have made from your participant-observation."[5]

As any good field researcher knows, one can't know what questions to ask until one infers cultural patterns through observation (and as Charles Briggs [1986] demonstrated, when fieldworkers conduct a long-term study, they must learn the cultural rules of *how* to ask as well). Thus, the interview paper assignment begins with students deciding "what tentative conclusion or major question" they are left with after writing their observation paper. The students write down this question along with other smaller questions about observed behaviors that follow from the overall question. Next, they choose informants based on "what kind of information and perspective they can reasonably be expected to provide given: a) their role in the culture or group, and b) your own relationship with them." They then translate their "big research question" into a series of ethnographic questions for their interviews. As students move through these beginning stages of developing questions, we also examine student models of the interview paper to see how others have constructed their questions. In addition, we discuss Chiseri-Strater and Sunstein's (2002) demonstrations of the holistic process and goals of ethnographic interviewing. Despite these activities and discussions, some students encounter another bout of anxiety at this stage in their field research. Mostly they are unsure how to devise ethnographic questions that are open ended enough to allow informants to interpret their own realities, but can also provide concrete responses to their research questions. When a few years ago one brave woman in my class openly recommended that I provide some general sheet of questions, I complied by drastically simplifying James Spradley's (1979) principles and drawing on what had worked for me in the past:

Ethnographic Interview Questions

Testing your hunches from your observation paper
(e.g., behaviors, rituals, who people talk about, social structures, power relations)

Can you describe a time when?...

Can you give me an example of...?

When would you say...? To whom?

How would you respond if...?

I noticed that _____ was doing _____, can you tell me what that was about?

Tour Questions (for their overall perspectives and to lead to examples)

Tell me what you would do during a typical _____?

Who would you do it with? Talk with? For what purposes?

Tell me about the different places involved in _____ activity?

Who do you associate with/hang around with the most? Why?

Insider Cultural Knowledge and Informal Role Membership

If I wanted to be accepted as a member (insider) of the group, what would I need to know? How to act? How to talk? In different places and times? What to watch out for?

How would you describe your role in the group?

What makes you part of the group?

Do you think there is more than one group here?

If I were new here, what would I not notice? What would label me an outsider?

What would I need to learn that wouldn't be taught directly?

Attitudes and Values

How do you feel about your being part of this activity?

What do you like about this group or place? Tell me of a time
  you particularly enjoyed?

What do you dislike? Specific examples?

How do you cope with the problems you find in the group or
  place?

What would you want to change about the group or its unspoken social rules?

Recognizing the difference between personal and cultural questions

What do most of the housekeepers do when they are on break?

What do <u>you</u> do during your breaks?

Note the differences between what people *do* and *what they say
  they do*!

As Spradley suggests, these questions focus on the how and what
of people's cultural practices and knowledge that allow for interpretations to emerge from talk rather than questions of "why"
that might force the interview participant toward particular
"answers." After students practice interviewing each other and
assessing what they want to do differently with their field interviews, they workshop their interview questions, concentrating on
developing open-ended questions, the sequential logic of their
questions, and phrasing their questions in the language of their
participants. In this workshop, some students choose to adapt
questions from my template for the situations of their own fieldsite and social group. Of course I also make clear that the questions are only the foot in the door that they can only open further
with careful listening, follow-up questions, and open conversational style. Just as this template and workshop for developing
interview questions encourages attention to differences between
observations and interviews, so do the guidelines for writing
response notes after each of their interview sessions:

Write Response/Analysis Notes

For each interview session (including each follow-up),
write one set of response/analysis notes.
Consider:

- What surprised you?
- What views seemed to confirm and/or contradict your
  observations?

- What do you notice about power relations within the interview?
- What do you notice about the language choices your informant uses?
- What new insights seem to emerge from your interview data?

What concepts or ideas from our readings or class discussions can help you detect patterns in the perspectives from your informant?

Leslie's study of Asian-American students who hung out at WSU's Asian American Hispanic Native American Center demonstrates well the complications and benefits of these contradictions encouraged by these response prompts. Despite the center's name, which attempts to include all world majority students compared with the campus' Bolinga African American Center, mostly Asian-American students, primarily of Indian and Filipino origin, study and socialize there. When Leslie wrote her research proposal, she made clear that the center—a space with a few tables, chairs, and computers—was also her campus home and that the women, and a man or two, who hung out there were her close friends who would only occasionally refer to her White American background to crack an intimate joke among their small group. As her friend Deepak, who is president of the Asian-American student association, put it to her, "you are not White. You are Asian. No one sees the White in you anymore."

In her first observations, however, Leslie grew frustrated, exclaiming that "all we do is study." But, as often happens, by the time of her observation paper, she had noticed a pattern, having paid careful attention to exactly who did and did not study when at the center. Leslie identified that the students who tended to socialize most were the premed majors who were the majority of the group, whereas the minority nonpremeds would attempt to study there, sometimes only to be drawn into the premeds' "goofing off" (to use Leslie's term). Through her study of some of these conversations, Leslie claimed their talk enacted a subtle tension of competition between these two groups. Because Leslie was one of the nonpremeds, she wondered whether her premed friends' comments were a tacit attempt to assert status—an interpretation that left her uncomfortable—but she was nonetheless interested in pursuing. In her observation paper, Leslie writes, "It always seemed as though the premed students see themselves as more important and better than the other students. They always claim to be studying but I never see any books in front of them. One premed friend, for example [. . .] doesn't even bring her books to school, instead of studying she sits around all day until it is time to go home."

Yet when Leslie tactfully pursued this thesis in her interviews, she found little evidence of competitive feelings or social hierarchy among the women, initially leaving her flummoxed. In her questions for developing her interview paper, however, she also wanted to ask about the influence of the women's parents on their choice of majors. Inferring from previous talk with her friends, she presumed that the women majoring in premed had the more controlling parents, often from strict Muslim backgrounds—an assumption that her interviews thoroughly verified. In our conference, she wanted to scrap her first focus on the studying entirely because she was wrong about a group hierarchy. But I thought of Gita, the student from Rashmi's class I featured in chapter 4, and asked Leslie what connection there might be between the behaviors of the women with more controlling parents when they were at the center and their lives at home. Her eyes lit up as she thought of her experiences visiting these friends and witnessing the many restrictions they faced. She now could articulate why these women "goofed off" at school and particularly in the safe haven of the center. In her final paper she writes, "The control dictated how the students reacted and interacted during the school day. The more parental control, the more goofing off I saw during the day."

Leslie's revision of her project led her to the social contexts of gender roles, culture, and values of education. She writes of one premed friend, "[. . .] once she comes home from school, she can't leave again. Her time spent at school is seen as her time to be a kid. At home she is expected to cook and clean for her family then to study once the chores are done." Leslie's follow-up interviews also helped some of her Asian-American premed friends reflect on this situation. For instance, one states: "I never really thought about it that way before. I would rather be at school because then I don't have to deal with my brothers."

Whereas some students encounter complications between observations and interviews, as Leslie did, others may face problems mediating between the experiences of the group and the processes of writing a cultural analysis of the group. These inescapable problems of written mediations, however, fortuitously create what Nancy Mack calls a "built-in ethical moment." Inevitably during class or conferences, students will raise the rhetorical issues of power and cultural representation on their own because they must continually make these ethical decisions of how or what to represent in regard to actual people. Often the students have a stake in the continuance of their relationships with these people—whether it is a workplace or social group—making these concerns of power and cultural representation all the more concrete.

For decades now postmodern anthropologists have acknowledged that ethnographic writing does not, nor as any writing cannot, show the whole nature of lived experience on the page or any other medium. In partial response to these assessments of ethnography's limits of representation, other ethnographers, particularly those inspired by feminist critiques of objectivity in the social sciences, have emphasized that the ethnographer should write for the researched community as well as about them. Early in the course, I discuss the value of this ethical obligation of also writing the study for, or *as if* for, your research participants as a way to maintain your focus on the insiders' perspectives. But it is the students who later bring up their troubled considerations of sharing power in their written representations, and never with reference to the comments I made earlier in the course. For instance, as they begin to develop cultural themes from their observations, some students rightly raise concerns about cultural stereotyping. In contrast, some cultural studies writing teachers tend to foist the issue on students through readings or writing prompts that are less likely to emerge from an immediate embodied situation. The students' concern for ethnography's potential to overgeneralize about groups offers a more persuasive moment for us to discuss the inescapable politics of representation and the necessity to address individual participants' variations within and against the field researcher's analysis of group behaviors.

In my work with students' projects, the problems of mediation tend to fall into three situations. First, some of them wrestle with how they represent the group in their cultural analysis. Second, others question the way that academic researchers or popular sources represent the group they are studying. And third, some question their representations of their social group when the act of ethnographic research makes group members perceive the identity of the student ethnographer in unanticipated ways.

Alex raised this first concern of how he was representing his fellow workers in his study of the divisions of labor in a car wash. Early in his participant-observation, he identified the tensions between the full timers, who worked out front "finishing off" the cars in full view of customers, and the part-time rookies, including himself, who did all the "prep work" on the cars out back. Because the full timers were the ones who directly dealt with customers, they were the ones who received the tips, leading to inevitable tensions between the two groups of workers. The differences of the two groups' economic situations heightened these tensions at times. Unlike the older full timers, who worked hard to survive and raise families, the much younger part-time rookies sometimes chose to goof off because they could make no tips and were still supported by their parents. Alex described resentment on both sides; rookies would often do poor prep jobs because they resented the full timers getting all the tips, which would then lead to the full timers' resentment of the required extra work for them.

I was impressed with the complexity of Alex's analysis of the tensions within this social structure and the scenes he depicted from his observations to demonstrate his claims. Yet as Alex conducted interviews with a full timer and observed more, he grew uncomfortable with this portrait of antagonists. He pointed to moments of teamwork between front and back on the high-volume weekends, compared with the far less busy weekdays and now claimed he got it wrong and was not showing his coworkers fairly. Judging from the particulars of his fieldnotes and analysis, I suggested that his first interpretations must be partially right, which ultimately helped Alex articulate the set of conditions that would often determine whether the groups operated in tension or cooperation. Specifically, he then analyzed how the weekend's surge in number of specialty customers would necessitate some of the rookies doing parts of the full timers' jobs to help them keep up with the work—a move that would consequently motivate the full timers to split the tips. He also showed how a full timer would help a rookie "even the odds" when dealing with the complaints of difficult irate customers, particularly when a rookie has earned the chance to work up front in hopes of becoming a full timer. As Alex developed these situations into his study, his main analysis evolved to analyze the tensions while also arguing how the workers do unify "when both groups see it as necessary."

Although Alex grew uncomfortable with his first written representations, Rachel found discomfort in the scarcity of academic representations (at the time) on the issues of social class in the group she studied. Rachel set out to learn about her mother's bowling league team. In her first observations of the team, Rachel was surprised to see her mother's teammates' raucous and some times rude behavior toward the teams of older, retired women. As one woman put it to her team, "Guess what, ladies? We are bowling against those old bitches tonight. Remember to be as obnoxious as you can be to piss them off." Unlike the older women, who treated the game seriously like a job, the middle-aged women implicitly viewed their bowling as an opportunity to escape the conventional social roles of mothers in the home and workers in the factories and in other working-class jobs. Preferring to act like girls Rachel's age, they would challenge each other to sneak jello-shots past the snooty older ladies. In the course of her observations and interviews, Rachel came to interpret her mother's friends' behaviors as responses to larger issues of power and control in the work and domestic domains of their lives—domains in which they most often had to answer to men. Yet when she sought out secondary research for her study of the women bowlers, she was surprised at the scarcity of academic research on White working-class women, particularly on their leisure choices. As a result of this frustration, she came to see herself as a spokesperson for these women's lives.

Whereas Rachel came to question the academic researchers, Audrey, whose work memoir I discussed in chapter 5, found herself questioning her initial ethnographic portrayal of the full-time workers at the local GM plant where she worked part time. Audrey's father had worked his way up from line worker to labor management in the corporation, so Audrey was both familiar with and wary of working on the line. Yet it was only when Audrey compared her social position to the full-time workers that she fully acknowledged their ambivalent responses to her as a "college hire." Audrey writes, "Anytime I would introduce myself to someone new, I was instantly asked about school. Rather than telling me the inside 'stuff,' I was quizzed on my intelligence [. . .] it is as though they assume that if they don't justify to the college hire why they do what they do, we won't approve of them." When Audrey carefully reflected on these ambivalences, she refocused her study on issues of labor and education from the perspectives of how the "factory workers are viewed by management, the ways they are viewed by the general population, and by the way they view themselves." At the time, I encouraged Audrey to focus more on the cultural behaviors that emerge from the workers' ambivalent attitudes rather than comparing all these perspectives. Looking back over her project, however, I admire her for keeping the focus that most disturbed her and that she wanted others to better understand.

ETHNOGRAPHY'S FUTURE
CRITICAL USE VALUE

I believe many of these students in my ethnography writing classes actively engaged in their own theory building and critical
analysis of cultures. Even so, as I have looked over the fence at
other writing teachers' work with community-based learning and
other more directly activist approaches, I have nagged myself that
the students' ethnographic research doesn't lead to social action
in response to the issues they analyze in their fieldsites. Yet over
the past year, I have come to view the ethnographic habit of mind
as critical literacy for life-long learning. Maintaining an ethnographic lens helps us read and name the power relations within
group dynamics, social structures, and social networks whenever
we encounter new situations, particularly workplaces. Of equal
importance, applying tenets of ethnographic methodology to situations in our lives helps discipline us to defer critical judgments
until we understand more of the cultural, historical, and material
contexts from insiders' perspectives. Once we better understand
that local and embodied knowledge, we can locate moments of
agency in which we may have more persuasive authority with
possible allies toward needed ethical changes depending on each
situation.[6] Of course any person's interest in drawing on this
habit of mind in future situations depends on individual motivation in the embodied moment of social interaction. So as a
teacher I cannot expect or know when people from my classes
may loosely draw on this methodology in their future.

Although this view of ethnographic approaches as life-long
learning was clearly an implicit part of my motives for teaching,
as I described them in this chapter, I only came to name and
articulate this understanding several months after the events of
September 11, 2001. As a left-minded Jew, I wanted to talk face
to face with American Muslims—to begin to understand some
Muslims as complex individuals who perhaps, like me and other
Jews I know, did not perceive their identity as one simple religious or cultural category. From a selfish standpoint, I wanted to
replace the nameless fears drawn from the airwaves with the
memories of a personal encounter. Because I belonged to a
Jewish Havurah men's group, I arranged a meeting of our group
with Salah, the husband of one of our graduate students, and
two of his friends from the Dayton Islamic center. I had never met
Salah, but when Shahrazad, his wife who is from Libya, thanked
me for the opportunity to take a class with an "open-minded"

Jewish teacher, I then asked whether her husband would be interested in this dialogue with other men. I was not raised with any Jewish religion and had only joined this men's group 2 years earlier, so negotiating the details of our meeting to everyone's satisfaction already required the knowledge I had gained of the group's dynamics and social networks. Also, as I considered questions to ask at the meeting, I found myself asking what questions I would want someone to ask me that would not confine me to the role of spokesperson for all Jews.

When I related all of these negotiations and concerns of ethics in the situation to a colleague at school, she remarked that I was practicing ethnographic action in my life. I then thought of my wife, Daniele, a preschool teacher (with a B.A. in anthropology) who has weathered many a dysfunctional institutional school culture by carefully reading and maneuvering its power relations and critically analyzing each institution's larger ideological assumptions. Once I took this view of ethnographic use value, I could see how many of the students were already responding analytically and physically to social issues and power relations they encountered in their field sites. Among the students in my class this past year, Jeff's and Kristen's responses to their field research particularly illustrate how and why students may draw on ethnographic habits in their future. Yet their situations also show why critical writing teachers must also consider how the social positioning of students in their local situations may limit the realistic possibilities of social action.

As a first-year acting major in a competitive theater arts program, Jeff wanted to better understand the social structure of people in his program and what he hopes his profession will be. In the first weeks, Jeff enthusiastically related his observations from the vantage points of his acting classes and the backstage socializing during the run of a mainstage production in which he had a walk-on role. Jeff quickly surmised the social hierarchy measured by who snubbed him and who frequently gave him and some of his friends' cold shoulders. At first he identified the juniors and seniors at the top and musical theater first-year students enjoying higher status than the acting first-year students and theater studies majors (a program that doesn't require auditions) given the least status.

But as Jeff paid more attention to the social networks that developed around the partying of people in the mainstage production, he perceived how some partiers could achieve higher status in the students' theater hierarchy regardless of their class year. In his observation paper, Jeff offers a telling moment of dialogue that took place one night after a performance of the main-stage play. Tim, one of the main actors in the play, casually asks Jeff and his friend Nate, another first year, whether they are headed to the party. When Jeff and Nate reply that they are "really tired," Tim advises them:

> Tim: Well, the parties are where you get to know peo-ple.
>
> Nate: So if we go to the party and get drunk people will talk to us?
>
> Tim: (gives a dirty look and turns away)
>
> Nate: No I'm asking, I want to know.

Jeff then writes about a few students who do rise in status by this method. He describes the treatment toward a first-year the-ater studies major who he heard got roaring drunk at the last party: "I noticed the upperclassmen talking to her, sitting by her, and really pulling her into their circle." At the time, Jeff speculat-ed that by partying one could "show them that you aren't all business like you might be in class." In the conclusion of his observation paper, Jeff openly states his discomfort with the hier-archy that was invisible to him before his fieldwork. He writes, "Now I am very disturbed by it. I want to break it down and find a way to make everyone equal. I guess ignorance is bliss." Although Jeff had been a successful actor before entering WSU, he told me after he wrote the observation paper that he was questioning his career decision.

As Jeff continued with his interviews and further observa-tions of his daily experiences, he theorized how much the per-ceived threat of competition from others in the program shaped many people's behaviors. To develop his analysis, he drew on experiences of other first-year and second-year students, includ-ing him, who encountered poker faces from upperclassmen (Jeff's term), only to find out later from others that these same upper-classmen appreciated their sense of humor; they just wouldn't let on to their face. Speaking of one such moment like this that hap-pened to him, Jeff states, "They just didn't want to lose their sta-tus above me by admitting that I was funny. It is like most people in this program feel that they must carry a certain persona when at school and around classmates." At the end of his interview paper, Jeff again articulates his frustrations: "You want to be able to look up to the people that came before you, but when they put on these masks that make you think they don't like you, it makes it hard. The worst part about it is that they are all such good actors; they never have to let down their walls. They can keep it going as long as they want."

From this view, Jeff analyzed more thoroughly the tensions of the partying scene as a location where theater people could let down their guard, but it was also another way to scope out the competition, particularly those who knew how to entertain various informal audiences. In his final paper, Jeff writes about the parties, "After all the watching and talking about the partiers, it almost seemed to be another job to me. [. . .] At parties, you still have to have your mask on. You must be funny and well liked among the people at the party."

Once Jeff had interpreted the intricacies of competitive behaviors in his program, he examined the larger contexts of competition in other university theater programs and in the profession. He writes in the conclusion of his final paper, "After everything is said and done I really had to sit down and think about what all this means. [. . .] If I knew how the program worked before I came here, would I still have come?" Jeff concluded both in his life and on paper that the power games he encountered in the social structure and social networks of the program were just a "small taste" of what he would encounter in the professional theater world. In my margin comments, I wrote back, "Sadly, you are likely right."

Although at times I truly wondered whether Jeff might leave the acting program, his ethnographic research and writing helped him locate moments of agency within these power games. From his physical participation in this research, he was able to develop strategies for forging allies that could help him cope with the rhetorical situations he would continue to encounter. At the end of the paper, Jeff reports that he now makes an effort to attend the parties and has become friends with people who initially ignored him. From the most cynical view, he has learned how to play the system. Yet Jeff's positioning within this culture's power structure leaves him few other options. To assume that Jeff must organize some kind of social or collective action in response to these problems strikes me as arrogance driven solely by critical theories. Kristen's situation, in contrast, offered some other options in response to her research.

As a first-year nursing major, Kristen chose to research her participation in a required service learning course that would provide respite care to families of children, ages 0 to 3 years, with disabilities. To be eligible for respite care, families must have four or more institutionally determined risk factors. Although Kristen recognized that she and her respite care partner would likely have to negotiate strong racial and cultural differences because the family lived in a poor African-American neighborhood in Dayton, she looked forward to their first respite visit. Kristen's eagerness soon drained, however, when her respite care situation turned out to be fraught with socioeconomic and psychological tensions way beyond the control of Kristen and her respite care partner.

Kristen and her partner, Ashley, were supposed to provide a domestic break for Shannon, a 19-year-old single mother with one 6-month-old boy with developmental delays and a two-and-a-half-year-old girl. Instead they walked into an ongoing battle between Shannon and her cousin, Monica, also 19 with a young boy, who seemed to be living in the small apartment as well. From what Kristen and Ashley could see of the apartment, they could find no toys, and the children seemed to crave their attention. Although they were told by their nursing teacher and service coordinator that they were to help around the house and not principally play the role of babysitters, Shannon gave up all parenting duties when Kristen and Ashley showed up. Whenever Ty, Monica's son, desired to join the play of Kristen and Ashley with Shannon's girl, Riley, Monica would pull him back, curse out Shannon, and throw cold looks at Kristen and Ashley, making clear her discomfort with these White girls. On top of all this conflict, Kristen believed that Shannon showed signs of some mental disabilities, often acting like a child herself. In her observation paper, Kristen describes the situation:

> Shannon and Monica seemed to yell back and forth about Ty and Riley. "You keep away from my babies or I'm gonna spank him!" Shannon yelled. "If she even touches him, she is gonna get it," Monica yelled in reply. Monica didn't want Riley to be around her or play with Ty. The same with Shannon. It was as if Ashley and I being there was a prize which Shannon did not want to share at all. It seemed that there were many tensions between Monica and Shannon and that Ashley and I were causing more.

On their third scheduled visit, Shannon was not home, and Monica shut the door in their face. Soon after, the program director, having found out some more disturbing news about the situation in this home, told Kristen and Ashley they were not to go back. Near the end of the quarter, Kristen told me in class that her nursing teacher had recently assigned her and Ashley to another family situation with a child who threw fits of physical and verbal abuse, and the parents would not take control of their child. Kristen and Ashley were soon pulled from this respite care family as well.

As Kristen tried to make sense of these experiences, she first wanted to acknowledge how privileged her own upbringing had been. Although I recognized this as a necessary response, I asked her what can her analysis of these experiences tell her about the difficulties with the respite care program in the context of a first-year service learning course? In other words, Kristen had the opportunity to develop an institutional critique from an insider's perspective. Kristen then shifted the focus of her research to question whether respite care does or does not help. At the same time, I continued to suggest that a more qualified and practical question might be, "Under what conditions does the program work best?" If she examined this question, she would also be analyzing the ethics of the program. Kristen's interview paper implicitly explored this question by comparing her and Ashley's experience to the more positive experiences of another respite care pair from the class. By the final paper, which also brought in contexts of other respite care programs to compare with these local experiences, she was better able to articulate these necessary conditions.

Just as important, as Kristen interpreted and analyzed the interview remarks of Ashley and the other respite care pair, she came to appreciate the microdynamics of what she and Ashley could do for Shannon. In her final paper, Kristen writes,

> Being a young mother of two children and not having anything to do but sit in the home all day can be very stressful, especially in the winter. By having us there, Riley didn't bother Shannon as much. [. . .] She was content to have someone else there to play with her and visit her. [. . .] As for Julie and Alice [the other respite care pair Kristen interviewed], they knew the relief they provided. It was laid out plain and simple for them. Ashley and I had to dig a little deeper.

This process was aided by Kristen's ethnographic research and writing. This ethnographic habit of mind may help Kristen tap into further insights necessary for sustaining herself when she faces future complicated personal interactions in her projected field of nursing. Yet she also used her larger analysis of her project to make well-considered recommendations for improving the service learning program. Among other rationales for her recommendations, she shows why the program needs to conduct more extensive evaluations in the family homes before placing first-year nursing students and why the service coordinators need to discuss the program's boundaries and expectations in far greater detail with the families before the nursing students are allowed to enter the homes. Near the end of the quarter, Kristen told me that her nursing professor was preparing a presentation about the program for a conference, and she was soliciting stories from her students to see how to improve the program. Although Kristen told me her teacher is continually busy, she may get an opportunity to influence the institutional situation that she researched.[7]

Throughout this chapter, I demonstrated how inductive theorizing and ethnographic methodology helps students defer critique until they have a stronger critical understanding of insiders' perspectives. To conclude, I want to briefly address how these approaches also help discipline me, the teacher, to remain attentive to the continually shifting terrain of the students' perspectives as well.

NOTES

1. Over 2 years I collaborated with my colleagues, Julie Lindquist, who created the course, and Gloria Nardini on all aspects of the curriculum design. As I address later in this chapter, we organized the course on what we saw as the research process of ethnographers, particularly the differences one finds between conducting participant observation and ethnographic interviewing. Although we developed this course before Elizabeth Chiseri-Strater and Bonnie Sunstein (2002) published their textbook *FieldWorking*, this chapter builds on their pedagogy, and I am indebted to their work as well as Jim Zebroski's (1994), Nancy Mack's (1995, 1992), and Julie Cheville's (2001) writings on teaching ethnography. All of them have enriched my own teaching.
2. In addition to Chiseri-Strater and Sunstein, see Appendix A in Cheville (2001) for other heuristics of ethnographic observation.
3. Both Owens (2001) and Johnathon Mauk (2003) describe their commuter students experiencing this sense of dislocation from the surrounding local space that the campus culture, particularly Mauk's community college, implicitly fosters. Owens read these

students' feelings of dislocation in their college experiences as well as their own neighborhoods as part of the larger problem of post-modern corporate society's instrumental disregard for the necessary sustainability of local environments. Mauk views the problem as a disparity between a changing population of largely commuter students and university culture's conventional understanding of what constitutes academic space. Owens offers teaching approaches for students writing on, and later critiquing, "the conditions and limitations of one's immediate environment" (p. 37). Mauk suggests research writing projects that encourage a dialectical "third space" between the conceptual and physical academic space and students' local spaces, often by students directly integrating the views and concerns of people in these local spaces (p. 380).

4. Jim Zebroski (1994) also addresses the students' frustrations with ethnographic projects and offers ways to help students through these anxieties.

5. Although I have changed aspects of this assignment over the years, I owe much of its structure and original language to my collaboration with Julie Lindquist on early versions of this course at the University of Illinois at Chicago.

6. I would compare this purpose for the ethnographic frame of mind to Kenneth Burke's view of rhetoric's major function in everyday life. Foss, Foss, and Trapp (1985) summarize Burke's view of this rhetorical function: "Rhetoric, in other words, helps the rhetor maneuver through life, directs the movements and operations of life, and provides ways of feeling more at home in the chaos of the everyday world" (p. 161). Like the everyday ethnographic analysis I suggest, Burke views this rhetorical function as a series of interpretive acts. See Seitz (2002) for discussion of students' ethnographic study of local rhetorics.

7. Seth Kahn (2002, 2003) points to the potential for grassroots social action when student ethnographers can distribute and share their field research to research participants or institutional representatives who have some power to influence change within the community or institution. Although Kahn understands this goal is not often possible for students who are not in positions of power, he demonstrates how it can persuade student ethnographers that this research approach can have social effects in their world.

Afterword

Who Should Be Building the Theory?

When students adhere to the inductive processes of ethnographic methodology that I have discussed, the method helps them continually reexamine conventional assumptions with each new contradictory interview, observation, or cultural inference. When I also hold myself to this methodology in my teaching of ethnographic research writing, I wait for what comes out of the students' interpretations of the group's cultural meanings rather than impose a particular critical lens on their data. Thus, I am forced to habitually reevaluate my conventional teachers' repertoire of critical theories on class, race, gender, and other forms of cultural and social formation. So when I adhere to methods of inductive theorizing in my teaching of critical writing, it helps constrain my theoretical arrogance. What I give up is control. What I gain, most of the time, is continual interest in students' insights and what can be made from them. For me this process fosters my disposition of humility that makes room for students' own internally persuasive critiques. In this last section, I illustrate the workings of this process, and my role within it, by briefly discussing the process of two students' ethnographic projects. I have also come to view inductive theorizing in teaching critical writing as a philosophy of teaching more than one method or strategy. So I want to end by identifying the conditions of inductive theorizing in teaching critical writing that I believe are necessary for the possibility of students' internal persuasion.

Once we identify these necessary conditions, we can point to some other teachers' approaches outside of ethnographic frameworks that put some of these conditions into practice.

In a section of my English 101 class that focused on values of work, both Gwen and Beth explored the functions of language within the social structure and social network of their respective predominantly female workplaces. Nevertheless, they came to very different conclusions. Gwen, whose work memoir I discussed in chapter 5, examined how gossip among employees at a local department store functioned in different ways depending on where you were positioned in the social structure. Beth, in contrast, came to see how people's language practices in the college admissions office where she worked supported an open social network that kept most people from feeling any dominance of a social hierarchy. Gwen's conclusions were a social critique; Beth's showed a model for better office relations. I could not have concluded where either of these studies would go until very late in the game.

In Gwen's participant-observation on the job, she couldn't help noticing the gossip, especially among the older women she had to supervise at the store. It was a constant struggle between the ways they might end up gossiping about her and the disdain the women managers showed toward the gossiping workers. As I discussed in chapter 5, Gwen comes from a working-class background that has made her deeply sensitive to the power of bosses, which made her both somewhat ambivalent in her role as supervisor of older women and strongly cognizant of the social power of talk in work situations. Gwen's insight about gossip and social power at the store came when she reflected more on why the women she supervised continued to gossip despite her managers' abhorrence of the practice. Didn't these women want to be liked by their managers? Up until now, she had only thought about her situation caught between the managers and the women whom she was supposed to supervise.

Through our conferences, Gwen came to analyze how the women she supervised used gossip as power—the only power they really had. If the supervisors did not treat their employees with respect, these women would gossip about their supervisors. The women at the bottom of the hierarchy knew that they would never be promoted to supervisors, much less managers, that it was the unspoken policy to hire management from outside the store. Gossip, then, was their only way to make life bearable—of controlling their work environment as much as they could.

When Beth was in the process of analyzing her participant-observation with her study of the college admissions office, she called me over during class to express her frustration. "There are no tensions in my field site," she groaned, "everyone gets along great." At first I thought to probe her more about possible contradictions, in the manner of my earlier approach to teaching at UIC that I described in chapter 1. Yet seeing Gwen across from Beth in her group, I thought of her approach to language and power in her fieldsite. I asked Beth, "What do you think people do to create that good will? Does language use have anything to do with it?" I realize now that I was trusting Beth's reading of the cultural patterns in this workplace—a trust she gained by the earlier processes of her research.

From a rhetorical perspective, when ethnographers set out to understand situated insider perspectives, they are consenting to be persuaded by the people whom they talk to, participate with, and observe. In a sense, they are looking to change their mind, to see how they need to rethink their worlds and perceptions of their reality based on a dialectic with the approximated perspectives of others. Most good teachers try to do this, but I have found that this focus on inductive research also provides a discipline to this credo. Moreover, Beth didn't need to write a damning social critique of her workplace to practice critical analysis in her project. Ethnographic research of local situations allows for interpreting what works socially, culturally, and ethically in a given group dynamic as well as what doesn't.

Gwen then explained to Beth more about her research focus on language and social structure. Although Beth still felt frustrated when she looked for patterns between the observation and interviews, she came to see how everyone's talk at work about their families helped to break down social hierarchies in this office. But it was only after she began to theorize this pattern that she then could see the tensions she now believed were there all along. In contrast to the administrators, counselors, and student workers, the two receptionists were not forthcoming about their lives outside the office, making them the misfits—an attitude that played into the ways others treated them.

Of course I am urging students toward a critical analysis of their observations, both through what I suggest they look for and the set of ethnographic terms to help them see what they observe as systemic behaviors rooted in local knowledge. The important difference is this more inductive work aims to validate the students' ways of theorizing. Gwen could clearly read the social dynamics at play; she only needed to shape them within a sociological framework. In contrast, some cultural studies approaches only serve to validate students' experiences and often as later grist for the critical theory mill.

Inductive methodology is not imposed as explicit politically interested critical theory from above by teachers or critical texts. Ideally, these ways of reading culturally and rhetorically are structurally built into the practices of the inductive methodology. Although I will have the class read some critical texts, alongside model student papers, that raise systemic issues of social power, I offer them as supplements to the students' own inductive work, heuristic guides, rather than as the required theoretical lens. Moreover, these texts, like Spradley and Mann's (1975) *The Cocktail Waitress*, emphasize concrete examples of the concepts that the students are trying to form as they gather social or cultural practices. In this way, the methodology helps withhold the necessity for applying criticism; the critique builds by inferences and becoming attentive to patterns.

Ultimately I see inductive theorizing in the teaching of critical writing as more than one particular method or strategy. Rather than a teaching philosophy, it is about the conditions that must be active within a teacher's critical pedagogy if she wishes to promote students' internal persuasion of social critiques. To that end, I have identified these four necessary conditions:

1. The processes of the assignment sequences allow for a level of unpredictability. As Wallace and Ewald (2000) have also argued, mutuality between students and the teacher, another condition necessary to some degree within the learning situation for internal persuasion, requires the critical teacher to give up a priori fixed theoretical assumptions about students' social critique or resistance.
2. The process requires the students to build their own cultural and social theories, rather than primarily apply the critical theories of others.
3. The process draws from students' knowledge and possibly their practices of making knowledge that are outside textual and academic domains.
4. The course recognizes a recursive and revisionary process of inquiry and writing.

With these conditions in mind, critical writing teachers can enact teaching strategies that require some inductive theorizing even if they do not work within an ethnographic framework. To that end, I want to point to some examples of other critical writing teachers' strategies within different approaches to teaching composition that meet some, if not all, of these four conditions. These examples are by no means exhaustive, but rather representative of some approaches available that may mesh with different teachers' motives and preferences.

For instance, like McComiskey's (2000) criticisms, my problems with critical pedagogies based on students' deductive applications of theories certainly point the finger at David Bartholomae and Anthony Petroskey's (2002) pedagogy featured in *Ways of Reading* (an approach to composition that nonetheless I have learned much from over the years). Yet I would contend that much of their basic reading and writing course, described in *Facts, Artifacts, and Counterfacts* (1986), emphasizes this inductively oriented inquiry as beginning college writers learn how to build their own theories of adolescence, work, or literacy, among other possible generative themes that teachers have used for this course model, based on the collected narratives of the class and the course readings. Moreover, teachers like Donna Qualley (1994) and Gwen Gorzelsky (2003) have adapted some of the principles of Bartholomae and Petroskey's theories of reading and culture, allowing for more student control and unpredictability through methods of reflexive collaboration (Qualley) and Taoist approaches to teaching critical writing (Gorzelsky).

From another perspective on cultural studies and composition, Joe Harris and Jay Rosen's (1995) textbook, *Media Journal: Reading and Writing about Popular Culture*, emphasizes students slowly developing theories of their pleasure and identification with various entertainments. In conjunction with reading cultural studies texts, this process occurs through group discussions of media journals they keep of their viewing practices and those of others they observe. Unlike most composition textbooks on popular culture, *Media Journal* organizes assignments around what people *do* with pop culture, rather than analyzing particular kinds of media or cultural artifacts. This approach foregrounds people's complex production of meanings from their physical and intellectual experiences with popular culture, rather than assuming a more passive notion of mass consumption.

Some teachers' pedagogies emphasize an inductive approach to help convince student writers that they must pay critical attention to social contexts when writing second-hand research. David Jolliffe's (1999) textbook, *Inquiry and Genre*, also encourages an inductive approach toward college research writing through the inquiry contract. This structure requires students to approach their sustained inquiry of a subject through a process of multiple writing genres. Students do not come to their conclusions or applications until they have clarified their focus, informed themselves about the subject's field of debate, and explored questions that resist closure, each step a different written genre and working paper along the way. Dennis Lynch, Diana George, and Marilyn Cooper (1997) offer a similar pedagogical model that takes an inductive approach to argumentation and understanding its social contexts that allows for the process of the students' own discoveries. Moreover, Lynch, George, and Cooper encourage students to investigate the power politics of who has access to publicly make their arguments—a critical view that I think would resonate with working-class, minority, and immigrant students.

In the field of teaching professional writing, Helen Ewald (Wallace & Ewald, 2000) builds an inductive approach on students' writing in the genre of case analyses. In Ewald's MA level class, students must develop their own theoretical analysis of a specific case narrative of professional communications by drawing on their own experiences and understanding and choosing particular theoretical readings from each week's set of readings to incorporate into their analysis. Ewald asserts that the genre of the case analysis "helps students see that there is no one right representation of disciplinary knowledge and to prepare students to actively participate in the reconstruction of disciplinary knowledge in class discussion and written assignments" (p. 75). By reconsidering these theories of communication in light of the material details of the case narratives and their own experiences, Ewald's students more actively engage in the "reconstruction of disciplinary knowledge," which allows them greater "interpretive agency" (as Wallace and Ewald define it) that may foster more internally persuasive learning.

In the field of community-based learning, Linda Flower's (1997) work with community problem-solving-based dialogues in Pittsburgh endeavors to draw from community knowledge for mutually valued solutions to community problems. More important, her focus on "rivaling" (a method that seeks multiple perspectives toward the community problem) and listening carefully to the "story behind the story" allows for counterinterpretations from community members that can foster critical humility for teachers and college students who must literally share the same table with people from different parts of the community. I also appreciate Nancy Welch's (2002) critique of Flower's model of community problem solving. Welch suggests how the "pressure to produce in just eight weeks a solutions oriented document or media text may prevent students from being more ethnographically attentive to community member's social critiques embedded in their everyday rhetorical performances" (p. 251).

Finally, I am not claiming that methodology alone can prevent the reinstatement of primarily deductive practices, the favored approach of critical academics. Indeed, I can imagine two ways that writing teachers might turn ethnographic practice of research into a deductive act of thinking. First, the focus of the course could fall into a slavish attention to instructing students in disciplinary methods that would lean toward losing track of the larger critical questions emerging for students in their projects. Second, a course that adheres to the necessity of students conducting some a priori concept of critical ethnographic or qualitative research could also fall into the trap of deductive analysis and unreflective reproduction of a theoretical stance. Instead I would argue that the purpose of the inductive practices of methodology should be to keep both teacher and students attentive to the situations before them, particularly in the connections between the students' research and the multidimensional dynamics of the critical writing classroom. As I described earlier, I see my interactions with Gwen and Beth and their developing theories as a small example of this attentiveness.

For all cultural studies teachers' talk about subjectivity, I don't think many of them fully engage people's continual flux in culture and identity, evident in my ethnographic research and my students' projects. If we emphasize inductive theorizing in critical pedagogy, we are more likely to treat culture as a process of emergent meanings and knowledges, rather than a set of positions and texts. When I emphasize inductive methods of research with my students, I force myself to be more attentive to this constantly shifting terrain as ethnographers must do. Does this attentiveness ensure most students will see the use value of analyzing their critical reflections in life? Who can know for sure. But it forces me to continually rethink the appropriate ways to imagine that possibility so I can better know a teachable moment when I see one.

Appendix

Syllabus From Rashmi's Class

The University of Illinois at Chicago
English 161: Women in the Third World
Spring 1995
Tue and Thurs
9:30 - 10:45 a.m./165 BSB
11 a.m. - 12:15 p.m./ 265 BSB

Instructor: Rashmi Varma
Department of English
2022, University Hall
Phone: 413-2242
Office hours: Tue and Thur 12:30-2p.m.

Required Texts:
Sara Suleri, Meatless Days (1989)
United Nations, The World's Women 1970-1990: Trends and Statistics (1991)
Xeroxed course packet available at Comet Press, 812 W. Van Buren, Chicago, IL 60607.   Tele: (312) 243-5400
Films shown in class
A slim spiral notebook for journal entries

Recommended:
Cervone, et al., Guide to UIC Resources
Clifford, Gould and Veit, eds., Reading, Writing, Research *why the choice of this text?*

Books on Library Reserve: There are several books that have been placed on reserve for in the library to assist you in your research and extra reading. Please consult the binders kept near the Reference Section on the First Floor of the Main Library for a detailed list of books relevant for this course. A couple of weeks after the course begins, you will also be provided with a bibliography.

Journals: Get an early start by browsing through some of these journals on a regular basis –
Signs, Feminist Studies, Tulsa Studies in Women's Literature, Ms., National Women's Studies Association Journal, Women's Studies International;
World Development, Third World Quarterly, Modern Asian Studies, Journal of African Studies, Journal of Latin American Studies and other regional journals

Course Objectives: This course will attempt to develop the reading, writing and research skills of its students. As such, the course will approach all three activities as inter-related. Simultaneous with the process of gaining a broad and global historical and theoretical understanding of Third World women and their concerns will be a series of local and specific studies. This method will give students a chance to see how theoretical arguments are constructed and then presented in research. The readings will be inter-disciplinary, cutting across history, cultural studies, anthropology, literature, film, arts and social sciences, and the methodologies will be multiple: oral history, field research, literary criticism, film analysis, archival research, etc.

Course Requirements:
Attendance -- 10 points. (A= full attendance; B= 1-2 absences; C= 3-4 absences; D= 5-6 absences; F and failure in the course = more than 6 absences). Students can obtain prior permission for excused absences, or submit a written request when they come back to class.
Class participation – 10 points. You are expected to do all the readings and come prepared to class to contribute in class discussions. In addition, each student will take responsibility for

APPENDIX A (continued)

opening class discussion atleast once during the semester. Finally, you will be expected to present and share your research in class, underscoring the idea of the class as a community of researchers. **Conferences** -- 5 points. Students are required to meet with the instructor atleast once before the Spring break and once before the final paper is due. Please inform me the day you are coming to see me.

2 Response papers/ 2-3 pages each -- 30 points (15 points each). These will consist of your responses to the readings as well as to issues raised in the class discussion, and will be based on your journal entries. Detailed handouts will further clarify this and other subsequent assignments.
1 Review paper/ 3-4 pages -- 10 points. This assignment will consist of finding an article that might be a suitable addition to the course's reading list. The students will be required to summarise and incorporate the article of their choice in a paper both justifying the addition of the material in the reading list as well as drawing on a reading component or a complex issue brought up in class.
Prospectus and bibliography/ 4-5 pages -- 10 points
Final paper/ 10-12 pages -- 25 points. In the second half of the course students will move on to the stage of their individual research projects. Now you will learn how to identify, select and search for a topic for their independent research in consultation with the instructor and other students. Students will have the option of presenting their final project in a variety of ways drawing on a multi-disciplinary approach.

All papers are to be submitted with the following requirements: they should be typed double-spaced, with proper page numbers, and the pages stapled together. Your name and date should appear on the upper left or right hand corner of the first page. Only in the case of your final paper you require a cover page. Late papers will not be accepted without penalty. You will lose 1 point per day that the paper is late. For example, if the paper is worth ten points, and you have obtained 8 points or a B, but you gave in the paper two days late, your actual grade will be 6 points, or a D.

Academic Dishonesty: The use of ideas or language taken from some source other than your own without giving proper credit (according to academic conventions which this course is supposed to teach you), is specifically known as plagiarism. The penalties for plagiarism range from failure in the course to expulsion from the University.

Class Schedule

Jan 10 Introduction to the course -- requirements, questions and goals.
Jan 12 Core concepts: Third World, Development, Sex/Gender, Feminism, International Division
       of Labour, Sexuality, Identity, Representation, Agency, Activism.
       Wolfgang Sachs, "Development: A Guide to the Ruins" (*New Internationalist*, June 1992);
       3pp.
       Maria Mies, "The Myth of Catching-Up Development" (Mies and Shiva, eds.,
       Ecofeminism, 1993); 12pp.
       Chandra Mohanty, "Cartographies of Struggle" (Mohanty, Russo and Torres, eds., Third
       World Women and the Politics of Feminism, 1991); 41pp. Begin reading this
       article.
       Trip to the Writing Center (112 Burnham Hall)
Jan 17 Momsen and Townsend, "Introduction" to The Geography of Gender in the Third World
       (1987); 45 pp.
       Finish reading Mohanty, "Cartographies of Struggle"
Jan 19 Barbara Ehrenreich and Annette Fuentes, "Life on the Global Assembly Line";
       Film: Women in the Global Assembly Line (58 mins.)

APPENDIX A (continued)

Jan 24 Maria Mies, "Housewifization International: Women and the New International Division of
          Labor" (Patriarchy and Accumulation on a World Scale, 1986); 31pp.
     Sara Suleri, "Excellent Things in Women" (Meatless Days, 1989); 20pp.
     Films: Women and work in Latin America (25 mins.)
Jan 26 Karen Hossfeld, "'Their Logic Against Them': Contradictions in Sex, Race and Class in
          Silicon Valley"; 12pp.
     Cynthia Enloe, Extract from Bananas, Bases and Patriarchy; 9pp.

*Jan 31 First Response paper (2-3 pages)
     Gerda Lerner, "Reconceptualising Differences Among Women"; 8pp.
     Vandana Shiva, "Gatt, Agriculture and Third World Women" (Ecofeminism); 13pp.
     Bina Agarwal, Patriarchy and the Modernising State (Agarwal, ed., Structures of
          Patriarchy: The State, the Community and the Household, 1988)); 27pp.
Feb 2   Bina Agarwal, "Neither Sustenance Nor Sustainability" (Structures of Patriarchy); 32pp.
     Film: Small Happiness: Women of a Chinese Village (50 mins.)

Feb 7   Rey Chow, "Violence in the Other Country" (Third World Women and the Politics of
          Feminism); 17pp.
     Suleri, "Meatless Days" and "Mustakori, My Friend" (Meatless Days); 51pp.
Feb 9   Library Orientation (LUIS). Meet in Room 330, First Floor, Opposite Circulation desk,
          Main Library

Feb 14 Library Orientation (IBIS). Meet same place in the Main Library.
Feb 16 Vandana Shiva, "Women, Ecology and Health" (Shiva, ed., Close to Home, 1994); 9pp.
     Dankelman and Davidson, "Human Settlements: Women's Environment of Poverty" and
          "Women and Conservation" (Women and Environment in the Third World, 1988);
          23+ pp.
     Film: Interview with Wangari Mathai (24 mins.)

Feb 21 Hanna Papanek, "The Ideal Woman and the Ideal Society: Control and Autonomy in the
          Construction of Identity" (Valentine Moghadam, ed., Identity Politics and Women,
          1994); 28pp.
     Evelyne Accad, "Sexuality and Sexual Politics... in the Middle East" (Third World Women
          and the Politics of Feminism); 9pp.
Feb 23 Nirmala Sathe, "Women's Health is Women's Concern" (Third World, Second Sex, 2);
     Maria Mies, "New Reproductive Technologies: Sexist and Racist Implications"
          (Ecofeminism); 21pp.

Feb 28 Trinh T. Minh-ha, "Difference: A Special Third World Women Issue" (Woman, Native,
          Other, 1989); 28pp.
     Film: Minh-ha, Sur Name Viet, Given Name Nam (104 mins.)
*March 2 Review paper due (3-4 pages)
     Nawal el Saadawi, "The Circumcision of Girls" (The Hidden Face of Eve, 1980); 10pp.
     AAWORD, "Statement on Genital Mutilation" (Miranda Davies, ed., Third World, Second
          Sex 2); 3pp. Review paper due.

Spring Break

March 14 Yayori Matsui, "Sexual Exploitation of Women" (Women's Asia, 1987); 12pp.
     Mahasweta Devi, The Witch-Hunt (Kalpana Bardhan, ed., Of Women, Untouchables,
          Peasants and Outcastes, 1990); 29pp.
     Suleri, "Goodbye to the Greatness of Tom" and "The Right Path" (MD); 35pp.
     Film: Rites (52 mins.)

*March 21 Proposal Due
    Kumari Jayawardena, Introduction to Feminism and Nationalism in the Third World, 1986; 24pp.
    Amal Jou'beh, "Women and Politics -- Reflections from Nairobi" (Report of Palestinian Union of Women's Work Comittee, Third World, Second Sex 2); 3pp.
March 23 Madeleine Tress, "Halakha, Zionism and Gender" (Identity Politics and Women); 17pp.
    Gloria Anzaldua, "Speaking in Tongues: A Letter to Third World Women Writers" (Anzaldua and Moraga, eds., This Bridge Called My Back, 1983); 8pp.

March 28 Ding Ling, Extract from "Sketches from the 'Cattle Shed'"; 23pp.
    Film: No Longer Silent (57 mins.)
March 30 V.Kannabiran and K. Lalitha, "That Magic Time: Women in the Telangana People's Struggle" (Sangari and Vaid, eds., Recasting Women, 1987); 23pp.
    Mahasweta Devi, Draupadi (Lakshmi Holmstrom, ed., The Inner Courtyard, 1990); 16pp.

*April 4 Second Response paper due 3-4 pages
    Kamla Bhasin, "Literacy for Women -- Why and How?" and "Women, Development and Media" (Third World, Second Sex 2); 15pp.
    Joan French, Organizing Women Through Drama in Rural Jamaica (ibid.); 6pp.
    Bessie Head, Extract from The Collector of Treasures; 21pp.
    Films: Two short films on women and activism in India and Nicaragua (24 mins.)
April 6 Gloria Anzaldua, "Towards a New Consciousness" (Borderlands, 1987); 14pp.
    John Krich, "Here Come the Brides" ; 11pp.

April 11 Shamita and Sayantini Dasgupta, "Journeys: Reclaiming South Asian Feminism (South Asian Women Collective, eds., Our Feet Walk the Sky; 1993); 7pp.
    Cherrie Moraga, "From a Long Line of Vendidas"
    Suleri, "The Immoderation of Iffat"; 19pp.
April 13 Minh-ha, "Not You/Like You: Postcolonial Women and the Interlocking Questions of Identity and Difference (Anzaldua, ed., Making Face, Making Soul, 1990); 5pp.
    Film: Bhaaji on the Beach (97 mins.)

April 18 bell hooks, Third World Diva Girls (Yearning: Race, Gender and Cultural Politics, 1990); 13pp.
    Charlotte Bunch, "Prospects for Global Feminism"; 3pp.
April 20 Suleri, "What Mamma Knew" and "Saving Daylight"; 35pp.
    Rashmi Sadana, "Making a Space for Women in the Third World: Displacement and Identity in Suleri's Meatless Days (Our Feet Walk the Sky); 4pp.
    Film: Mitsuye and Nellie (58 mins.)

April 25 Class Presentations
*April 27 Class Presentations
    Final Paper due

Appendix Ⓑ

Main Assignments for English 161:
Women in the Third World

Assignment 1

English 161/Response Paper (due Jan 31)

Please Refer to syllabus for directions on format

Write a two-part essay in which the first part consists of your mapping out of the world as it looks from where you are "located" (for instance, in the sense in which Mohanty talks of it in pp. 1-7 of her article). Begin by summarizing Mohanty's notion of "cartographies" in that section. Then write a personal account of how you see <u>your</u> location/s contributing to your understanding of both yourself and other peoples and their cultures.

In the second part of the essay, present a critique of any of the reading or concepts that have been discussed so far—pointing out how it/they either enabled you to understand certain issues or were examples of weak or strong arguments. As far as possible, give concrete examples, citing sources as you do so.* A good idea would be to focus on a specific section of an article or choose one concept among the following:

- women and work
- who are Third World women
- the idea of development
  (compare and contrast with that of those articles you read)
- the geography of gender
- issues in research

*e.g. (Mohanty, 8) or (Sachs, 3) or (Mies 1994, 56)

241

Assignment 2

Review Paper (due March 2)

Find an article that is not included in your reading packet on the special topic of this course: Women in the Third World. The article you choose could be on any aspect of women's lives in the Third World that has been covered in the syllabus or even that has been left out of it. Unless you are reviewing a book, please make a copy of the article and attach it to your paper.

Write a 3- to 4-page paper in which you do the following:

- Summarize the main points of the article;
- Connect or relate it to at least one article that you read in your course packet and at least one issue that has been discussed in class;
- Comment on the ways in which the authors have conducted their research or presented their point of view;
- Explain how and why the article you chose adds, alters, or expands our knowledge of the topics discussed so far; and
- Argue for its inclusion in the syllabus of this course.

Make sure you cite your sources in the format provided in your handbooks, and make a list of references at the end of the paper. All other format guidelines are provided in your syllabus.

Note: For the other main assignments, Rashmi wrote out guidelines on the blackboard for the second response paper, prospectus, and final paper. For the prospectus and final paper, she then gave time for students' questions and concerns. The following are my notes copied from the board.

Assignment 3 Final Research Paper

3/2 Notes on Board about prospectus and final paper:

   Over Spring Break—
   Start thinking about your final paper.
   You will need at least two journal articles and one article from a book or full book, two articles from the course packet, or one article and *Meatless Days* (the autobiography of Pakistani feminist critic Sara Suleri, a required book for the course)

3/16
Prospectus
Due Thursday, March 23rd

1. Thesis statement/argument
2. How do you intend to support it? (some kind of outline)
3. Your research methods
4. Bibliography

Arrange conference with me regarding your final project.

Assignment 4: In-Class Response Essay

Note: Instead of assigning another response paper, Rashmi organized the writing as an in-class essay. Beforehand, she told the class she might choose one of three essays for their response writing. She chose the bell hooks essay, "Third World Diva Girls," and she wrote the following on the board, addressing students' questions before she told them to begin.

I have included contextual annotation to my notes.

4/18
Using your own words, comment on the significance of:
hooks' paragraph on p. 90 that begins, "Faced with the choice of assimilating or returning to my roots, I would catch the first train back home."

In your response, discuss:

a. the context of hooks' essay—the psychic tensions when relating to our own and/or different races
(multiple power relations of: White and Black women, Third World women and Black women, Black women and Black women)
b. context of this course (the students "studying" women in the Third World)
c. context of your relationship to this course/English class.

Appendix  C

Interview Questions and Contexts

During the semester of Rashmi's class, I conducted short interviews lasting on the average a half hour with most of the participants I discuss in the following chapters. At those moments, I mostly asked for their responses to the course and brought up some specific questions about their reading, writing, and talking within it. Over the summer, I developed a series of questions for an extended general interview with the eight major participants. In general, I meant these questions to open up discussion in the following areas, listed here in the order I asked participants:

- work experiences and how they perceive and value "work"
- school experiences and how they perceive and value "education"
- religious practices (if applicable) and in relation to education
- speech communities—differences of discourses among neighborhood, peers, college classes
- implicit practices of critical thinking (in neighborhood/school contexts)
- participants' sense of and valuing of "class consciousness"
- "impact" of Rashmi's class—its persuasive authority
- critical reading of the media/perceptions of political activism
- emic views of writing papers; expressing and performing critical thought within institutional context

General Interview Questions (conducted up to 12–15 months
after the class)

1. Who are the members in your family, and what do
    they do?
2. How long have you lived where you are now? Where
    did you live before that?
3. Do you think you have obligations outside school? To
    what? Whom? Does this make problems? What kinds?
4. What are your goals? What kind of jobs do you want
    to have? The way you want to live?
5. Are you working now? What do you do? For how many
    hours?
6. What other jobs have you had?
7. What are the best and worst things about these jobs?
8. Did you consider the reading, writing, and thinking in
    Rashmi's class "real work"? Compared to other class-
    es?
9. If someone from your family asked you what you were
    studying in Rashmi's class, what would you say?
    Friends from outside school?
10. Where did you go to school?
11. Were your experiences in school generally positive or
    negative?
12. What's the most important thing you learned in
    school? Least important?
13. Have your parents encouraged you in your education?
    How have they told you about their school experiences?
14. What do you think can and cannot be learned in
    school? Why?
15. Do you think college is important for economic suc-
    cess? If it cannot guarantee "upward mobility," is there
    a reason to attend?
16. How would you describe an educated person? How do
    you know such a person when you see him or her?
17. What does "thinking critically" mean to you? When do
    you think you do it?
18. Do you think your attitudes about how to live in the
    world and think about society come from school or
    your daily experiences?
19. How would you compare yourself to other students at
    UIC? People who were in our class?
20. Do you consider yourself religious?
21. What religion are you?

22. Is practicing religion important in your life?
23. Do you think about your religious beliefs in other parts of your life? In what parts? In school? Writing, reading, discussions in classes?
24. How do people get to know each other in your neighborhood?
25. How do you know when you've got your message across to someone else?
26. How do you know when to be suspicious of someone else?
27. Do you think there's such a thing as "Good English"? How do you define it? Do you speak it?
28. Do you make judgments about people based on the way they talk? What can you tell about a person by his or her speech?
29. Do you find yourself talking differently in class and in your neighborhood? What are the differences?
30. Do you act differently or behave differently in class discussions compared to other parts of your life? What about in Rashmi's class?
31. Do you talk with people outside of class/school about issues/ideas discussed in your classes? In what situations? Did you talk about stuff from Rashmi's class?
32. What do you like about your neighborhood?
33. Do you see any problems there? Where do you think these problems stem from? What are their root causes?
34. How would you describe "talking like a teacher?" (high school? college?). Talking like a sociology book?
35. How would you describe "thinking like a teacher"?
36. Do you think it has any value outside of school? Why? What about thinking about the issues discussed in Rashmi's class?
37. Can you describe some situations when your views are most likely to conflict with other people you know?
38. What are your biggest differences in views from your parents? What "issues" do you argue with them most about?
39. Who are your heroes? What are the things you admire about them?
40. Who in our class struck you as smart, articulate?
41. Do most people you know seem to be upper/middle/or working class, and how do you know? Is it the kind of jobs or the money they make?
42. Do you think Rashmi's class has changed your think-

ing in any way?

43. What topics or issues do you remember from the class? Why are they memorable?

44. Have you found yourself thinking about problems discussed in Rashmi's class any times outside of school?

45. Would you think differently about issues of research and writing about cultural problems because of this class?

46. Nowadays, people are claiming they are part of various social groups in an effort to fight for rights and (political power). For instance, African Americans, Gay rights, Native Americans. What groups do you think need most to organize as a group to gain better rights? Do you think there are groups that shouldn't be doing this?

47. Do you know anyone that is "politically active"? Explain how.

48. How do you get most of your information about current events? TV, radio, papers?

49. How do you recognize (bullshit or more polite phrase)? What makes you suspicious when you see it?

50. Do you ever bullshit/fake it on papers for school? When? How different from your other papers?

51. Did you do bullshit/fake on papers for this class or felt like you were?

52. Possible follow-up: When is a paper not (bullshit/faking it)? Was there any writing and thinking you did for this class where it meant something more to you than "just getting the job done?"

53. Have you had teachers suggest ways to make your writing of ideas or arguments more "complex?" What do you think they meant?

54. Have you ever written anything where you wanted to speak for your "community" (cultural group, etc.)? About their values? What was your purpose for this?

55. How would you compare writing about your ideas and experiences to talking to others about them?

56. Did anything you wrote for school (or otherwise) ever make you rethink your thinking and values?

Although these areas may seem more compartmentalized as listed here on the printed page, I intended for participants to discuss where they perceived places of possible overlap and conflict between them. For instance, I wanted to see how they compared their valuing of work and education and in what ways they might see education, and Rashmi's class, as "work" and vice versa. I designed or borrowed many of the interview questions to compare each participant's talk of tacit critical actions or beliefs in various domains outside schooling to what they thought some teachers expected of their thinking. So in addition to asking indirect open questions to elicit their critical perceptions of their life worlds, I also asked a few direct questions to get their definitions of critical teachers' priorities.

When conducting and later analyzing these interviews, I viewed them as contextualized speech events particularly because they took place outside the participants' neighborhoods or communities that I asked them to discuss with me. As speech events, the interviews had their own complex interactions of roles, status, and interpretation depending on the interlocutors and content of discussion (Briggs, 1986). In effect, I did not assume a transparency of truth within our communication. Much of the content of the participants' talk was emeshed in how they represented themselves to me through their choices in language. Because I was interested in what ways they tend to orient themselves to institutional identities, I could often learn much from how they imagined my social identities and institutional affiliations. What subject positions of my ethos stood out for them? Did they chiefly me see as White and male? as a success in higher education? as middle-class? as leftist or liberal? To an extent, I could read what I represented to individual participants by their relative openness or reticence and the ways they chose to talk about these topic areas. In conjunction with the positions they espoused and the experiences they related, the ways the participants related to their images of me helped me interpret their various psychological investments in mainstream institutions. Moreover, it demonstrated what kinds of cultural capital, in both mainstream and local cultures, they might acknowledge and value.

CONCERNS OF RECIPROCITY AND WHAT THEY SUGGEST

Researchers drawing from postmodern feminist ethics have stressed the contexts of the researcher(s)' and participants' multiple subject positions throughout the research process (Brodkey, 1987; Fine, 1992). They have also argued for mutually beneficial reciprocity between researchers and participants at all stages of inquiry. I have tried to offer a meaningful reciprocity with my featured participants dependent on their different interests while investigating power dynamics within these relationships. To those participants I was following who were having difficulty with Rashmi's course, for whatever reasons, I offered whatever kind of tutoring they thought would help their writing. Only Shianta and Xiao took me up on this and only at the most stressful points of producing their final paper. Lilia accepted my tutoring assistance for an incomplete she had from her organizational psychology class two semesters later.

Although these tutoring sessions were more like "giving back" than acts of conscience, I also spoke for some students to Rashmi and offered advice and advocacy for other institutional situations when they asked me. In one situation, I acted as liaison in a grade dispute between Min Wei and her business writing teacher, a friend and colleague in my department. During our interviews, Min Wei told me she believed the teacher was culturally prejudiced toward her. Her perception turned out to be based on several misunderstandings between teacher and student over paperwork and grades, which was later resolved. Nevertheless, my tutoring produced little effect on these students' final work.

Moreover, I saw participants' responses to my different offers of reciprocation as another way to infer their orientations toward Rashmi's course, education, and social class, and how they imagined my institutional roles. For instance, Shianta and Lilia, who did accept my offer of tutoring, fully identified with values from mainstream education, although in separate ways (as they articulate in chap. 6). In contrast, Mike never showed any concern that he was receiving Cs in the class, and the one time I offered some help as a way to give back he essentially ignored it. I believe his behavior toward my possible role as tutor concurs with his views of achievement through mainstream institutions (as examined in chaps. 3, 6, and 7). In the first week of class, when I casually offered the possibility of tutoring to Peter, should he later feel the need, he gave me the thumbs up—a gesture that now puzzles me. Although he grumbled to me about the Bs he was getting in the course, he never took me up on my original offer for advice, often keeping an emotional distance from the rest of the class. After hearing his perspectives on school and race issues, which I describe in chapter 4, I was not surprised by his abstentions from more academically intellectual involvement. In the end, only one participant—Gita—expressed interest in visiting a class that I taught. After one of our interviews, Gita sat in on my advanced writing course and later offered her views of my teaching and interactions with students compared with Rashmi's class. Her interest in a participatory meta-analysis of teaching provided further evidence of her complicated orientations toward critical pedagogies she has encountered in school settings. It also gave her a chance to critique me and open another way to voice her perceptions of my social positioning within the university.

When I began asking students' consent for interviews, I offered a small stipend to those I assumed I would feature in the dissertation, not having enough funding to pay all my interviewees. To my initial surprise, more students in this group off-handedly declined the possibility of payment than the offer of tutoring, although all of them worked in jobs and were not particularly well off. I now see that I offered the funds as a commodity exchange on the table. In comparison, most of these participants might have viewed their involvement as a sharing of a resource not to be associated with the commodity exchange of work labor. Several of them replied they liked helping people out when I asked them why they consented to talk with me. Although I offered these kinds of reciprocation for my participants' time and thought, some also told me they simply enjoyed the opportunity to talk and reflect on their lives or indirectly indicated this through their enthusiasm once they got going. In this respect, the opportunity for self-reflection or an attentive listener was for most participants its own kind of benefit.

References

Adler, Patricia & Peter Adler. (1987). *Membership roles in field research.* Newbury Park, CA: Sage.

Anderson, Virginia. (1997). Confrontational teaching and rhetorical practice. *College Composition and Communication, 48,* 197–214.

Anyon, Jean. (1980). Social class and the hidden curriculum of work. *Journal of Education, 162*(1), 67–92.

Anzaldua, Gloria. (1987). *La conciencia de la mestiza: Toward a new consciousness. Borderlands: La Frontera—The New Mestiza.* San Francisco: Aunt Lute Books.

Aronowitz, Stanley. (1992). *The politics of identity: Class, culture, social movements.* New York: Routledge.

Balester, Valerie. (1993). *Cultural divide: A study of African-American college level writers.* Portsmouth, NH: Boynton Cook.

Bartholome, David. (1985). Inventing the university. In M. Rose (Ed.), *When a writer can't write: Studies in writer's block and other composing problems* (pp. 134–165). New York: Guilford.

Bartholome, David & Anthony Petrosky. (1986). *Facts, artifacts and counterfacts: Theory and method for a basic reading and writing course.* Portsmouth: Boynton Cook.

Bartholome, David & Anthony Petrosky. (2002). *Ways of reading: An anthology for writers.* Boston: Bedford/St. Martins

Bean, Janet. (2003). Manufacturing emotions: Tactical resistance in the narratives of working class students. In Laura Micciche & Dale Jacobs (Eds.), *Ways to move: Rhetorics of emotion and composition studies* (pp. 101–112). Portsmouth, NH: Boynton Cook.

Belenky, Mary Field, Blythe McVicker Clinchy, Nancy Rule Goldberger, & Jill Mattuck Tarule. (1986). *Women's ways of knowing: The development of self, voice, and mind.* New York: Basic Books.

Bellah, Robert N., Richard Madsen, William M. Sullivan, Ann Swindler, & Steven M. Tipton. (1985). Finding oneself through work. In Rise B. Axelrod & Charles R. Cooper (Eds.), *Who are we?: Readings on identity, community, work, and career* (pp. 98–104). New York: Bedford St. Martins.

Berlin, James A. (1984). *Writing instruction in nineteenth century American colleges.* Carbondale: Southern Illinois University Press.

Berlin, James A. (1987). *Rhetoric and reality: Writing instruction in American colleges, 1900-1985.* Carbondale: Southern Illinois University Press.

Berlin, James A. (1996). *Rhetorics, poetics, and cultures: Refiguring college English studies.* Urbana, IL: NCTE.

Berlin James A. & Michael Vivion, (Eds.). (1992). *Cultural studies in the English classroom.* Portsmouth, NH: Boynton Cook.

Bizzell, Patricia. (1984). William Perry and liberal education. *College English, 46*(5), 447–454.

Bizzell, Patricia. (1991). Marxist ideas in composition studies. In Patricia Harkin & John Schilb (Eds.), *Contending with words: Composition and rehetoric in a postmodern age* (pp. 52–68). New York: Modern Language Association.

Bizzell, Patricia. (1994). Contact zones and English studies. *College English, 56*, 163–169.

Bourdieu, Pierre. (1984). *Distinction: A social critique of the judgment of taste* (Richard Nice, Trans.). Cambridge, MA: Harvard University Press.

Briggs, Charles L. (1986). *Learning how to ask: A sociolinguistic appraisal of the role of the interview in social science research.* Philadelphia: University of Pennsylvania Press.

Brodkey, Linda. (1987). Writing critical ethnographic narratives. *Anthropology and Education Quarterly, 18*(2), 67–76.

Brooke, Robert. (1987). Underlife and writing instruction. *College Composition & Communication, 38*, 141–153.

Chase, Geoffrey. (1988). Accommodation, resistance, and the politics of student writing. *College Composition and Communication, 39*(1), 13–22.

Cheville, Julie. (2001). *Minding the body: What student athletes know about learning.* Portsmouth, NH: Boynton Cook.

Chiseri-Strater, Elizabeth. (1991). *Academic literacies: The public and private discourse of university students.* Portsmouth: Boynton-Cook Heinemann.

Chiseri-Strater, Elizabeth & Bonnie Stone Sunstein. (2002). *Fieldworking: Reading and writing research* (2nd ed.). Boston: Bedford/St. Martins.

Clark, Suzanne & Lisa Ede. (1990). Collaboration, resistance, and the teaching of writing. In Andrea Lunsford, Helene Moglen, & James Slevin (Eds.), *The right to literacy* (pp. 276–285). New York: The Modern Language Association of America.

Clifford, James. (1988). *The predicament of culture: Twentieth-century ethnography, literature, and art.* Cambridge, MA: Harvard University Press.

Connors, Robert. J. (1991). Rhetoric in the modern university: The creation of an underclass. In Richard Bullock & John Trimbur (Eds.), *The politics of writing instruction: Postsecondary* (pp. 55–84). Portsmouth, NH: Boynton Cook.

Cooper, Marilyn M. & Michael Holtzman. (1989). *Writing as social action.* Portsmouth, NH: Boynton Cook.

Crapanzano, Vincent. (1986). Hermes' dilemma: The masking of subversion in ethnographic description. In James Clifford and George Marcus (Eds.), *Writing culture: The poetics and politics of ethnography* (pp. 51–76). Berkeley: University of California Press.

Crowley, Sharon. (1995). Biting the hand that feeds us: Nineteenth-century uses of a pedagogy of taste. In John F. Reynolds (Ed.), *Cultural studies, rhetoric and literacy* (pp. 11–20). Hillsdale, NJ: Lawrence Erlbaum Associates.

Daniel, Jack L. & Geneva Smitherman. (1976). How I got over: Communication dynamics in the Black community. *Quarterly Journal of Speech, 62,* 26–39.

DeCerteau, Michel. (1984). *The practice of everyday life.* Berkeley: University of California Press.

Delpit, Lisa. (1995). *Other people's children: Cultural conflict in the classroom.* New York: The New Press.

Durst, Russel. (1999). *Collision-course: Conflict, negotiation, and learning in college composition.* Urbana, IL: NCTE.

Eagleton, Terry. (1983). *Literacy theory: An introduction.* Minneapolis: University of Minnesota Press.

Eckert, Penelope. (1989). *Jocks and burnouts: Social categories and identity in the high school.* New York: Teachers College Press.

Ehrenreich, Barbara. (1989). *Fear of falling: The inner life of the middle class.* New York: Pantheon.

Ehrenreich, Barbara & Annette Fuentes. (1993). Life on the global assembly line. In Allison Jaggar and Paul Rosenburg (Eds.), *Feminist frameworks* (pp. 359–366). New York: McGraw.

Ellsworth, Elizabeth. (1989). Why doesn't this feel empowering? Working through the repressive myths of critical pedagogy. *Harvard Educational Review, 59*(3), 297–324.

Faigley, Lester. (1992). *Fragments of rationality: Postmodernity and the subject of composition.* Pittsburgh: University of Pittsburgh Press.

Fine, Michelle. (1992). *Disruptive voices: The possibilities of feminine research.* Ann Arbor: University of Michigan Press.

Fishman, Stephen. (1993). Explicating our tacit tradition: John Dewey and composition studies. *College Composition & Communication, 44*(3), 315–330.

Fitts, Karen & Alan France. (1995). *Left margins: Cultural studies and composition pedagogy.* Albany: State University of New York Press.

Flower, Linda. (1997). Partners in inquiry: A logic for community outreach. In Linda Kassner, Robert Crooks, & Ann Watters (Eds.), *Writing the community: Concepts and models for service learning in composition* (pp. 95–117). Washington, DC: American Association for Higher Education.

Flynn, Elizabeth. (2001). Strategic, counter-strategic, and reactive resistance in the feminist classroom. In Andrea Greenbaum (Ed.),

Insurrections: Approaches to resistance in composition studies (pp. 17–36). Albany: SUNY Press.

Foley, Douglas. (1990). *Learning capitalist culture: Deep in the heart of Tejas.* Philadelphia: University of Pennsylvania Press.

Fordham, Signithia. (1988). Racelessness as a factor in Black students' school success: Pragmatic strategy or pyrrhic victory? *Harvard Educational Review, 58*(1), 54–84.

Foss, Sonja K., Karen A. Foss, & Robert Trapp. (1985). *Contemporary perspectives on rhetoric.* Prospect Heights, IL: Waveland.

Foster, Michelle. (1989). It's cookin' now: A performance analysis of the speech events of a Black teacher in an urban community college. *Language and Society, 18*(1), 1–29.

Foucault, Michel. (1976). *The archaeology of knowledge.* (A. M. Sheridan Smith, Trans.). New York: Harper.

Foucault, Michel. (1979). *Discipline and punish: The birth of the prison.* (Alan Sheridan, Trans.). New York: Vintage.

Fox, Helen. (1994). *Listening to the world.* Urbana, IL: NCTE.

Fox, Tom. (1990). *The social uses of writing: Politics and pedagogy.* Norwood, NJ: Ablex.

Fox, Tom. (2001). Race and collective resistance. In Andrea Greenbaum (Ed.), *Insurrections: Approaches to resistance in composition studies* (pp. 71–88). Albany: SUNY Press.

Freire, Paulo. (1970). *Pedagogy of the oppressed.* New York: Continuum.

Fu, Danling. (1995). *My trouble is my English: Asian students and the American dream.* Portsmouth, NH: Heinneman/Boynton-Cook.

Geertz, Clifford. (1987). *Works and lives: The anthropologist as author.* Stanford, CA: Stanford University Press.

Gibson, Margaret A. (1988). *Accommodation without assimilation: Punjabi Sikh immigrants in an American high school and community.* Ithaca, NY: Cornell University Press.

Gibson, Margaret A. (1997). Exploring and explaining the variability: Cross national perspectives on the school performance of minority students [Special Issue]. *Anthropology and Education Quarterly,* 1–17.

Giroux, Henry. (1983). *Theory and resistance in education.* Granby, MA: Bergin & Garvey.

Giroux, Henry. (1991). Postmodernism as border pedagogy: Redefining the boundaries of race and ethnicity. In Henry Giroux (Ed.), *Postmodernism, feminism, and cultural politics: Redrawing educational boundaries* (pp. 217–256). Albany: SUNY Press.

Goffman, Erving. (1973). *The presentation of self in everyday life.* Woodstock, NY: Overlook Press.

Goodburn, Amy. (1998). It's a question of faith: Discourses of fundamentalism and critical pedagogy in the writing classroom. *JAC: A Journal of Composition Theory, 18*(2), 333–353.

Gordon, Suzanne. (1991). *Prisoners of men's dreams: Striking out for a new feminine future.* Boston: Little, Brown.

Gorzelsky, Gwendolyn. (2003) Redefining resistance: Rereading critical pedagogy. *Reader: A Journal of Reader-Oriented Theory, Criticism, and Pedagogy, 48,* 51–86.

Goto, Stanford. (1997). Nerds, normal people, and homeboys: Accommodation and resistance among Chinese American students. *Anthropology and Education Quarterly,* 70–84.

Graff, Harvey. (1991). *The literacy myth: Cultural integration and social structure in the nineteenth century.* New Brunswick, NJ: Transaction Books.

Halloran, Michael. (1993). Rhetoric in the American college curriculum: The decline of public discourse. In Victor J. Vitanza (Ed.), *Pretext: The first decade.* Pittsburgh: University of Pittsburgh Press.

Hairston, Maxine. (1991). The postdisciplinary politics of lore. In Patricia Harkin & John Schilb (Eds.), *Contending with words: Composition and rhetoric in a postmodern age.* New York: Modern Language Association.

Hairston, Maxine. (1992). Diversity, ideology, and teaching writing. *College Compositon and Communication, 43,* 179–195.

Harkin, Patricia. (1991). The postdisciplinary politics of lore. In Patricia Harkin & John Schilb (Eds.), *Contending with words: Composition and rhetoric in a postmodern age* (pp. 124–138). New York: Modern Language Association.

Harris, Joseph. (1995). Negotiating the contact zone. *Journal of Basic Writing, 14,* 27–42.

Harris, Joseph & Jay Rosen. (1995). *Media journal: Reading and writing about popular Culture.* Needham Heights, MA: Allyn & Bacon.

Heath, Shirley Brice. (1983). *Ways with words: Language, life, and work in communities and classrooms.* Cambridge: Cambridge University Press.

Heath, Shirley Brice & Milbrey W. McLaughlin. (1993). *Identity and inner city youth: Beyond ethnicity and gender.* New York: Teachers College Press.

Helmers, Marguerite. (1994). *Writing students: Composition, testimonials, and representations of students* (pp. 97–118). Albany: SUNY Press.

Herrington, Anne J. & Marcia Curtis. (2000). *Persons in process: Four stories of writing and personal development in college.* Urbana, IL: NCTE.

Herzberg, Bruce. (1991). Composition and the politics of curriculum. In Richard Bullock & John Trimbur (Eds.), *The politics of writing instruction: Postsecondary* (pp. 97–118). Portsmouth, NH: Boynton Cook.

Hochschild, Arlie Russel & Annie Machung. (1989). *The second shift: Working parents and the revolution at home.* New York: Viking.

hooks, bell. (1990). *Third World diva girls. Yearning: Race, gender, and cultural politics.* Chicago: Third Side Press.

Horkheimer, Max & Theodor Adorno. (1972). *Dialectic of enlightenment.* New York: Herder & Herder.

Hymes, Dell. (1974). *Foundations of sociolinguistics: An ethnographic approach*. Philadelphia: University of Pennsylvania Press.

Jacoby, Russel. (1987). *The last intellectuals: American culture in the age of academe*. New York: Basic Books.

Jarratt, Susan. (1991a). *Rereading the sophists: Classical rhetoric refigured*. Carbondale: Southern Illinois University Press.

Jarratt, Susan (1991b). Feminism and composition studies: The case for conflict. In Patricia Harkin & John Schilb (Eds.), *Contending with words: Composition and rhetoric in a postmodern age* (pp. 105–23). New York: Modern Language Association.

Jolliffe, David et al. (Eds.). (1988). *Purposes and ideas: Readings for university writing*. Dubuque, IA: Kendall Hunt.

Jolliffe, David. (1999). *Inquiry and genre: Writing to learn in college*. Boston: Allyn & Bacon.

Kahn, Seth. (2002). *Grassroots democracy in process: Ethnographic writing as a site of democratic action*. Unpublished doctoral dissertation, Syracuse University.

Kahn, Seth. (2003). Ethnographic writing as grassroots democratic action. *Composition Studies, 31*(1), 63–81.

Kirsch, Gesa & Peter Mortensen. (1993). On authority in the study of writing. *College Composition and Communication, 44*, 556–572.

Kleine, Ted. (1994). Living the Lansing dream. In Eric Liu (Ed.), *Next: Young American writers on the new generation* (pp. 95–109). New York: W.W. Norton and Co.

Knoblauch, C.H. (1991). Critical teaching and dominant culture. In C. Mark Hurlbert & Michael Blitz (Eds.), *Composition and resistance* (pp. 12–23). Portsmouth, NH: Boynton cook.

Kochman, Thomas. (1981). *Black and white styles in conflict*. Chicago: University of Chicago Press.

Lee, Amy. (2000). *Composing critical pedagogies: Teaching writing as revision*. Urbana, IL: NCTE.

Levinson, Bradley & Dorothy Holland. (1996). The cultural production of the educated person: An introduction. In Bradley A. Levinson, Douglas E. Foley, & Dorothy C. Holland (Eds.), *The cultural production of the educated person: Critical ethnographies of schooling and local practice*. Albany: State University of New York Press.

Lindquist, Julie. (2002). *A place to stand: Politics and persuasion in a working class bar*. Oxford, England: Oxford University Press.

Loeb, Paul. (1994). *Generation at the crossroads: Apathy and action on the American campus*. New Brunswick: Rutgers University Press.

Lu, Min-Zhan. (1992). Conflict and struggle: The enemies or preconditions of basic writing. *College English, 54*, 887–913.

Lynch, Dennis A., Diana George, & Marilyn Cooper. (1997). Agonistic inquiry and confrontational cooperation. *College Composition and Communication, 48*(1), 61–85.

Lyotard, Francois. (1984). *The postmodern condition*. Minneapolis: University of Minnesota Press.

Mack, Nancy. (1995). Writing for change: When motive matters. *The Writing Instructor, 15*(1), 20–33.

Mack, Nancy. (1998). *From social activity to self-regulation: Writing as identity formation.* Conference on College Composition and Communication, Chicago IL.

Mack, Nancy & James Thomas Zebroski. (1992). Ethnographic writing for critical consciousness. In C. Mark Hurlbert & Samuel Totten (Eds.), *Social issues in the English classroom: Theory and practice* (pp. 196–205). Urbana, IL: NCTE.

Mahalia, Daniel. (1991). Writing utopias: Writing across the curriculum and the promise of reform. *College English, 53*, 773–789.

Mahiri, Jabari. (1998). *Shooting for excellence: African American and youth culture in New Century Schools.* Urbana, IL: NCTE.

Marcuse, Herbert. (1964). *One dimensional man: Studies in the ideology of advanced industrial society.* Boston: Beacon.

Marshall, Margaret. (1997). Marking the unmarked: Reading student diversity and preparing teachers. *College Composition and Communication, 48*(2), 231–248.

Mauk, Johnathan, (2003). Location, location, location: The "real" (e)states of being, writing, and thinking in composition. *College English, 65*(4), 368-388.

McComiskey, Bruce. (2000). *Teaching composition as social process.* Logan: Utah State University Press.

Mckay, Sandra L. & Sau-Ling Wong. (1996). Multiple discourses, multiple identities: Investment and agency in second-language learning and Chinese adolescent immigrant students. *Harvard Educational Review, 66*(3), 577–608.

McLaughlin, Thomas. (1996). *Street smarts and critical theory: Listening to the vernacular.* Madison: University of Wisconsin Press.

McLeod, Susan H. (1997). *Notes on the heart: Affective issues in the writing classroom.* Carbondale: Southern Illinois University Press.

Miller, Richard. (1994). Fault lines in the contact zone. *College English, 56*, 389–408.

Miller, Susan. (1991). The feminization of composition. In Richard Bullock & John Trimbur (Eds.), *The politics of writing instruction: Postsecondary* (pp. 39–52). Portsmouth, NH: Boynton Cook.

Miller, Susan. (1992). The feminization of composition. In Richard Bullock & John Trimbur (Eds.), *The politics of writing instruction: Postsecondary,* (pp. 39–54). Portsmouth, NH: Boynton Cook.

Miller, Thomas P. (1997). *The formation of college English: Rhetoric and Belle Lettres in the British cultural provinces.* Pittsburgh: University of Pittsburgh Press.

Milroy, James. (1992). *Linguistic variation and change.* Oxford: Blackwell.

Moffatt, Michael. (1989). *Coming of age in New Jersey: College and American culture.* New Brunswick, NJ: Rutgers University Press.

Mohanty, Chandra. (1991). Cartographies of struggle: Third World women and the politics of feminism. In Chandra Mohanty, Ann

Russo, & Lourdes Torres (Eds.), *Third World women and the politics of feminism* (pp. 1–47.). Bloomington: Indiana University Press.

Moss, Beverly. (1992).Ethnography and composition. In Gesa Kirsch & Patricia A. Sullivan (Eds.), *Methods and methodology in composition research.* Carbondale: Southern Illionois University Press.

Myers, Greg. (1986). Reality, consensus, and reform in the rhetoric of composition teaching. *College English, 48,* 154–174.

Newkirk, Thomas. (1996). Seduction and betrayal in qualitative research. In Peter Mortensen & Gesa E. Kirsch (Eds.), *Ethics and representation in qualitative studies of literacy* (pp. 3–16). Urbana, IL: NCTE

Newkirk, Thomas. (1997). *The performance of self in student writing.* Portsmouth, NH: Boynton Cook.

North, Stephen. (1987). *The making of knowledge in composition.* Portsmouth, NH: Boynton Cook.

Ogbu, John. (1987). Opportunity structure, cultural boundaries, and literacy. In J. Langer (Ed.), *Language, literacy and cultural issues in schooling.* Norwood, NJ: Ablex.

Ogbu, John, & Margaret A. Gibson (Eds.). (1991). *Minority status and schooling: A comparative study of immigrant and involuntary minorities.* New York: Garland.

Ohmann, Richard. (1976). *English in America: A radical view of the profession.* New York: Oxford University Press.

Ohmann, Richard. (1979). Use definite specific concrete language. In Gary Tate, Edward P.J. Corbett, & Nancy Myers (Eds.), *The writing teachers' sourcebook.* New York: Oxford University Press.

Ohmann, Richard. (1990). Graduate students, professionals, intellectuals. *College English, 52,* 247–257.

Owens, Derek. (2001). *Composition and sustainability: Teaching for a threatened generation.* Urbana, IL: NCTE.

Peckham, Irvin. (2003). *Going north, thinking west: The crossroads of social class, thinking,and writing instruction.* Unpublished book manuscript.

Penticoff, Richard & Linda Brodkey. (1992). Writing about difference: Hard cases for cultural studies. In James A. Berlin and Michael J. Vivion (Eds.), *Cultural studies in the English classroom* (pp. 123–144.). Portsmouth, NH: Boynton Cook.

Perry, William G. (1970). *Forms of intellectual and ethical development in the college years; A scheme.* New York: Holt, Rinehart and Winston.

Peverly, Susan. (1996). *University of Illinois teaching assistants handbook.* University document. Unpublished.

Philipsen, Gerry. (1992). *Speaking culturally: Explorations in social communication.* Albany: State University of New York Press.

Picket, Nell Ann. (1997). The two year college as democracy in action. *College Composition and Communication, 49,* 90–98.

Pratt, Mary Louise. (1991). *Arts of the contact zone. Profession 91.* New York: Modern Language Association.

Qualley, Donna J. (1994). Being in two places at once: Feminism and the development of "both/and" perspectives. In Patricia A. Sullivan &

Donna J. Qualley (Eds.), *Pedagogy in the age of politics: Writing and reading in the academy* (pp. 25–42). Urbana, IL: NCTE.

Rand, Elizabeth A. (2001). Enacting faith: Evangelical discourse and the discipline of composition studies. *College Composition and Communication, 52*(3), 349–367.

Riggs, Marlon. (1995). *Black is—Black ain't: A personal journey through Black identity* [motion picture]. Independent Television Service. San Francisco: California Newsreel.

Rodriguez, Richard. (1981). *Hunger of memory: The education of Richard Rodriguez: An autobiography.* Boston: D. Godine.

Rosaldo, Renato. (1989). *Culture and truth: The remaking of social analysis.* Boston: Beacon.

Rose, Mike. (1990). *Lives on the boundary: A moving account of the struggles and achievements of America's educational underclass.* New York: Penguin Books

Rosen, George. (1980). *Decision-making Chicago-style: The genesis of a University of Illinois campus.* Urbana: University of Illinois Press.

Rosenblatt, Louise. (1938). *Literature as exploration.* A publication of the Progressive. In Richard Bullock & John Trimbur (Eds.), *Education association.* New York, London: Appleton-Century.

Roth, William F. Jr. (1989). On the meaning of work. In Janet Marting (Ed.), *Making a living: A real world reader.* New York: HarperCollins.

Royko, Mike. (1971). *Boss: Richard J. Daley of Chicago.* New York: New American Library.

Saville-Troike, Muriel. (1982). *The ethnography of communication: An introduction.* Baltimore: University Park Press.

Schwegler, Robert. (1991). The politics of reading student papers. In Richard Bullock & John Trimbur (Eds.), *The politics of writing instruction: Postsecondary* (pp. 203–226). Portsmouth, NH: Boynton Cook.

Scollon, Ron & Susan Wong Scollon. (1995). *Intercultural communication: A discourse approach.* Cambridge, MA: Blackwell.

Seibel Trainor, Jennifer. (2002). Critical pedagogy's "other": Constructions of Whiteness in education for social change. *College Composition and Communication, 53*(4), 631–650.

Seitz, David. (1998). Keeping honest: Working class students, difference, and rethinking the critical agenda in composition. In Chris Anson & Christine Farris (Eds.), *Under construction: Working at the intersections of composition theory, research, and practice* (pp. 65–78). Salt Lake City: Utah State Press.

Seitz, David. (2002) Rhetoric in action: An ethnographic view. In Cindy Moore & Peggy O'Neill (Eds.), *Practice in context: Situating the work of writing teachers.* Urbana, IL: NCTE.

Seitz, David & Julie Lindquist (forthcoming). Between ethnographic and virtual worlds: Toward a pedagogy of mediation. In Pamela Takayoshi & Patricia Sullivan (Eds.), *Labor, writing technologies, and the shaping of composition in the academy.* Cresskill, NJ: Hampton.

Severino, Carol. (1996). An urban university and its academic support program: Teaching basic writing in the context of an "urban mission." *Journal of Basic Writing, 15*, 39–56.

Severino, Carol. (1997). Teaching and writing "Up Against the Mall." *College English, 59*(1), 74–82.

Shor, Ira. (1987). *Critical teaching in everyday life.* Chicago: University of Chicago Press.

Shor, Ira. (1996). *When students have power: Negotiating authority in a critical pedagogy.* Chicago: University of Chicago Press.

Skorczewsi, Dawn. (2000). Everybody has their own ideas: Responding to cliché in student writing. *College Composition and Communication, 52*(2), 220–239.

Smith, Jeff. (1997). Students' goals, gatekeeping, and some questions of ethics. *College English, 59*, 299–320.

Sommer, Robert. (1988). Hard architecture. In David Jolliffe et al. (Eds.), *Purposes and ideas: Readings for university writing* (pp. 230–239). Dubuque, IA: Kendall/Hunt.

Sommers, Nancy. (1982). Responding to student writing. *College Composition and Communication, 33*, 148–156.

Spellmeyer, Kurt. (1991). Knowledge against knowledge: Freshman English, public discourse, and the social imagination. In C. Mark Hurlbert & Michael Blitz (Eds.), *Composition and resistance* (pp. 70–80). Portsmouth, NH: Boynton Cook.

Spellmeyer, Kurt. (1993). *Common ground: Dialogue, understanding, and the teaching of composition.* Englewood Cliffs, NJ: Prentice-Hall.

Spradley, James P. (1979). *The ethnographic interview.* New York: Holt, Rhinehart & Winston.

Spradley James P. & Brenda J. Mann. (1975). *The cocktail waitress: Woman's work in a man's world.* New York:Wiley.

Sprecher, Jill. (1997). Clockwatchers [motion picture]. United States: Fox-Lorber.

Stack, Carol B. (1974). *All our kin: Strategies for survival in a Black community.* New York: Harper & Row.

Steinitz, Victoria Anne & Ellen Rachel Solomon. (1986). *Starting out: Class and community in the lives of working-class youth.* Philadelphia: Temple University Press.

Sternglass, Marilyn S. (1997). *Time to know them: A longitudinal study of writing and learning at the college level.* Mahwah, NJ: Lawrence Erlbaum Associates.

Stuckey, Elspeth J. (1991). *The violence of literacy.* Portsmouth, NH: Boynton/Cook.

Terkel, Studs. (1967). *Division street: America.* New York: Avon.

Tobin, Lad. (1993). *Writing relationships: What really happens in the writing class.* Portsmouth, NH: Heinneman/Boynton-Cook.

Trimbur, John. (1989). Consensus and difference in collaborative learning. *College English, 51*, 602–616.

Trimbur, John. (1991). Literacy and the discourse of crisis. In Richard Bullock & John Trimbur (Eds.), *The politics of writing instruction: Postsecondary* (pp. 277-296). Portsmouth, NH: Boynton Cook.

Van Mannen, John. (1988). *Tales of the field: On writing ethnography.* Chicago: University of Chicago Press.

Varma, Rashmi & David Seitz. (1995). *Social positioning in the classroom.* Presentation at the 31st annual English Articulation Conference, Urbana, IL.

Villanueva, Victor. (1993). *Bootstraps: From an American academic of color.* Urbana, IL: NCTE.

Vitanza, Victor. (1991). Three countertheses: Or, a critical in(ter)vention into composition theories and pedagogies. In Patricia Harkin & John Schilb (Eds.), *Contending with words: Composition and rhetoric in a postmordern age* (pp. 139–172). New York: Modern Language Association.

Walker, Alice & Pratibha Pamar. (1993). *Warrior masks.* New York: Harcourt Brace.

Wallace, David L. & Helen Rothchild Ewald. (2000). *Mutuality in the rhetoric and composition classroom.* Carbondale: Southern Illinois University Press.

Weis, Lois. (1990). *Working class without work: High school students in de-industrializing economy.* Boston and London: Routledge.

Welch, Nancy. "And now that I know them": Composing mutuality in a service learning course. *College Composition and Communication, 54*(2), 243–263.

Wheeler, Susan. (1993). Exercises for discovery, experiment, skills, and play. In Thomas Newkirk (Ed.), *Nuts and bolts: A practical guide to teaching college composition.* Portsmouth, NH: Boynton–Cook.

Yee, Marian. (1991). Are you the writing teacher? In C. Mark Hurlbert & Michael Blitz (Eds.), *Composition and resistance* (pp. 24–30). Portsmouth, NH: Boynton Cook.

Young, Linda W.L. (1994). *Cross-talk and culture in Sino-American communication.* Cambridge: Cambridge University Press.

Zebroski, James Thomas. (1994). *Thinking through theory: Vygotskian perspectives on the teaching of writing.* Portsmouth, NH: Boynton-Cook.

Author Index

Subject Index

Cultural and social capital, 13-14,
58, 62-63, 63-64, 67, 68, 81,
82-83, 89, 142, 144, 182-183,
185
Cultural relativism, 181-182, 182-
183, 192
Cultural Reproduction, 5, 11, 22-
23

D

Dewey, John, 8
Difference, 7, 10, 14-15, 25, 49,
108, 139-141, 144-148, 151-
154, 158-159, 224
Distinction, 13-14, 147, 169

E

Education
and attitudes, 57-59, 60-61, 78-
79, 81-83, 86, 91-92, 99, 141-
142, 148-149, 162-164, 182-
183, 216-217, 219
and connected education, 11-13
and literacy myth, 79
Embodied cognition, 200, 202-203
English studies and ideology of
emotion, 94
Ethnography
and critical use value, 220-221,
223, 225-226
and ethnographic interviewing,
199, 209, 212-15, 345-49
and participant observation, 10,
39-40, 196-197, 199-202
and pedagogy, 26, 195-202,
205-209, 226, 229-232
and research methodology, 42-
43, 45-46, 51-52, 142, 196-
197, 220-221, 229-232, 249-
251
and written mediations, 216-
219
Ethos, 13, 23, 58
and working class identity, 36-
37

F

Feminism, 4, 12, 66, 113, 139,
154-156, 167, 179, 183
and environmentalism, 90-91
and international labor, 96-98
and gender, 22, 79-81, 85-86,
101-102, 149-151, 166-167
Frankfurt School, 53-54
Friere, Paulo, 7, 23
Foucault, Michel, 30

H

Habermas, Jurgen, 12, 55

I

Individualism 55
and working class students, 25,
141, 145-148, 153-154, 168
Inductive Theorizing, 26, 112, 197-
199, 211-212, 232-235
and ethnographic methodology,
229-232
Instrumentalism, 11-13, 24-25,
49, 53-57, 64, 174-175
and composition studies, 56-57,
59
as technical rationality, 53-55,
72
as communicative practice, 55-
57, 64
and student motives, 54-55, 57-
59, 103-104
and working class students, 61-
64
and minority students, 60-61,
66-67
and immigrant students, 75-78,
88-89, 96-97
Immigrant students, 18-19, 20-22,
37-38, 47, 48, 98-100
and dual frame of reference, 75-
78, 91-92, 96-98
and gender, 79-81, 98-102,
215-216

Printed in the United States
21305LVS00005B/52